D0378130

crashing the party

An American Reporter in China

SCOTT SAVITT

DISCARD

SOFT SKULL PRESS

AN IMPRINT OF COUNTERPOINT

SANTA CLARA PUBLIC LIBRARY
2635 Homestead Road
Santa Clara, CA 95051

Copyright © 2016 by Scott Savitt

All rights reserved under International and Pan-American Copyright
Conventions. No part of this book may be used or reproduced in any
manner whatsoever without written permission from the publisher,
except in the case of brief quotations embodied in critical articles and
reviews.

Library of Congress Cataloging-in-Publication Data is Available

Cover design by Faceout Studio
Interior design by Tabitha Lahr

ISBN 978-1-59376-652-8

Soft Skull Press
An Imprint of Counterpoint
2560 Ninth Street, Suite 318
Berkeley, CA 94710
www.softskull.com

Printed in the United States of America
Distributed by Publishers Group West

10 9 8 7 6 5 4 3 2 1

You say that sheep will always be sheep, obediently walking in line to the slaughterhouse. And pigs, which struggle and squeal and must be dragged to their death, in the end cannot escape fate. Is their resistance not in vain?

But this is to say that even when faced with death, one should behave like a sheep; thus the world will be in peace.

Very well, but have you ever considered wild boars? With their tusks they can keep even experienced hunters at bay. In fact, all that an ordinary pig need do is escape the pen where the swineherd keeps it locked, and reach the forest—and in no time it will grow such tusks.

—Eminent Chinese writer and rebel Lu Hsün,

Parables, 1926

prologue

You can't truly know a nation until you've been inside its prisons.
—Chinese contemporary artist and activist Ai Weiwei

Artillery Alley, Beijing, August 2000

I'm lying on a bamboo mat on the concrete prison floor. My torn T-shirt is tied around my eyes to block the bare ceiling bulb that burns day and night. Sweat drenches my shirt from summer temperatures that soar above 100 degrees. The cell is six-by-eight feet, windowless, with a food slot in the iron door.

The humidity is suffocating.

I roll my head from side to side, desperate to get some rest. The drone from the light blends with the buzz of mosquitoes in my ears. I'm too tired to slap the insects away. My skin is covered in a rash of bites.

I untie the blindfold and put the T-shirt back on. Blinking to adjust my eyes to the glare, I glimpse faded Chinese characters carved into the plaster walls. Most are just names, probably of the poor souls locked in here before me. One inscription reads:

Wo zhen caodan [I'm really fucked].

Yes I am, I think and can't help smiling.

Then my smile fades and despair returns.

I'm locked in this cell and no one, not my family or friends, knows where I am. I have no idea how long I'll be held here. I'm so numb and exhausted I can't even cry.

To ease my fear and calm myself I do *qi gong*, a traditional deep-breathing exercise I learned from my martial arts teacher. I inhale deeply through my nose then exhale through my mouth, over and over. I feel the internal energy—*qi*—flow down the front of my body and up my back in a continuous cycle. My heart rate slows and anxiety eases. The mosquitoes are still distracting, but the noise grows fainter until I'm only conscious of the rhythm of my breath.

"*Yi, er, san, si.* . . . One, two, three, four. . . ."

Clang.

The sound of the door bolt startles me. I must have finally fallen asleep. The door flap swings up and I see the familiar black boots of the prison guard.

"*Matong* [shit bucket]," the officer barks.

I crawl over and push the red plastic bucket through the hole. It contains nothing but water as I've refused to eat for the four weeks I've been locked up here. I hear the officer empty it. Then he kicks it back inside, splashing drops of urine on me. Before the slot closes I glimpse pale red light in the hallway, marking the start of another day. Then the slot slams shut.

I can't take much more of this. I'm prepared to do something desperate, but there's not even a piece of metal or shard of broken glass in here to cut myself with. Could I strangle myself with my own bare hands or smash my head against the wall?

I close my eyes and replay scenes from the prison films I've been obsessed with since childhood: *The Bridge on the River Kwai, Papillon, The Deer Hunter, Apocalypse Now.* I imagine my heroes William Holden, Steve McQueen, Robert De Niro, and Martin Sheen patiently enduring prison waiting for an opportunity to escape. But there's no escape from this hellhole. They never let me out of this cage unshackled.

Without natural light it's impossible to measure the passage of time.

and my independent English-language newspaper *Beijing Scene*.[6] I understood the risk of getting in bed with these corrupt bureaucrats. My hope was to continue to produce a critically and commercially successful newspaper and make money for my Chinese partners. That's the only reliable insurance policy here anyway. And this too is a double-edged sword. The moment they decide they can run the newspaper without me, I'm expendable.

I didn't make things easier for myself by continuing to publish articles critical of China in the international press. Most foreigners would have just shut up and made money. But I was taught that a writer's responsibility is to give voice to the voiceless. Now I'm silenced too.

I spend another sleepless night tossing and turning. *How the hell am I going to get out of here?*

The outer cell door creaks open. Dawn is visible through the crack. The guard takes my waste bucket and empties it, but instead of shutting the door growls, "*Gen wo zou* [Come with me]."

I stand up on wobbly legs, extend my arms through the bars so he can handcuff me, and then follow him out.

My plastic prison-issue flip-flops scratch on the cement floor as I hurry to keep up. I steal glances into the crowded cells lining the hallway, packed with prisoners squatting with their hands clasped behind their heads, the painful position they're required to maintain all day.

How can they keep that up for so many hours without keeling over? I wonder when the guard spins around and kicks me in the shin.

"*Tamade!* Goddamn it!" I shout as I fall to the floor.

"I told you to keep your fucking eyes forward!"

Blood oozes from the gash left by his steel-toed boot. I press the wound, but there's no time to examine it. I hurry to my feet and keep moving so he won't kick me again. He enjoys exercising this total control over a foreigner. He's kicked and punched me regularly since my arrival.

At the end of the hallway is a small office with barred windows. I'm

---

6. I'd started as an underground black-and-white rag produced in my Beijing living room by my photographer-designer girlfriend and me.

interrogated here daily. Sometimes I'm brought in the middle of the night, sometimes just before dawn, to disrupt my already erratic sleep patterns I guess.

The guard shoves me through the door and onto a rickety wooden stool. Then he salutes the officers and stands at attention by the door. I squint into the spotlight and can make out the portly profile of Sergeant Wang and his skinny young assistant in their rumpled green police uniforms. They're sitting behind a long interrogation table, smoking cigarettes and scribbling in their notebooks.

Sergeant Wang sees my bloody shin and asks, "Did you have an accident?"

Then he makes eye contact with the guard and cackles.

I stare straight ahead, too exhausted to be angry.

Sergeant Wang repeats the same questions he's asked me every day since my arrest.

"What happened to all your newspaper's money?"[7]

"The *People's Daily* took US$5,000 a month as a management fee [*guanli fei*]—political protection for our newspaper. That was all our profit. The rest of the income covered expenses. All revenue passed through their advertising company. I never touched any money."

"Who were your accomplices?"

"I'll only talk about myself. If you want to know about other people, you'll have to ask them yourself."

Be polite to cops, but don't be a rat. My attorney father drilled these lessons into me since early childhood. *Say 'yes sir,' 'no sir,' and give vital personal information. Otherwise keep your mouth shut.*

"Who else did you bribe? We want names!"

I remain silent.

"We have all the time in the world," Sergeant Wang says. "Nobody knows where you are, and we can keep you here as long as we want."

---

7. The police confiscated US$50,000 in cash and hundreds of thousands of dollars in computers, cameras, and printing equipment when they raided our office. I assume with this line of questioning that they are seeking more assets to seize.

His words hit me like a punch in the gut. I know what he says is true, but I refuse to show I'm afraid. So I press my lips tight and continue to stare straight ahead.

When Sergeant Wang concludes he's not going to get any new information from me, he flicks his wrist, signaling the end of the interview. The guard yanks me off the stool and pushes me back toward my cell. As I approach the door I see a pen lying on the floor. I pretend to stumble, fall to my knees, and palm the ballpoint in my hand. If I'm caught I know I'll be beaten and probably have my incarceration extended. But I don't care. I'm determined to take this shred of control back into my own hands.

Locked in my cell again, I feel resurrected. Now I have a means to endure this torment, by documenting all I've experienced in my decades as a reporter here. Maybe through telling my story I can prevent others from being subjected to this same cruel treatment.

I squat with my back against the bars so I'll hear if anyone's coming down the hallway. The roll of scratchy, parchment-like toilet paper is just the right stiffness, and it's the only paper I have access to. I write in minuscule script, my hand trembling.

My sanity saved by a roll of toilet paper and cheap ballpoint pen, I laugh to myself, then start scribbling.

When I'm done with a session I stash the pen and paper in my underwear. I'll worry about how to smuggle it out later. I've concealed film up my ass past police checkpoints before. As I scratch words on this crude scroll, I feel a kinship with the Chinese rebels I've known who've paid dearly—some with their lives—for their resistance to political repression. I can only hope that the ink in this pen holds out. Of that I'm confident. My health, on the other hand, I'm less sure of.

But writing gives me something to hold onto. I begin chronicling all I've witnessed since arriving in China eighteen years ago, and the fateful decisions that have led me to this cell.

chapter one

如影隨形
ruying suixing
INSEPARABLE AS EACH OTHER'S SHADOWS

It's my first day in Beijing.

I'm a nineteen-year-old student on a year abroad from Duke University. China and the U.S. only normalized diplomatic relations three years ago, so student exchanges are still brand new. I'm one of the first Americans to live and study for a school year at Beijing Teacher's College, and am determined to make the most of this opportunity.

My dozen American classmates and I eat our first meal in a screened-off corner of the campus cafeteria. Our foreign appearance would attract too much attention if we ate out in the open.

This segregation makes me uncomfortable.

Our first meal consists of steamed rice, stir-fried Chinese cabbage spiced with red chili oil, and a boiled chicken with its head and feet still attached—to demonstrate freshness, the cook explains.

"Even if you arrive late, you still get a head," I wisecrack.

A Chinese-American member of our group, Elizabeth Chen, pops the chicken head into her mouth and chews with gusto.

"We eat this all the time at home," she explains, licking her fingers.

After dinner, instead of resting in our dorm with my classmates to recover from the round-the-world trip here, I stroll across the campus strumming my prized Guild guitar, a gift from an old blues musician in

North Carolina. The setting sun feels warm and soothing on my back. The scene is peaceful, the only sounds are crickets chirping and birds singing, punctuated by occasional muted voices. The air is filled with the comforting smell of *zhima shaobing* [sesame flatbread] baking in out-door brick ovens.

Painted big-character propaganda slogans—now weathered and fading six years after Chairman Mao's death and the end of his Cultural Revolution—cover the sides of every building. With my basic Mandarin and pocket Chinese-English dictionary, I slowly decipher them:

> *Mom and Dad can't compare with Chairman Mao. The great-ness of heaven and earth can't compare with the great kind-ness of the Communist Party.*

> *Resolutely support the anticolonial struggles of all peoples of the world.*

> *Revolution is not a crime, to rebel is justified.*

> *Down with Yankee Imperialism!*

And here I was thinking that the whole world loved America.

Everyone I pass stares at me. It's not every day that a bearded for-eigner in cut-off jeans walks through the center of their campus strum-ming a guitar.

"*Ni hao ma?* [How are you?]" I say as people pass. They nod, but are too shocked to respond.

Fresh-faced Chinese students stream past kicking soccer balls, chat-ting and laughing. I see from a dorm sign they're heading toward public showers that are strictly rationed with one hour of hot water a day.

I've always taken hot water for granted. I never considered how expensive it is to produce. I vow to never waste hot water again. Now I'll have to get used to timing my showers.

I find a patch of grass, sit down, and look around at where I'm going to be living and studying for the coming school year. The buildings are low-slung, unadorned red brick boxes. The tree-lined paths and quiet atmosphere remind me of a small college campus back home in New England.

I start to fingerpick a slow blues tune on my guitar. A young athletic-looking Chinese guy stops to listen. He's six feet tall, with prominent cheekbones and a warm smile. His muscular physique and rugged features are typical of Northern Chinese, I know from my background reading. Northerners are generally bigger and sturdier than their slighter southern cousins who make up the majority of Chinese immigrants to the U.S.[8]

He listens to me play for a minute, then asks in halting English, "Where are you from?"

"*Meiguo* [Beautiful Country or America]," I say in carefully enunciated Mandarin.

"You're the first American I've ever met."

I nod in surprise. "*Ni hui tan ma?* [Do you play the guitar?]"

He smiles but shakes his head 'no.'

I continue strumming and after a few minutes set the guitar aside to wipe sweat from my forehead. I didn't realize how hot it would be in Beijing in the summer. It's closer to the high humidity of North Carolina where I go to college than the cooler climate in Connecticut where I grew up.

"Can I take a look?" he asks in English.

"Sure," I say, and hand him the guitar.

He cradles it to his chest and starts to pluck out a Beatles song with note-for-note accuracy. Then he sings in a high clear tenor:

Blackbird singing in the dead of night
Take these broken wings and learn to fly
All your life
You were only waiting for this moment to arise
Blackbird fly, into the light of the dark, black night.

---

8. Most Americans are surprised when they see how big and brawny Northern Chinese men are.

When the final note fades, I applaud in amazed appreciation. How does this guy even *know* about the Beatles, never mind play and sing a complicated song like "Blackbird" perfectly?

"What's your name?" I ask.

"John, like my favorite singer, John Lennon. It also sounds like my Chinese surname Zhang."[9]

"You're an amazing guitar player and singer."

"*Nali nali*, not at all," he says modestly, then adds: "All young Chinese love rock and roll."

I arch my eyebrows in surprise. They didn't teach this in my *Introduction to the Chinese Revolution* seminar.

"Where did you learn to speak such good English?"

"From BBC and Voice of America shortwave radio broadcasts. It's illegal, but we still listen in secret at night."

"Do you have a guitar?"

"Yes, I made an electric guitar and amplifier out of spare parts in our school's electronics workshop. It was a *piece of cake*," he says proudly, showing off his best, if slightly dated, American slang.

As John continues talking in increasingly confident English, I feel a strong, unexpected bond with him. He tells me he gets together with his friends every evening to play Beatles, Bob Dylan, Simon and Garfunkel, and traditional American and British folk songs—also learned from banned international radio broadcasts. And they've started to play at campuses around the capital and are building up a word-of-mouth following.

"We also just finished recording an album," he adds in a conspiratorial whisper. "We're going to sell it on the black market."

I'm thrilled. It's my first day in Beijing and I've stumbled upon its rock and roll underground.

"DIY[10] in the PRC!" I joke, but when I see John doesn't get my punk rock reference, I change the subject and ask: "Isn't what you're doing risky?"

"*When you ain't got nothin', you got nothin' to lose*," he croons like Bob Dylan and smiles.

---

9. Pronounced *J-ahng*.

10. Do It Yourself, the new punk ethos taking root in the U.K. and U.S.

I laugh out loud. I really like this guy. A Beijing local who plays virtuoso guitar, can quote Bob Dylan lyrics on cue, and looks like he could use a native-English-speaking rhythm guitar player and background singer. I think I just made my first Chinese friend.

In the next few weeks John shows me around Beijing. With my capable guide, I feel like an eyewitness to history as the Middle Kingdom emerges, blinking, into the modern world. Forget entering the technological age, China hasn't even been through the *industrial* revolution yet. There are more horse carts on Beijing's wide empty boulevards than cars.

"These military-grade roads were made for tanks, not automobiles," John explains. "Mao used to conduct military reviews on *Chang'an*—the Avenue of Eternal Peace—and the Chairman loved to roll out the armor."

The only motor vehicles on the road now are a few imported Japanese taxis carrying newly-arrived foreign business executives, Soviet-modeled Red Flag limousines ferrying Communist Party officials to and from endless meetings, camouflaged military trucks, and diesel-spewing public buses crammed so full that the doors have to be pried open and closed with crowbars by the attendants.

The majority of people ride bicycles. An endless stream of identical black steel-framed Flying Pigeon bikes glide quietly past, bells chiming, steered by stern-faced men and women in baggy, unisex Mao suits.

The capital's residents are just emerging from the hangover of Mao's rule. Olive drab and proletarian blue military uniforms are still the daily dress of most men and women. But there are signs of change everywhere. Some young women dare to dress more fashionably and wear makeup, short skirts, and high heels in public—grounds for a labor camp sentence just a few years ago. Girls are even starting to drink alcohol and smoke cigarettes in public, unimaginable in Mao's day.

Young couples stroll side by side in public parks, hands occasionally brushing. Handholding is still deemed an immodest public display of affection.

When I offer to buy John a meal off-campus he tells me that I can't, there are no private restaurants. Food is served in public canteens at schools and workplaces during tightly restricted hours. Ration coupons are required for daily necessities including cooking oil, rice, eggs, sugar, flour, salt, and cotton cloth. John takes me to the campus general store to see the meager selection: wilted carrots, cabbage, potatoes, and mealy apples. Other than a few canned goods, the shelves are bare.

"All the best food, clothing, and imported goods go to Communist Party officials in special shops off-limits to ordinary people (*laobaixing*),"[11] John tells me as the screen front door swings shut behind us. "Only the leftovers go to us *masses*," he adds, sneering the Communist Party catchphrase.

"So much for socialist equality," I murmur under my breath, not wanting to hurt John's feelings.

It's difficult to imagine these people ever attaining the standard of living I'm accustomed to in the States. Private automobiles are unimaginable. Traffic could never maneuver through the maze of narrow alleyways (*hutongs*)[12] that crisscross the capital anyway.

John and I spend all our free time together. He shares my adventurous spirit and mistrust of authority, and we bond like brothers. We're a treasure trove of knowledge for each other. I'm a living encyclopedia of all things American, and he's the best resource on Chinese language and culture—especially underground youth culture—I could hope for. We joke that our friendship is a local-foreign joint venture—*zhongwai hezi*—the only business structure permitted for foreigners investing here.

Every day after school I meet John and his Beatles-loving buddies in the bleachers of a weed-strewn, dirt soccer field and share bottles of warm Beijing beer (refrigerators are also a luxury reserved only for officials). Several dozen male and female students gather to watch the novel sight of an American and a bunch of Chinese guys play guitars and sing together. This is the first time that American and Chinese youth have interacted freely since the Communists came to power in 1949.

---

11. *Laobaixing* (literally "Old 100 surnames" or common people).

12. *Hutong* is a Mongolian word meaning "water well," and was used to describe Beijing's narrow back alleys (the site of public wells) during the Mongol-led Yuan Dynasty (1271–1368).

Our fathers' generation fought each other in the Korean War—literally as both John's and my father served in their nation's army there—then remained sworn enemies through three decades of Cold War.

Now I'm drinking beer and playing music with a bunch of Red Chinese rock 'n' rollers. It's a scene our fathers couldn't have dreamed of.

John's English name really suits him. He plays guitar and sings just like John Lennon. From angry, growling blues to slow, moving ballads, he's a natural entertainer. I'm captivated by his charm, and so are the girls on campus judging by their ever-increasing numbers at our jams.

I teach John and his comrades a new song every day. They especially like the line from the Beatles song "Revolution": "*And if you go carrying pictures of Chairman Mao, you ain't gonna make it with anyone anyhow.*" In return they teach me racy Chinese street rhymes and revolutionary war songs. One day I bring my Walkman tape recorder and play them Jimi Hendrix's feedback-laden, electric guitar version of "The Star-Spangled Banner" at Woodstock. They go crazy. The next day they reciprocate with an improvised, revved-up version of China's national anthem "March of the Volunteers."[13]

"China's answer to 'God Save the Queen,'"[14] I joke.

John urges me to explain this, so I tell them about Johnny Rotten, Sid Vicious, and the Sex Pistols' brilliant parody of British royalty. Then I teach them the song.

"*God save the queen, the Fascist regime,*" they shout in unison, flailing on their guitars and convulsing in laughter.

I'm a one-man spiritual pollution campaign,[15] I think to myself and smile.

---

13. "March of the Volunteers" memorializes China's resistance to Japan's brutal 1930s invasion:
Arise, ye who refuse to be slaves;
With our very flesh and blood
Let us build our new Great Wall!
The Peoples of China are in their most critical time,
Everybody must roar defiance.
Arise! Arise! Arise!
Millions of hearts with one mind,
Brave the enemy's gunfire,
March on! Brave the enemy's gunfire,
March on! March on! March on, on!

14. The Sex Pistols' punk anthem.

15. *Jingshen Wuran* (literally: Spiritual Pollution). Communist Party term for Western cultural corruption.

One night after our usual jam session John invites me to meet his family. I eagerly accept. I follow him to a cluster of run-down red brick rowhouses at the back of campus. He unlocks a rusty wrought-iron gate, and we step through a small vegetable garden into his apartment.

Electricity is a recent and unreliable luxury. Rather than waste scarce resources on it, these frugal people light candles after dark. A middle-aged woman is sitting in the glow, knitting a sweater. As the screen door slams she rises to greet us.

"*Huanying, huanying* [welcome, welcome]," she says in a resonant, Beijing-accented voice. Her eyes are wide with excitement, but also a hint of worry.

"She's never met a foreigner before," John explains.

"Hey, Ma," he says loudly. "He's not from outer space!"

Her cheeks flush with embarrassment.

"*Bie zheteng* [Quit being a pain in the ass]," I say, using one of the first slang terms John taught me.

His mom smiles. My local humor seems to make me less foreign and put her at ease.

I can see where John gets his good looks. His mom is strikingly beautiful. She has the same smooth, golden skin and well-defined features as her son. But worry lines etch her eyes and forehead.

"I apologize for our humble circumstances," she says, bowing her head in traditional modesty.

"*Meiyou* [not at all]," I assure her. "Your home is clean and comfortable."

I glance around the room again and am shocked by how small it is. No more than a hundred square feet, the single square space serves as bedroom, living room, and dining room for the whole family. A plank bed with a straw mattress is pressed against the back wall. The only other sizable piece of furniture is a tall wooden wardrobe. There's no space for anything else. Tucked in the back corner is a tiny makeshift kitchen with a two-burner hotplate, cold-water spigot, and concrete basin. A closet-sized bathroom with a hole in the floor serves as both toilet and shower. A plastic showerhead is duct-taped to the sink's cold-water spigot.

So this is what my immigrant grandparents, who arrived in New York from Eastern Europe in 1900, meant by a cold-water, walk-up flat.

A woman in her late twenties sits silently in a chair by the wall.

"That's my older sister," John says. "She can't talk. Red Guards kidnapped her during the Cultural Revolution because of my family's educated class background. While being interrogated she 'fell' out a third-story window. She's brain damaged and mute."

I've read about student radicals incited to violence by Chairman Mao injuring and killing innocents, but this is the first time I've met people who've suffered the horror themselves. It makes me painfully aware of my own privileged upbringing, and shocks me into silence.

Then John adds: "My father's fate was worse."

I cringe at what I'm about to hear.

"He was a literature professor, a 'stinking intellectual'[16] Mao called them. After they took my sister the Red Guards ransacked our house, burned all our books and other valuables, and marched my father off in a dunce cap. We never saw him again. They told us he died under interrogation. We still don't know what really happened."

"I'm sorry," is all I can say.

"*Meishi*, it doesn't matter," John says with a wave of his hand, but I can see deep pain in his eyes.

"Now you know why my friends and I dislike politics. We don't believe in Marx or Mao. Our faith is simpler, more American: Believe in yourself."

I love this guy's spirit. It's no surprise that the Communist Party feels threatened by his independent-minded new generation.

John's mom can't follow our rapid blend of Chinese and English we call *Chinglish*, but she instinctively gets the gist of what we're saying and to lighten the mood asks if I'd like to stay for dinner.

"I don't want to impose," I tell her.

"It's no trouble, we're just having *jiachangcai* [a simple family meal]."

John signals to me with a nod that his mother won't take no for an answer, so I say: "*Feichang rongxing* [I'm honored to accept]."

She guides me to the dining table, turns on the fluorescent overhead

---

16. *Chou zhishifenzi* Mao's label for the exploitative intellectual class.

light, and hands me a copy of the *Beijing Evening News*. Then she and John busy themselves in the kitchen preparing the meal. I offer to help but they won't let me do anything. So I sit back and relax to the rhythm of their iron cleavers chopping vegetables on wooden cutting boards and read.

As they finish preparing the food, the electricity goes out and the room is plunged into darkness. They shrug it off as a familiar inconvenience. I view it as a welcome relief from the fluorescent buzzing. They light candles and place them on the table. We sit down and I share our American custom of joining hands, bowing heads, and saying grace.

"Bless this food to our use and us to thy service. Thank you for your abundance and these wonderful new friends. Amen."

"Amen," John repeats mockingly, and we both grin.

As the honored guest, no one will start eating until I do. So I pick up a piece of tofu with my chopsticks, take a bite, and nod with approval. Only then does the family dig in. There are platters of stir-fried shoestring potatoes with spicy green pepper slices, silken tofu stew laced with numbing Sichuan peppercorns, and clear watercress and tomato soup. Then John produces a plate of pan-fried scallion pancakes. All the dishes are delicious. I'm not sure if there's no meat because I've told John I'm vegetarian or because it's too expensive.

The meal is accompanied by heaping bowls of steamed white rice, the staple for all Chinese—at least those who can afford it.

We eat in silence. Then after a couple of minutes John's mother says, "I'm sorry to serve such a simple meal to so honored a guest."

"*Nali nali* [you're too kind]. It's one of the most delicious meals I've ever eaten," I say and mean it.

At the end of the meal, I follow John's lead and lift my bowl to my lips, scoop the remaining grains of rice into my mouth, then fill the bowl with soup and drink it. Not a single grain of rice or precious drop of oil goes to waste.

"Let me help," I say as I try to clear the table and wash the dishes, but John and his mom won't let me lift a finger.

So I sit back down with the newspaper and reflect on how lucky I am to have this front-row seat on the world's oldest civilization opening its doors wider to the outside world than at any time in its history.

chapter two

玉不琢不成器，人不学不成才
yu bu zhuo bu cheng qi, ren bu xue bu cheng cai.

JADE MUST BE CARVED AND POLISHED BEFORE IT BECOMES A GEM. A PERSON MUST BE TRAINED BEFORE THEY CAN FULFILL THEIR POTENTIAL.

My mornings are spent in language classes, diligently memorizing Chinese characters and practicing the tricky tones of Mandarin. It's nothing like learning a Latin-based language, which at least has some correlation to English. This requires the adoption of a beginner's mind—*chuxin*—and imitating native speakers the way a child does.

I learn more outside the classroom with John and his friends than from my textbooks.

After school I explore the historical and scenic sights of Beijing with John: Tiananmen Square, Forbidden City, Summer Palace, Temple of Heaven, museums, art galleries, public parks. I even teach him how to backpack and camp out—highly illegally—on the Great Wall. We barely avoid getting arrested by the park police.

And every evening John and I continue to play music with his friends.

While I represent 200 years of American history, John feels obliged to impart the essence of thousands of years of Chinese culture. He teaches me to memorize and recite Tang Dynasty[17] poetry, considered the quintessence of Chinese culture. I love the simple but profound verses of the Zen poet Cold Mountain (*Han Shan*).[18] John also introduces me to the timeless wisdom of the Taoist sages Lao Tzu and Chuang Tzu, and helps me memorize the four-character proverbs all educated Chinese sprinkle their speech with.

"*A gem can't be polished without friction, nor a person perfected without trials. All worthwhile undertakings are difficult,*" is the phrase John quotes to me most often.

He and his friends also instruct me in traditional Chinese health practices. Every day we rise before dawn and run to the school's sports field where his *kung fu* buddies teach me martial arts and meditation exercises. We do *t'ai chi*, push hands (*tuishou*), and spar freestyle (*sanda*). It's more fun than Western boxing because in addition to punching you can kick, joint lock, and wrestle. This is mixed martial arts before the term has been coined. It feels great to get the adrenaline flowing first thing in the morning, and no one gets more than a few cuts and bruises.

After working out, we return to John's house and drink the first of many cups of steaming green tea to stay well hydrated. He also teaches me acupressure massage tricks we periodically do on each other to stimulate our immune systems, and if we feel a cold coming on we ingest medicinal Chinese herbs to nurture our body's *yin-yang* balance and maintain health.

I take to this lifestyle instinctively, as if I were a Zen monk in a past life. I've always woken well before dawn, making me an oddity among my fellow young Americans who relish late nights and sleeping in. In China, rising early is a necessary virtue. Sunlight is precious. One never knows when the electricity might be cut off.

---

17. 600–900 AD.

18. 寒山 (*Han shan,* literally "Cold Mountain") was a legendary Tang Dynasty poet. He's considered an incarnation of the Bodhisattva of Wisdom in Zen lore.

Late into the night, John and I sit up in the back corner of his apartment—long after his mom and sister have gone to bed—discussing the dramatic transformation we're witnessing. Even as a naïve American teenager I can recognize the signs of rapid social change. The new Communist Party leader, Deng Xiaoping, has replaced Mao's catastrophic policy of "permanent revolution" with a call for reform and opening to the outside world (*gaige kaifang*). This is a radical about-face for China.

It means dismantling Mao's peoples' communes, and returning the land to the peasants to grow their own crops as they'd successfully done for millennia. The forced collectivization of agriculture after the revolution led to the Great Leap Forward famine of 1959–1961 in which tens of millions starved to death.

Deng's reforms have revitalized China's economy after decades of stagnation. Foreign investment is pouring in, and a free-market economy is taking root. And implicit in this new approach is also reform of the Communist Party's rigid political system to accommodate the rapid social changes.

"We call them 'Black Cat, White Cat' reforms," John explains. "It doesn't matter if the cat is black or white—capitalist or socialist—as long as it catches mice."

"Deng's aware of the tidal wave of change he's unleashed," John continues. "His hope is that the Communist Party can ride out the wave of reform instead of being toppled by it."

"*Shui ke zaizhou ye ke fuzhou.* Water can raise a boat or sink a boat," he adds this pithy proverb for emphasis.

"But what about democracy?" I start to ask but John anticipates my question and cuts me off.

"After Mao's chaos, most Chinese will tolerate ongoing Party dictatorship as long as it improves their standard of living. But if they stop delivering on their promise . . . ," he says, shaking his head as his voice trails off.

Over the course of the semester I sense a collective weight lifting as reforms gain momentum. People seem more relaxed and animated in their daily lives. Women start to shed their Mao suits and dress in more colorful and stylish clothing as fashions produced for export enter the local economy.

Once sparsely trafficked streets are now lined with bustling outdoor free market stalls selling a diversity and quality of products unimaginable even a year ago—fresh fruit like oranges and bananas, greenhouse-grown broccoli and tomatoes, foreign-brand high-end products like Sony electronics and Nike and Adidas sportswear. Gone are the days of cabbage[19] being the staple of every meal for everyone but Communist Party officials.

John and I browse quasi-legal private bookstalls set up on sidewalks, selling everything from traditional Chinese literature banned by the Communists—the Ming Dynasty pornographic novel *The Golden Lotus* (*Jinpingmei*)[20] is a best-seller—to translations of works by officially blacklisted authors Kafka, Orwell, Solzhenitsyn, and Havel.[21]

New business opportunities—import and export trading, real estate development, political fixing, and antique smuggling—dominate conversations. Entrepreneurship is now permitted for the first time since the Communists came to power and abolished private ownership. As an American I recognize the buzz of increased economic opportunity and personal freedom. The Chinese have had every aspect of their lives dictated to them for decades. Now they're collectively removing their shackles and a vibrant society is sprouting up between the cracks.

John and I agree that this is going to pose a real challenge to the Party's monopoly not just on power, but people's hearts and minds. Now that they've gained this measure of hard-won freedom, they won't surrender it lightly. On the contrary, they'll continue to demand more of it.

"Deng's policies are an attempt to resolve the centuries-old dilemma of *ti* (essence) and *yong* (function)," John explains. "The challenge is to

---

19. Dubbed 爱国菜 (*aiguocai*—the "patriotic vegetable") because eating it was considered the patriotic duty of every nation-loving citizen.

20. Novel composed in vernacular Chinese during the late Ming Dynasty (1368–1644). The earliest known versions of the novel were handwritten; the first block-printed book was only released in 1610. Its explicit sexuality garnered a level of notoriety in China akin to Lady Chatterley's Lover in English literature.

21. Václav Havel (1936–2011) was a dissident Czech playwright who became that country's first post-communist president.

reconcile advanced Western technology with time-honored but time-worn Confucian traditions of social hierarchy and filial piety (essence).

"*Mozhe shitou guohe*—We have to cross the river by feeling for stones," he adds with a wry smile, mocking the Communist Party slogan.

"Just be careful you don't trip on the rocks and drown," I wisecrack, and he whacks me with his pillow, sparking a pillow fight. In the scuffle we knock over his alarm clock, and I notice that it's after midnight.

"*Cao!* [Fuck!] My dorm is locked. I'll have to wake up the night watchman and he'll report me."

"Sleep here," John says, unconcerned by the illegality of what he's proposing. "We'll get up and leave before dawn. No one will notice."

Why not? It's better than getting busted, I reason.

I squeeze in beside him on his narrow military cot and clutch my side of the scratchy woolen blanket. We sleep head to toe. Despite the discomfort, it has the thrill of the taboo. Like illicitly staying overnight in an all-female dorm back home.

We wake up and leave the house for our morning workout well before dawn. As John predicted, no one notices.

After that first night, I sleep at John's house more frequently, unable to tear myself away from our late-night political discussions. Eventually I pack my belongings and move into his apartment. John's mother is a member of the local Neighborhood Committee [*juweihui*], nicknamed the Old Ladies with Bound Feet Brigade [*xiaojiao lao taitai zhenjidui*].[22] These networks of senior citizens extend Communist Party control into every household in China. Their duties include tracking women's menstrual cycles to enforce the draconian one-child birth control policy, issuing official marriage, divorce, birth, and death certificates, coordinating community crime watch, mediating domestic disputes, and generally serving as the eyes and ears of the government at the grassroots level. She was given this job by the authorities as a concession for the terrible suffering her family endured under Mao. She'll know in advance if my presence causes problems and will be able to intercede.

---

22. Bound Feet is a metaphor for being old busybodies. Their feet aren't really bound; that barbaric custom of binding a young girl's feet until her toes were crushed and she could barely walk ended with the fall of the Qing Dynasty (1911).

This small act of defiance is her way of resisting the pervasive Communist Party control that's taken such a terrible toll on her family. She smiles as John and I slip out each morning, silently encouraging our act of subversion.

Now that we live together, John sets about training me physically and spiritually to be a good, humble Chinese lad. He teaches me to *chi ku*—'eat bitter' or endure suffering—a necessary virtue in this ruthless society. After we rise at 4 AM and do our physical training, we shop for the day's food. Without refrigerators, people have to shop every day for fresh produce. When we return home we sponge-bathe in the bathroom—washing with cold water is considered healthy as it stimulates the body's immune system—then prepare breakfast. John's mom looks after his sister who can't dress herself. After eating a simple meal of millet porridge, homemade pickled vegetables, and steamed wheat buns, I head to Chinese class and John bikes to the nearby high school where he teaches history and physical education.

I feel like I'm in basic training for my new Chinese life. I take pride in my physical, cultural, and Mandarin language progress. I've never worked harder, but it isn't just learning by rote, instead it's what John calls *xiuxing* [cultivating spirit].

We have a winter break at the end of the semester. After consulting with John and his mom, I decide to test my new survival skills and travel alone. I bike the ten kilometers to the downtown Beijing railway station, leave my bike in the parking shed next to the station entrance, and purchase a third-class hard-berth seat to the impoverished neighboring province of Shanxi.

chapter three

少見多怪
shaojian duoguai
RARE EVENTS APPEAR MARVELOUS

The train is choked with cigarette smoke, so I spend most of the overnight ride in the exposed section between cars, propped against my backpack. It's freezing but well ventilated. I catch up on much-needed sleep after the long semester. With a fur-lined green army cap pulled down over my eyes, and big scarf covering my face, no one can see that I'm a foreigner so no one approaches me to practice English.

Before dawn the steam engine whistles. The scarred black locomotive slows to a halt at the small landing in *Wutaishan*[23]—Five Peaks Mountain—near China's border with Mongolia, 250 miles west of Beijing.

I empty the remaining hot water in my tin teacup out the train window, stuff my book of Tang Dynasty ghost stories and well-worn pocket journal into my knapsack, and descend to the platform.

The clock on the station wall reads 4:14 AM.

Vendors are selling hot tea, breakfast buns, herbal remedies, newspapers, and magazines to the predawn travelers. I need to keep moving to get my blood flowing after spending the night sitting up so I head for the exit.

The station leads out onto a dirt track with no lights or street signs. I know my destination lies uphill, so I pull my scarf tighter around my neck, lower my head, and start hiking.

---

23. Pronounced *Woo-tie-shahn*.

The air is bitter cold. Food hawkers' diesel lamps illuminate a dense ground fog. I can't tell if this is natural haze or pollution from the coal burned for heat and power here. The stench of sulfur burns my nostrils.

This region is known as China's Appalachia because of its rugged mountains, heavy reliance on coal mining, and endemic poverty. It was only recently opened to foreigners.

After a few minutes of hiking I smell a cooking fire. I look up and see a man standing over a glowing oil barrel.

The flame illuminates his face. He's gaunt, with a calm gaze. Salt-and-pepper stubble covers his chin, and a grey felt cap is pulled down over his ears. His leathery skin and upturned eyelids make him look more Mongolian than Chinese. He's stirring stew in a big iron wok with a wooden paddle that looks like a boat oar. My stomach grumbles. I haven't eaten since boarding the train twelve hours ago.

I don't recognize what he's cooking, surprising after a year of adventurous street eating in Beijing.

I address him in my most formal Mandarin: "Elder Master, what succulent dish are you preparing?"

The old man continues his rhythmic stirring and says in a thick local dialect: "*Xue Doufu* [Blood Tofu]."

Blood . . . ?

I remember reading about a regional delicacy made from coagulated pig's blood. The square chunks floating in the thick, wine-colored stew do resemble tofu cubes, but instead of being white they're the scarlet color of fresh blood.

Ruxiang suisu, I think to myself. *When on the road follow the local customs.*

My vegetarianism is trumped by hunger and I order a large bowl. I pull a crumpled one-*yuan* note (twelve U.S. cents) from my pocket and wave for the man to keep the four cents change. He nods and ladles the steaming soup into a chipped porcelain bowl. I take the dish with both hands and relish the warmth radiating through my numb fingers.

Squatting on the pavement like a local, I bring the bowl to my lips and take a sip. The strong, almost rancid odor of the pig's blood makes me retch. I haven't eaten meat in years. A generous helping of fresh ground pepper cuts the gamey smell, and I slurp down the rest of the soup.

"*Nar que, nar bu* [what's deficient must be supplemented]," the old man rasps, citing the traditional health precept that eating blood remedies anemic fatigue.

A street peddler quoting 2,000-year-old medical principles in the freezing predawn should surprise me. But the more I see of China, the less strange it seems. And whether it's the pig's blood or my first meal in a day, I feel strength flow back into my limbs.

I stand up and return the empty bowl.

"How far to the mountains?" I ask.

He holds up a bony index finger and says: "An hour by foot." Then he points to a bicycle rickshaw parked behind him. I nod in thanks at his offer of a ride but decide to walk the five kilometers to stretch my legs and watch the sun rise.

Snow-capped peaks become visible against the reddening horizon. The diamond-shaped northern crag hovers above the rest. At more than 3,000 meters (10,033 feet), it's the highest point in northern China and the peak I plan to climb today.

After an hour of steady hiking I arrive at the foot of the mountains. I'm sweating and can finally feel my fingers and toes again. There's a small village with a cobblestone lane containing a noodle stand, teahouse, souvenir shop, and inn. No cars are allowed in this nature preserve, the only sound is birdsong. It's off-season for tourists before lunar Chinese New Year next month, when religious pilgrims and families will flock here.

A few monks and nuns go about their morning chores. Their identical clean-shaven heads would make it impossible to tell them apart if not for their distinctive robes—saffron for monks and maroon for nuns.

I stop at the teahouse to refill my water bottle. The woman behind the counter heaves a huge blackened kettle off the stove and pours a stream of scalding water into the thermos' narrow spout. I smile at her skill. Before I leave I ask to use the bathroom and she points to the back of the shop. A tattered plastic curtain surrounds a hole in the floor and a cracked, stained sink. Flies buzz around the foul-smelling pit. I hold my nose and squat. There's no toilet paper, so I fish a piece of newspaper out of the trash bin and use that. When I'm done I scrub my hands—I won't see another toilet today—then head back outside.

A trail map is posted on a utility pole. I find my location, and head to the northern peak path.

It feels great to be back in the mountains. I've missed nature after my school year in the noisy, crowded capital.

The trail leads up into a hardwood forest. Bright red, yellow, and orange leaves carpet the ground and muffle my footsteps. This rush of color is a welcome relief from the drab greys and browns of Beijing.[24] I hike at a steady pace and estimate it will take eight hours to climb the peak and get back down before dark. The last thing I want is to be stranded on this mountain overnight in the middle of winter.

Trees arch above my head in a natural cathedral. Chipmunks and squirrels chase each other through the underbrush and gather groundnuts. These are the first wild animals I've seen since arriving in China. There's no wildlife left in the capital. All animals were hunted to extinction during periods of food shortage[25] and pest eradication after the revolution. As I climb higher, the hardwood forest gives way to evergreens—cypress, cedar, spruce, and pine—gnarled like the ancient trees in traditional Chinese paintings.

After an hour of hiking I sit down to take a short rest. Swigging water from my thermos, I look down at the valley I just climbed up from. It's carpeted with jade winter wheat rippling in the wind. The train station is visible in the distance, its toy-like engines trailing wispy white clouds of steam.

I've finally made it to Wutaishan, I think with a sense of accomplishment. It's one of China's most sacred Buddhist mountains, believed by the faithful to be the abode of the Buddha of Wisdom.[26] Legend has it that the Enlightened One still returns here in human form.

---

24. My classmates and I have dubbed the capital "Greyjing."

25. Acute since the 1949 revolution, climaxing in the 三年困難 (three years of hardship, 1959–1961) following Mao's great leap forward of communalizing agriculture.

26. *Manjusri,* said in the scriptures to reside on this "clear cold mountain," hence Wutaishan's alternative name 清涼山 (Qingliangshan).

I've wanted to visit this place since reading about it in a world religion class in college. It's the leading center of Tibetan Buddhism in China—the more esoteric sister tradition to the homegrown, nature-based Zen that's more common in the rest of the country. This mountain is renowned for its ancient wooden temples and sexually explicit Tantric sculptures—male and female deities in divine embrace—enclosed in glass cases and now covered up with white sheets by the straitlaced Communist authorities.

I resume hiking and am making good progress, so decide to explore a little off-trail. I leave the main path and walk through a grove of tall pine trees. Rays of sunlight spill through the upper branches and shimmer on the forest floor. At the far end the trees open onto a clearing containing a stone hut and neatly tended garden. An old monk and young boy are gathering vegetables. They're wearing blue cotton robes and black cloth slippers, and their heads are newly-shaven.

"*Hei!* [Hey!]" I call out as I emerge from the woods so as not to startle them.

The monk and boy look up from their work and blink in surprise at this strange apparition: a white guy with a big black beard coming out of the forest shouting in Chinese.

Their wicker basket is full of typical cold-weather vegetables: winter squash, snow radish, cabbage, carrots, and beets.

"Your garden looks great," I tell them, giving the thumbs-up that all Chinese seem to know. The old man nods but his apprentice continues to stare at me in silence.

"He's never seen a foreigner before," the monk explains.

I press my palms together in front of my face and bow in the traditional Buddhist sign of respect and greeting.

The old man smiles at my knowledge of this custom. He asks if I'd like to join them for tea.

I nod and follow him through the hand-hewn wooden door.

The single room appears to serve as their kitchen, bedroom, and study. There's an altar by the door with sweet-smelling juniper incense burning in an iron pot, and an image of the Goddess of Mercy (*Guanyin Pusa*) is pasted to the mud wall. The old man bows, places the vegetables on the altar, and whispers: "Goddess of Mercy, we honor your generosity and abundance. Please bless this food."

I bow as I pass the altar and whisper: "Amen."

There's a fire blazing in the stone hearth in the middle of the room. Behind it is a traditional sleeping platform, a *k'ang*. The fireplace heats the bed and serves as a stove. There's no electricity or indoor plumbing. The old man tells me they chop their own firewood to cook and heat with, and pump water from an outdoor well.

He leads me to a carved wooden table with a sweeping view of the valley. The cloudless blue sky and steep drop-off make me dizzy, but as my eyes adjust I have the euphoric feeling of looking down from the top of the world.

The boy busies himself at the stove preparing tea. He hands me a steaming cup and I cradle it in my hands.

"What brings you here?" the old man asks.

"I study Chinese at a university in Beijing."

His eyebrows arch, then his mouth spreads into a smile. "So foreigners come here to study Chinese?" he says and bursts into laughter.

I grin at his odd response, and take another sip of tea.

When I look up the old man is staring into my eyes. His gaze is piercing, but his serenity relaxes me.

"Have you ever had your fortune told?"

"N-n-o-o . . ." I stammer, not sure I've heard him correctly. Then he repeats the word "*suanming*" (literally "calculate fate"), and before I have a chance to refuse, he's reaching for my hand.

He strokes my palm several times as if to wipe it clean. Then he inspects it carefully, tracing the lines and whispering: "I see you've suffered a tragic recent loss."

"What?!" I say loudly, shocked by his words. How could he know? I haven't told John or my American classmates, no one in China knows. Is the grief written on my face?

He ignores my response and continues to study my hand, then says: "You'll have dramatic swings in fate [*daqi daluo*]. This cycle started with your recent misfortune. In your zodiac year [*benmingnian*—every twelfth year of the Chinese astrological cycle—when I'm twenty-four, I'm now twenty] your career will take off. You'll continue to experience professional success but personal tragedy."

He stares into my eyes again to make sure I've understood his words, then releases my hand and takes a long sip of tea.

I'm so shocked by his first words that I barely pay attention to the rest.

I need to get outside. I gulp my tea and tell the old man I have to get back to climbing. The monk sits silently, staring past me out the window. I take his hand and shake it, thank them both for their hospitality, and say *bai* [bye] as I bolt out the door.

I run across the pasture into the pine grove and stagger against a tree. A wave of nausea wracks me and I begin to retch. The pig's blood comes up in a bright red spout. I feel light-headed and slump to the forest floor. Wiping my mouth with my jacket sleeve I struggle to catch my breath.

A tragic event last year that I've fled to the other side of the world to escape has finally caught up with me.

Sitting on this forest floor I recall every moment of it.

chapter four

憶苦思甜
yiku sitian

REMEMBER PAST SUFFERING TO BETTER
APPRECIATE THE PRESENT

The telephone rings in my freshman dorm room. It's after midnight.

"Hey, you," the soft voice says.

It's my girlfriend, Karen. We're both eighteen. She's about to graduate from our New Haven high school and attend Wellesley College. I'm finishing my first year at Duke.

"I just woke up and wanted to tell you my dream," she whispers. She sleeps in a room next to her strict Catholic parents. They don't allow her to talk on the phone at all on school nights, never mind after midnight.

"There was a light shining through my window. It was a pure-white rainbow that I could walk out on. I couldn't see where it led, but I really wanted to go and look."

"Just be sure to leave a trail of breadcrumbs so you remember how to get back," I joke.

She laughs and continues: "It felt so real! I had to resist with all my might to not walk out on it and disappear."

"You're not going anywhere," I say. "I'll be home next week."

I'm in my last week of school before final exams. Then I'll return to Connecticut where Karen and I have summer jobs teaching tennis and lifeguarding. We're looking forward to spending our last summer together before she goes away to college.

We chat a few minutes longer then say good-bye.

Overnight I develop a high fever, am racked with chills, and soak my bedclothes with sweat. I wake up drained and exhausted. I see in the mirror that my face is pale and drawn, and there are dark rings under my eyes.

I drag myself to the library to study, and by afternoon I have regained enough energy to go for my daily ten-kilometer run around the Duke golf course. As I arrive back at my room the telephone is ringing.

"Hi, Scott, it's Mom."

Why is she calling? I wonder. We usually talk only on Sundays.

"I don't know how to tell you this," she says. I'm concerned because my mom isn't dramatic. "Karen's very ill."

"What do you mean *very ill*?" I say, my voice rising. "I just talked to her last night."

"Her mother came home from work this afternoon and found her unconscious on the floor. She never left for school. They took her to Yale Hospital. She's in a coma."

My legs wobble and I reach for the dresser to support myself.

"They think it's meningitis.[27] They're still doing tests."

I struggle to make sense of her words. Maybe it's the kind of coma you wake up from? My mom's next words dash my hopes.

"She went without oxygen all day. There's likely brain damage."

I fall onto the bed. All I can think of is the white light Karen saw in her dream.

I beg to come home immediately. But my mom won't let me, telling me there's nothing I can do.

Unable to sleep, I wander across campus and end up in Duke's Gothic chapel. I'm not sure what I'm doing here, I don't even know if I believe in God. But I'm so desperate and scared I'll try anything. I sit

---

27. Swelling of the brain tissue.

down in the front pew, bow my head and fold my hands, and pray with all my might: *Please let her be all right.*

The next few days are torturous. I try to write papers and study for exams but can't focus on anything but Karen lying with a breathing tube down her throat, barely clinging to life. My mom gives me daily updates, but the prognosis isn't good. Karen's condition continues to deteriorate, and by the end of the week her organs start to fail. Sunday night after I return from my run the telephone rings.

"Scott?" It's my mom again. I don't have the strength to speak. She takes a deep breath then says: "Karen's kidneys stopped functioning this afternoon. They took her off life support and she passed away.

"I'm so sorry, honey."

A wave of anguish rushes over me. I collapse to the floor, tears flowing.

I hear my mom's voice: "Scott . . . Scott. . . . Are you all right?" But the phone drops from my hand and I curl up in a tight ball and sob myself to sleep.

The next morning I go see my dean to tell her the news. The school has special procedures for this kind of emergency. They contact my professors and my final exams are postponed. I take a taxi to the airport and get on the first flight home.

My mom meets me at the airport in New York and we're silent for the two-hour ride home. What can you say about the sudden death of a previously healthy eighteen-year-old girl?

We go straight to Karen's house. Her mom opens the door. Her eyes are red and swollen from crying. Her dad stands behind her in the hallway, his shoulders slumped. They look old. The last time I saw them they were happy parents preparing to send their only child off to college. Now they're experiencing what must be every parent's worst nightmare, losing their daughter this sudden, tragic way.

We sit in the living room surrounded by photos of Karen at her first communion, in school class pictures, at family holiday parties, and on ski trips with me.

I swore I'd be strong for her parents, but I'm the one who breaks down and starts sobbing. Her mom takes me upstairs to Karen's bedroom, where my graduation photo still sits on her nightstand. Nothing else has changed except she's not here. It's as if Karen could climb back in through the window and this would all be a bad dream.

We grew up together. In our teens we became a couple. We did everything together: play tennis, swim, backpack, strum guitars, and sing. People often mistook us for brother and sister. I was certain she was my soulmate and we would spend the rest of our lives together. People told me all the time how lucky I was to have found the right person in my hometown. Now this blessing has become a curse. This place I love so much will always be tainted with this tragedy.

Our 2,000-student New Haven high school is closed in mourning on the day of Karen's funeral. The service is held at Holy Infant, her family's Catholic church. Karen and I used to attend midnight mass here together every Christmas.

There are hundreds of people at the service and I know most of them. All the eyes in the church feel like they're on me. Everyone is thinking: *That's the last person in the world I'd want to be.* I feel the same way.

There's an open coffin. No one warned me and I catch a glimpse of Karen's corpse. Her cheeks are heavily rouged, and she's wearing the purple silk dress she wore to her senior prom with me less than a month ago. On her left hand is the gold heirloom ring I gave her before I left for college.

My mom encourages me to go over and "pay my last respects."

"Pay my last respects? That's just a dead body!" I half-shout, my voice cracking with sorrow. I can't bear to look and my mom understands.

Karen's gone. She walked out her window onto that white rainbow. That phone call was her way of saying good-bye to me. This is all just a show for the rest of these people. Other than her parents, I'm the person most devastated by this tragedy.

I curse myself for not returning home the moment Karen fell ill. If only I'd gone back and been with her, held her hand, talked to her, maybe she would have sensed my presence and it would have made a difference. It would have made a difference to me at least, to hold her hand and see her beautiful face alive one last time.

After the funeral I return to North Carolina to take my final exams on Duke's deserted campus. I feel numb. I'm going through the motions of daily life but not really living. Part of me died with Karen and I don't know if I can go on without her.

I walk across campus on a hot June morning and run into my old friend Greg Robbins, a Duke medical student. He asks me what I'm doing here so long after school ended, and I tell him I just finished my last exam because I had to go home for a family emergency.

"I hope everything's okay," he says.

I don't respond, and he sensitively changes the subject. "Hey, Duke has a new study abroad program I think you'd be perfect for. It's in China."

"China?" I say, picturing the one thing I know about the place, that it's on the opposite side of the world.

"They need reliable students because it's a harsh environment and they want to make a positive first impression. Your wilderness survival training is good preparation for the electricity shortages, limited food supply, and year without telephone contact with home. I know the professor in charge of the program and can recommend you."

"Thanks, that's really generous of you."

Greg was my freshman orientation instructor at the Outward Bound School in the Blue Ridge Mountains of western North Carolina, and we formed a tight bond on the two-week backpacking trip that included rock climbing, a three-day solo fast, and a half-marathon (thirteen-mile) run on the final day. He knows I have strong leadership skills and a high threshold for adversity.

As he details the difficulties of studying in China, I focus on the advantages: a fresh start in a new place as far away from Karen's death as possible. This could be the best thing for me.

I thank Greg again for his suggestion and head off to find the professor leading the trip, Arif Dirlik.

Dirlik is a renowned Chinese history professor at Duke, an immigrant from Turkey who was a student activist at Berkeley in the 1960s. I find him in his office and he invites me in. A life-sized black-and-white poster of Chairman Mao hangs on his wall. Dirlik looks a little like Mao himself. He's got a Fu Manchu moustache and a mischievous sparkle in his eyes.

He's very different from the tweedy, effete professors I'm used to meeting at Duke. He's wearing a flannel shirt, worn brown corduroys, and scuffed work boots. He serves me strong black tea and chain-smokes Camel cigarettes by his open window the whole time we're talking.

I tell him I'm interested in the China program he's leading, and he asks me questions about my personal background and career goals. After a few minutes we realize that we have a lot in common: a wry sense of humor, a rebellious streak, and a strong commitment to social justice. It's clear we'd make good travel companions.

Professor Dirlik, who insists I call him Arif, invites me to join the new Duke Study in China program. Requirements include taking his yearlong *History of the Chinese Revolution* seminar and intensive Mandarin every day at 8 AM. I tell him to count me in.

Back in Beijing—still in shock from my mountain climbing trip and unexpected encounter with the fortuneteller—I sit with John in his apartment and tell him everything about meeting the monk and the old man's clairvoyant description of Karen's death.

"Why didn't you tell me your girlfriend died?" John asks, hurt I didn't confide in him.

"For the same reason you don't go around talking about your father's death or your sister's crippling. What good does it do?"

He nods in sad agreement.

"Now I understand why you're so different from your American classmates. You've experienced death at a young age like me and so many Chinese."

I didn't think of this before, but he's right. There's been so much recent suffering here that every Chinese person I know has experienced some deep personal loss. My misfortune doesn't isolate me but makes me feel closer to these people. I'm among fellow sufferers who can really understand my grief.

As I reflect on this, John meets my eyes and says: "Take that fortune-teller's words seriously. He has *teyi gongneng* [special cognition]. Divination [*suanming*], intuitive healing [*reiki*], geomancy [*fengshui*], telepathy [*diliu ganjue*]—most Chinese believe in these unseen skills. The Communist Party[28] has tried to eradicate these traditional practices as superstition [*mixin*], but it's impossible to get rid of them. These beliefs are deeply rooted in our culture, the product of thousands of years of experience and faith."

He refills my teacup then continues: "That monk lives deep in the mountains and meditates hours every day. He's attuned to energy most of us can't feel or see. Maybe that's why he intuited things about your past . . . and future."

A shiver runs through me. I don't pretend to understand all this, but I'm struck again by how much more is going on here than first meets the eye. And I'm no longer willing to dismiss things just because I can't see them.

By the end of my second semester studying in China, with the Lunar Chinese New Year approaching, I'm seriously considering staying in Beijing. I'm learning much more here than in the privileged, sheltered environment of Duke, and everything and everyone at home still reminds me of Karen's death.

I decide to call my parents long-distance to discuss this.

We exchange weekly letters, but they take up to a month to arrive so it's difficult to discuss something as important as leaving college that way. I'd promised to phone home only in case of emergency, but I consider this an extenuating circumstance.

I bike to the Russian-built Beijing Telecommunications building near Tiananmen Square and pay ¥100 (US$20) to reserve an international phone line. The much more expensive actual phone call will be reverse-charged to my parents. It takes several hours for an international phone line to become available. I sit on the wooden wait-bench until the clerk calls my name. I slip into the soundproofed booth, pick up the heavy rotary receiver, and hear the Chinese operator ask my parents if they'll accept the charge. "Scotty?" I hear my mom's familiar voice. "Is something wrong?"

---

28. With its emphasis on Western (Marxist) Materialism.

"No, I just got homesick," I joke, but then quickly reassure them—my dad's on the other line—that everything's fine. But at the rate of US$10 per minute I get right to the point. I tell them I'm considering staying in China instead of returning to Duke, at least until the end of the school year, and maybe longer.

"What?" my father shouts, "You're crazy! What about your Duke degree?"

It's unspoken but clearly understood in our family that my father expects me to follow in his footsteps: Duke undergraduate degree, Duke Law School, and then a partnership in his law firm. I don't have the guts to tell him I'm considering different career plans.

My mom, ever the mediator between her no-nonsense, war veteran husband and free-spirited, idealistic son, proposes a compromise: "Why don't you come home and finish school, and if you still want to return to China after that we can discuss it?" This might not seem like much of a compromise, but even the possibility of my pursuing such an unorthodox career path qualifies as a major concession from my father. So I accept the offer and agree that her suggestion makes sense. Not wanting to drag out the expensive phone call that already costs more than US$100, I tell them that I'll see them in a couple of weeks and hang up.

It's a cold rainy morning when my American classmates and I prepare to leave Beijing and return to the States. John and his mom accompany us to the bus to the airport. The three of us huddle under one umbrella, pressing close for warmth. Before I get on board I hand John my cherished guitar in its homemade, hand-embroidered cotton case. I wait until this last moment because I know he'll refuse it. He tries to say no, but I insist. So he cradles the guitar to his chest like he's holding a baby.

"I'll take good care of it, I know you'll be back for it."

I laugh and sniff back tears as I climb the steps. Then I wave goodbye through the rain-streaked window as the bus pulls out of the school gate. I wonder if I'll ever see John and his mom again.

chapter five

浪子回头金不换
langzi huitou jin buhuan
RETURN OF THE PRODIGAL SON

The Duke Chapel towers over our graduation ceremony. Pink and purple azaleas are blooming, sugar magnolias perfume the air, and daffodils and tulips paint the landscape in a rainbow of colors.

It's been more than a year since my return from China, and in honor of my agreement with my parents I've made it to this day.

My whole family is here—my parents, older and younger brothers, and maternal grandparents. My dad's older brother and his three sons—all Duke alums—are also here. Today I join this proud family tradition.

This should be a day of celebration.

But I can't help thinking that it was a perfect May day just like this that Karen died. I still think about her constantly, feel her touch, smell her skin. Her devout Catholic mom told me that Karen would go on living through me. I thought she meant this figuratively, but now I believe it literally. She's with me in spirit like a guardian angel. I'm determined to be worthy of her. I know Karen would be proud of me today. But I can't help wishing she could share this.

Of course I can't leave Duke without stirring up controversy. Our graduation speaker is South African anti-apartheid activist and Nobel

Peace Prize laureate Archbishop Desmond Tutu. Some classmates and I organize an anti-apartheid rally in front of the Duke Chapel before our graduation. I carry a banner reading DUKE DIVEST FROM SOUTH AFRICA. Archbishop Tutu sees our protest and walks over to show his support. He puts his arm around me to pose for a photograph. Our picture appears together on the front page of both the Duke and local Durham newspapers.

My mom is taking snapshots of our demonstration, and my dad is fuming that his son can't graduate from his beloved alma mater without making a show of his liberal politics.

"Can't you do anything like normal people?" he asks sarcastically.

I just smile, knowing that he grudgingly respects me for standing up for my beliefs, however naïve he thinks they are.

Our graduation ceremony is in Duke's football stadium. Flasks of bourbon—an old commencement tradition—pass up and down the rows. I don't drink, but enjoy the festivities. Several classmates unexpectedly confide in me that they feel sad. They see graduation as the end of their youth, with only the drudgery of a job, marriage and family, bills, and other weighty responsibilities lying ahead. I sympathize with them, but don't share their view. I've already experienced the shock of losing my best friend and don't take a single day for granted. I'm determined to embrace life for myself and Karen. In this spirit I'm waiting for the right moment to share some big news with my parents.

We're walking across campus as we've done so many times for basketball and football games since my childhood. Ever practical, my dad raises the subject of law school again. "Why don't you just take the Law Boards [LSATs] so you'll have a backup plan?"

"I know what you're going to say, Scott . . ." my mom begins, but I interrupt her.

"I got a job."

My parents stop and stare at me.

"I got a job," I repeat. "Teaching English at the university in Beijing that I studied at. It comes with a round-trip plane ticket, free housing, and a two-hundred-dollar-a-week salary."

I know this amount of money is a pittance to my parents, but it's more than enough for me to live on in China, especially with my extreme frugality.

I watch their expressions turn from surprise to relief.

"Congratulations," my dad says, ruffling my hair. "I'm proud of you. You got a job. You graduated from college, you're an adult now, you're on your own."

When he was my age he joined the army, entered basic training, and then served in Korea for two years. Compared to that, teaching at a university in China isn't so daunting.

"Go and get China out of your system," he adds, and we all laugh, greatly relieved to shelve discussion of this contentious topic for the time being.

I know my dad still harbors hope that I'll change my mind, attend law school, and join his firm like my younger brother plans to do. But he knows I'm the least conventional of his three sons, and if he pushes I'll dig in my heels and insist on pursuing my own path, a stubborn streak I inherited from him. My parents accept that I have to make my own way in the world, and respect me for following my heart back to China even if they worry about what kind of career that will lead to.

I return to New Haven just long enough to pack for my trip. Everything here still reminds me of Karen. I visit her parents one last time, but seeing each other is too painful for all of us. I'm moving on, and they're frozen in the past, burdened by a loss they'll never escape. I promise to keep in touch, knowing it's going to be difficult. Mercifully I'll be living in a place with no affordable long-distance telephone service, and mail takes a month round-trip. If I had to stay in the States and be confronted by Karen's death every day, the pain might be unbearable.

My departure date arrives, and my mom offers to drive me to New York so I don't have to take a train to the airport. This is the first time we've had a chance to really talk since I broke my news about returning to China.

"You know I'm not cut out to be a lawyer," I tell her.

"I know you're not," she says. But then she adds something unexpected: "You'd better be prepared to support yourself. Once you leave the nest there's no coming back." This shocks me. I always thought I would have a safe place to return to if something went wrong. Now that safety net has been pulled out from under me. The stakes in my move to China just got a lot higher.

The plane lands in Beijing, and the first thing that hits me is the heat and humidity. My T-shirt is soaked with sweat before I reach the terminal. There's still no air-conditioning here. Mandarin flight announcements and tinny Taiwan bubblegum pop blare from wall-mounted speakers. The pungent odor of kerosene—used in mop water to keep the Gobi Desert dust down—combines with sweat, garlic, tobacco smoke, and human waste to create the distinct aroma that says 'Welcome to Beijing.'

I get in the customs line and have a panic attack: *What if I fail here?*

I let the anxiety pass through me, then take a deep breath and relax.

There's no turning back. I'm determined to become a writer. Moving to Beijing in the mid-1980s is like young American writers Hemingway, Fitzgerald, Eliot, and Pound moving to Paris in the beginning of the twentieth century.

I get to the window and see a female customs agent with bright brown eyes, shiny black hair, and a form-fitting navy blue skirt. I turn on the charm and practice my rusty Mandarin.

"*Renjia xinkule* [You're working really hard]."

She raises her eyebrows in surprise at my Chinese. Few Westerners speak it with anything approaching fluency. "*Mei you* [not at all]," she says.

Then she compliments me on my Mandarin even though I know I'm out of practice. I'm not worried, I'll regain fluency quickly.

Perhaps due to my flirting, or the "foreign expert" status on my work visa because I'm teaching at a university here, she quickly stamps my passport and waves me through.

"*Duo baozhong* [Take care]," she says as I head toward the exit.

I walk out the doors and am engulfed by the familiar sights, sounds, and smells of the capital. I love hearing Beijing-accented Mandarin. Then my nostrils are assaulted by the stench of diesel fumes as I take my place at the back of the taxi line. When I get to the front, I toss my backpack into the trunk of a beat-up Toyota Corolla and sit in the front seat next to the driver.

"*Beijing Shifan Xueyuan* [Beijing Teacher's College]," I say in my most carefully enunciated tones.

"*Wo cao! Laowai hui jiang zhongwen!* [Fuck, the foreigner speaks Chinese!]" He sticks his thumb up and adds in heavily accented English: "OH-kay!"

He hits the accelerator and leaves a cloud of exhaust smoke behind us. Then, as he merges with the high-speed traffic on the new airport expressway, I ask him to tell me about himself.

"My surname's Song, like the dynasty. I'm from Hebei (the province surrounding Beijing), but got sent to the capital when I joined the army twenty years ago. I've been driving supply trucks ever since. I just got demobilized,[29] and the army gave me this taxi to drive."

I love Beijing cabbies, I think to myself and smile. You can count on them for an interesting life story and opinions on everything. They're the real tour guides of this town.

"How do you like your job?" I ask.

"I don't mind driving, but rising prices are killing us," he says, and he launches into a lament I'll hear many times in the months ahead. "Taxi fares are frozen while government subsidies are lifted on fuel, maintenance, parts, not to mention the daily expenses of rent, food, utilities. . . . It's getting harder for us average workers to make ends meet. But corrupt officials keep getting fatter off our sweat and blood!"

I sigh and tell him it's not much different in the States.

"*Tianxia wuya yiban hei* [Crows are black everywhere]," I say, and he laughs at the sad truth of this proverb.

Then we lapse into silence and I stare out the window. There's been tremendous change even since I left a little over a year ago. Skyscrapers are going up everywhere, and construction sites cover what used to be farmland. Automobile traffic and street-level commercial activity have also greatly increased.

---

29. In Deng Xiaoping's early 1980s push to reduce China's standing armed forces.

We pull up at the Beijing Teacher's College gate, and I tell the driver to let me out. I want to surprise John, and cars on campus are so rare—used only by officials and VIPs—that they attract attention just by driving inside. So I walk the kilometer across campus to John's apartment.

Even though we've exchanged regular letters over the past year, I haven't told John and his mom about my new job and that I'm returning to live here.

I arrive at their door, put my backpack down, and rap out the Bo Diddley blues beat John and I used as our private code last year.

Bop-be-bop-bop, be-bop-bop.

"*Wode tian!* Oh my God!" I hear John's familiar voice shout.

The door swings open and I see his smiling face. A warm feeling rushes over me. *This is my second home.*

We hug each other like long-lost brothers, then he pulls me inside and guides me to the couch.

"What are you doing here?" he asks as he pours me a cup of tea.

"I got a job teaching English at your school, and wanted to surprise you."

"Well, I'm sure surprised! That's great!"

We sit drinking tea and sharing our experiences since we last saw each other. We're bursting with news. Our conversation is fueled by tea and then bottles of warm Beijing beer—John's family still can't afford a refrigerator.

"I can't believe they're providing me my own housing," I say between sips of the cheap but refreshing local German-style lager I've missed.

John slaps me on the back in congratulations and nods toward the corner of the room where our old army cot is tucked away.

"Your bed is still here if you want it."

"Thanks, I might just take you up on that."

We share stories past midnight, until we can barely keep our eyes open. Then I finally need to rest, and as John prepares for work I crash on his cot.

I wake up at noon and go to meet my new bosses in the English department. They help me move into my apartment in a guarded, gated guesthouse at the center of campus. It exclusively caters to foreigners and officials.

I unpack and start to set up my new apartment as a home office. A cinder block–sized, World War II–vintage manual typewriter supplied by the school sits on the wooden writing desk. Inside it I secrete the contraband shortwave radio I've smuggled in.

I'm anxious to get started with my new life and work here. My relatively light teaching load—five one-hour classes per week—will afford me plenty of time to pursue my ambition of becoming a published writer. I've secured work as a stringer for both my Duke student newspaper and hometown *New Haven Register.*

John and I resume our old routine of hanging out and playing music every night. He also informs me of the latest cultural developments in Beijing. His band is riding the wave of economic development, playing in newly opened five-star hotels catering to foreigners. This in spite of the fact that he and his bandmates, like all average Chinese, can't enter these hotels without a foreign escort. He makes more money in a single night playing music than he earns in a month in his job as a high school teacher. An average teacher makes ¥40 (US$5) a month, and with tips he can make ¥80 (US$10) a night playing music.

John also tells me about a new wave of literature that's sweeping the nation. It's known as Scar Literature (*shanghen wenxue*)—shocking revelations of the suffering people endured during the Cultural Revolution. He gives me mimeographed copies of some of the best new writing: *The Wall* by talented female poet Shu Ting. *Why Is Life's Road Getting Narrower and Narrower* by the female essayist Pan Xiao. *Black Walls*, a novella by renowned *People's Literature* magazine editor Liu Xinwu.[30] And celebrated artist Zhong Ah-cheng's picaresque masterpiece *The King of Children*—a novel about his experiences as a schoolteacher in the impoverished southwestern border province of Yunnan[31] during the Cultural Revolution. It's a literary renaissance, and many of the publications are reprinted as *samizdat*[32]—stapled mimeographs shared among youth in the capital and provinces.

---

30. *Black Walls*, a novella by Liu Xinwu.

31. Literally: South of the Clouds.

32. The clandestine copying and distribution of literature banned by the state, especially in Communist countries.

Many of these writers began publishing in the underground maga-zines *Beijing Spring, Exploration, Enlightenment,* and *Today* during the brief flowering of freedom that became known as the 1978–79 Democ-racy Wall movement.[33] Deng Xiaoping allowed this limited dissent when he first returned to power after Mao's death because the criticism of the old system helped him purge remnant leftists in the Party and consolidate his control. Then once his political objective was achieved, he ruthlessly cracked down on the independent publications, arresting the founders and giving them decades-long prison sentences.

"*Qiaoshan zhenhu,* shake the mountain to frighten the tigers," John says to describe this, shaking his head at the thought of all the youth-ful idealism extinguished. But underground publications have continued to circulate among students and politically engaged citizens hungry for uncensored writing.

The first poem John shares with me is "The Cry of a Generation" by Shu Ting:

I do not complain
About my misfortune
The loss of my youth,
The deforming of my soul.
Sleepless nights without number. . . .
So that innocent children
A hundred years from now
Need not guess at the history we leave behind.
For this blank in our nation's memory,
For the arduous path our race must travel,
For the purity of the skies

---

33. The Democracy Wall (西单民主墙 xī dān mín zhǔ qiáng) was a long brick wall at Xidan in-tersection in Beijing's Western District that became the focus for democratic dissent. In October 1978 democracy activists such as Ren Wanding, Xu Wenli, and Wei Jingsheng recorded news and ideas, often in the form of big-character posters (*dazibao*) and mimeographed homemade publications during a period known as the Beijing Spring. A shutdown was initiated in spring 1978 when the main organizers were arrested and Wei Jingsheng and Xu Wenli were both given fifteen-year prison sentences.

And the straightness of the road ahead
I Demand The Truth![34]

"Wow, that's powerful," I remark.

John next draws my attention to the poem "My Generation" by Gu Cheng:

The dark night has given me dark eyes,
I use them to seek light.[35]

This poetry is revelatory. It reassures me that it's not just John and I who see the hollowness of official culture, and that many of his generation are moved to express dissent. It gives me hope that more humane values—like those espoused by the writers and artists of the early-twentieth-century New Culture movement before the Communist

---

34. "The Wall" by Shu Ting
I have no means to resist the wall,
Only the will.
What am I? And it?
Perhaps it is
My slowly aging skin,
Numb to wind and sleet
Impervious to orchid fragrance.
Or I am just a plantain,
A pretty
Parasite lodged in one of its crevices,
My fortuity determining its necessity.
At night the wall begins to move
Stretching a soft imaginary foot,
Squeezes,
Twists me,
Forces me into a variety of shapes.
Terrified, I flee to the street,
To find the same nightmare
Hanging on every heel,
Each cowering gaze
An ice-cold wall.
Finally I know
What I have to resist first:
My compromise with walls, my
Insecurity in this world.

35. 黑夜给了我黑色的眼睛, 我却用它寻找光明.

revolution—can take the place of violent Maoist ideology. I'm eager to read more of this new literature and discuss it with John, but my English classes are starting.

I arrive early on the first day, eager to meet my new students. My two dozen pupils are all university faculty members, rewarded for their loyal service to the Party with the privilege of studying with a native-English-speaking American. I immediately see the promise and challenge of this work.

My students' English ability ranges from conversational to barely comprehensible. And to complicate matters, each class includes a political monitor (*banzhang*), a trusted Communist Party functionary responsible for maintaining discipline and reporting on everyone in the class to the school authorities. They're of course all forbidden to get too friendly with the foreign teacher. My class' commissar is a short, potbellied man with a thick southern accent and poor English. He approaches my desk before class, introduces himself, and notifies me that he'll be reporting on my performance, indeed all my activities, to the school authorities.

"It's for your security," Comrade Chen reassures me with a stiff smile.

Stunned, I remind myself that I'm living in a very foreign culture. This exchange also reminds me of how important it is to be constantly cautious. I need to keep my students at arm's length until I know which ones I can trust. John has drilled this lesson into me.

I give my students English names on the hunch that it might coax them out of their traditional timidity to speak in class. There's a Chinese saying that sums up this reticence: *bushuo bucuo*—if you don't say anything, then you can't say anything wrong. This teaching trick works. I let them pick their own names, and immediately they begin talking excitedly among themselves. The outcome is both hilarious and deeply revealing.

"My name is Betsy Ross," a matronly math professor stands up and says.

"That's an interesting choice, Betsy," I respond, resisting my urge to laugh. "Can you tell us why you picked that name?"

"Betsy Ross sewed the first American flag. I love America, and also love to sew," the white-haired woman says, blushing with embarrassment and then breaking into a broad grin.

The rest of the students come up with similarly imaginative names. Our class now contains a Robin Hood: "Because he took from the rich and gave to the poor, just like socialism." McDonnell Douglas: "It's my dream to fly an F-16 fighter jet." Magic Johnson: "I love the NBA." And Bible figures including Mary, Joseph, Matthew, Luke, and Paul.

I'm fascinated by the powerful attraction Western—especially American—culture holds for these people. The Chinese have been subjected to nonstop propaganda about how evil and corrupt the United States is, and religious worship is denounced as the "opiate of the masses." But I'm starting to realize that in China, just like back home, there's no better way to increase interest in something than to ban it. My students are living illustrations of this.

Since traveling abroad is an impossible dream for all but the most politically well-connected Chinese, interacting with an American teacher, learning English, and studying American culture is the next best thing. I'm an instant hit with my students, and am thrilled when I start receiving meal invitations to their homes. It's the kind of privileged access a young writer dreams of. It's hard to know who's more excited by these new friendships, my students or me.

I start bringing my guitar to class every day. At the end of each day's lesson we put our textbooks away and I teach them a new song. I hand out the lyric sheets and then play the tunes: "Blowin' in the Wind," "Country Roads," "This Land Is Your Land," "The Sound of Silence," "American Pie." We review the words and I explain their meaning.

Then I decide to test the boundaries and introduce the Beatles song "Come Together."

Betsy Ross stands up and says, in halting English: "I don't understand the words: '*He wear no shoeshine, he got toe-jam football, he got monkey finger, he shoot Coca-Cola.*'"

I can't help laughing, but quickly compose myself.

"I don't understand them either, but I guess the song is about drugs."

The class nods knowingly, aware that recreational drug use is a scourge of contemporary Western society. In China drugs are associated with the mid-nineteenth-century Opium Wars,[36] considered the height of humiliation in China's two centuries of subjugation by foreign colonial powers.[37] All Chinese schoolchildren are taught that this historical crime must be avenged. For this reason no self-respecting Chinese would consider taking drugs, not that they're available anyway.

---

36. British smuggling of Indian opium erupted into war (1839–1842), and China's defeat meant having to tolerate the drug trade and surrender "concessions" like Hong Kong.

37. The U.S., England, France, Germany, Russia, and Japan.

chapter six

石在，火種是不會絕的

As long as there shall be stones, the seeds of fire will not die
                              —Lu Hsün, December 1935

Scars

Let me tell you, world,
I—do—not—believe!
If one thousand challengers stand at your feet,
Count me as number one thousand and one.
I do not believe that the sun is red
I do not believe in the sound of thunder
I do not believe that dreams are in vain
I do not believe that death has no revenge.
        —"The Answer," Bei Dao, in *The Anthology of New Wave*
                Poetry, Beijing University Press, 1984

After my last class of the day, I stroll across campus to meet John at the soccer field. The autumn sun is setting, and in a grove of pine trees I see a group of students sitting in a circle around a candle. They're reciting poetry with quiet passion. I'm not in a hurry so I sit down to listen. The students take turns reading from the poem "Begin from Here" by Jiang He:

Begin from here then,
Begin from my own story,

Begin from the human aspirations
Of millions, dead and alive;
Begin from the name that thrilled through me before my birth.
That the forgotten,
The injured,
The lone,
May stretch from their huddled fearful numbness
Stretch out for life.

Then they start to recite "Believe in the Future" by Guo Lusheng:

When the cobwebs showed no mercy
and sealed up my hearth,
when the silent dregs of fires past
sighed poverty and despair,
I leveled out the hopeless ash
and traced there in a snowflake hand:
Believe in the future.[38]

---

38. . . . When my purple grapes fermented
into cold late-autumn dew,
and the flowers I had hoped to pluck
filled someone else's arms,
I dipped my finger in the frozen sea
and scrawled across this dreary land:
Believe in the future.
With these fingers, I will point the way
to waves on the horizon.
With these hands, I will grasp the seas
that bear the weight of the sun.
As morning's promise warms the shaft
of my most splendid writing brush,
I will scribble in a childish hand:
Believe in the future.
The reason I believe so firmly in the future
is that I trust her vision. I have faith in her eyes.
She has lashes to bat away the dust of history,
and pupils to see through the chapters of time.
What will they say about our rotting flesh—
the paths from which we strayed, our agonized defeats?
Some will be moved to tears and sympathy,
others will smirk and make of us a mockery.
But I trust that when they examine our spines—

I'm again mesmerized by the quiet power of this poetry. *I guess that great suffering begets great art.* I've seen John and his friends cleverly improvise blues lyrics, but this is some of the most creative imagery I've ever encountered in any language.

I ask a young woman with round wire-rimmed glasses and long brown hair if I can look at her book. To my surprise she answers in fluent English: "Of course you can, you can borrow it if you want to." She explains that the book, *The Anthology of New Wave Poetry*, has sold out several print runs totaling hundreds of thousands of copies. It was only published last year. It's unimaginable in America for a volume of poetry to sell so many copies so quickly.

She tells me that her English name is Lisa—because it sounds like her Chinese name Li Sha—and she's a teacher in the university English department too. She agrees to help me read the anthology in exchange for my helping her with spoken English. We make an appointment to meet at her dormitory the next evening.

My meeting with Lisa is my first introduction—other than my sessions with John—into Beijing's new generation of rebellious young writers. She's a talented poet in addition to being a self-taught scholar on this new literary movement.

Alarmed by the popularity of this subversive new poetry, the Communist Party has banned the collection from public sale and classified it as *neibu*—for internal circulation only. Lisa explains that's why the book can only be bought in campus bookstores in plain white paper covers.[39] I'm reminded of similar controversies in the U.S.—Henry Miller's *Tropic of Cancer* and Allen Ginsberg's *Howl* were both banned in the 1950s—and this cutting-edge writing resembles theirs.

---

after inquiries and missteps, triumphs and defeats—
we will be judged with humanity, objectivity and fairness.
I anxiously await their judgment.
Believe in this, my friend: your future.
Have faith in all your efforts,
have faith that youth can vanquish death.
Put your faith in the future
and hold fast to this, your life.

39. Hence its label *bai pi shu* (literally: white-cover book).

The Anthology of New Wave Poetry is so popular that students create and disseminate homemade copies, painstakingly transcribing the hundreds of pages of poems by hand.

"We believe that these words can heal our lost generation," Lisa tells me. "After the monstrousness of Mao, we've lost faith in our leaders. We want to create a pure new language of our own." Before I leave she bookmarks several of her favorite poems for me to read at home.

Beijing's official censors label the poetry *menglong*—obscure—and denounce it as ideologically unhealthy.

I'm elated to have made this new friend and look forward to exploring the deeper meaning of these poems with her.

As the weather gets colder and northern days shorter, I spend my days teaching classes and evenings playing music with John and his friends. But I also start to spend more time with Lisa in her dorm room, reading and discussing the significance of the impassioned new writing. Her roommate Amy, also an English teacher in our department, joins in our conversations.

They also tell me their stories of being sent to the countryside during the (1966–76) Cultural Revolution. Lisa started working on a communal farm at the age of fifteen. I ask if I can interview her about her life during that troubled time. She's hesitant at first, but then seems to set aside her fear and agrees.

I discover she's ten years older than me, a member of the *laosanjie*—Three Old Classes—students who were in high school when Mao launched his Great Proletarian Cultural Revolution in the summer of 1966. When the U.S. was experiencing another kind of Cultural Revolution of rock music, long hair, Vietnam War protests, and sexual freedom, Chairman Mao was in Tiananmen Square inciting his young shock troops—the Red Guards—to mass violence. Mao declared that China's old society had to be completely destroyed. Schools were closed and young people encouraged to "make revolution." They attacked authority figures—teachers, government officials, even their own parents—and this led to such brutality and chaos that Mao had to call in the army to restore order. To ensure the turmoil didn't continue, urban high school students were exiled to the countryside to "learn from the peasants." Lisa was sent to the poor south-western province of Yunnan—bordering Burma and Laos where purged members of China's imperial court were traditionally exiled.

We sit side by side at her dorm room desk, viewing old black-and-white photographs of her and her family as she describes her experiences in the countryside during those ten nightmarish years.

"At first I was excited. I believed in Mao's revolution and thought that working with the peasants was an honor and privilege," she recalls.

"But when I got to the village my eyes were opened to China's true circumstances. The peasants were so poor, lacking basic necessities like food, cooking utensils, and clothing. Meat was an unimaginable luxury that was only available on Chinese New Year. Otherwise we subsisted on corn gruel—the same thing we fed the pigs—and whatever vegetables we could forage in the forest.

"Most of the peasants were illiterate. I taught the village children in an outdoor classroom, and started them off with the most basic Chinese characters. The dropout rate was high as most peasants couldn't see the value of their children learning to read and write when they were just going to work on a collective farm anyway."

She pauses to drink some tea then continues: "I had to collect night soil from the village latrines and carry it to the fields. The heavy buckets had to be balanced on bamboo shoulder poles. I wasn't strong enough to carry them without stumbling, and urine and feces splashed all over me. The stench was nauseating. We were also required to help drain swamp-land. It was backbreaking labor. Every day I returned from work covered in foul-smelling muck. It was impossible to get clean. My fingernails were black the entire time.

"This way of life was a shock for city kids. The peasants didn't want us there, they were barely getting by as it was, and now they had to share their meager rations with us. The Communist Party boss let the female students know that he would grant special privileges for sex. Benefits included better work assignments, more food rations, and passes back to the city to visit family. Most of the girls succumbed. I resisted his advances but he raped me anyway," she says matter-of-factly.

"I stayed there for twelve years."

I'm shocked by her story, but don't interrupt.

She closes her eyes, takes a few deep breaths to compose herself, then continues: "In 1976, when Mao became debilitated, students began returning home on their own. My parents were university professors and were also sent to the countryside to labor on a Party cadre work farm.[40] Both of them died there. I wasn't informed until I returned to Beijing two years later. The authorities kept this information from me to spare my feelings," she says, shaking her head sadly.

I struggle to absorb the weight of her story. Lisa appears to find relief in confiding these traumatic memories to me. I'm aware of the tremendous responsibility that comes with being chosen to listen to her long-repressed confessions.

She shifts in her chair and resumes talking, her voice now trembling with emotion. "Now an orphan, I threw myself into my studies. When the universities reopened I passed the entrance exam to Beijing Teacher's College as a member of the first university class post-Mao.[41] I channeled my anger into my studies, and excelled in English. After graduation I was invited to stay on as a faculty member," she concludes, then sits back, takes a sip of tea, and brushes a tear from her cheek.

As Lisa and I spend more time together, a strong bond grows between us. I see her as an elder sister, even at her encouragement call her *dajie*—big sister. The mere thought of a romantic relationship is taboo. Premarital sex between young Chinese remains a crime, never mind an affair between a local and a foreigner. It would be reckless to get involved with a Chinese woman given the danger it would pose to my work at the university and her personal safety. I resolve to keep our relationship platonic, and Lisa and I develop a deep trust and friendship that's rare here.

---

40. Popularly known as May 7 Cadre Schools—*Wuqi Ganxiao*—named for the date in 1966 that Mao decreed purged officials must be sent to rural work camps to perform manual labor and undergo ideological reeducation.

41. The class of 1977—*qiqiji* in Chinese.

One evening after several hours of interviewing, Lisa turns to me and says, "I hope you're being careful with your notes."

"What do you think I am, a *shamao'r* [careless fool]?" I respond, using the gutter slang I'm learning from John that prim and proper schoolteacher Lisa disapproves of.

"Please don't get me in trouble. The worst that can happen to you is you get sent home. But I could be shipped back to the countryside, or worse . . ." her voice trails off in imagined dread.

"I promise to be careful."

Several weeks later I return from my morning classes to find my apartment door wide open and room ransacked. My desk and dresser drawers lie overturned on the floor. In panic I check if anything critical like my passport has been stolen, but suddenly realize what's missing: My notes documenting Lisa's Cultural Revolution experiences.

What a fool I am!

I run to find her. The door to her dorm room is open. Her roommate Amy is sitting on her bed with her head cradled in her hands.

She looks up in a daze and says: "Lisa's gone."

"What do you mean *gone*?"

"We woke up to pounding on our door. Before we could get out of bed uniformed guards rushed in. They grabbed Lisa and interrogated her about her relationship with you. Then they dragged her away."

Looking out at the dirty iron grate that covers their ground-floor window, Amy lets out a low moan.

"When the school officials returned to collect her belongings they said: 'Your roommate is a spy and you'll never see her again,' and warned me that if I discussed the incident with anyone—especially 'the foreigner'—I would suffer the same fate."

How could I be so stupid?

I want to scream or throw something at the wall. I should have kept my notes better hidden. But they were concealed in the dust jacket of my Bible. How could I know that wasn't safe enough? If they searched that carefully, no hiding place in that small room would have gone undiscovered.

I know from John about people disappearing into police custody like this, it happens all the time. You only have to criticize a Party official in the presence of a secret informant and you can be dragged off to a labor camp, only to return years later or not at all.

I tell Amy that I'm going to find out what happened. I run back to John's house and tell him everything and seek his advice. He gives me an angry look I've never seen from him before.

"Why did you keep those notes in your room?"

I have no answer. What can I say? That my sheltered suburban-American upbringing didn't prepare me to live in a police state?

John advises me to forget about Lisa.

"You'll never see her again," he says with quiet conviction.

"What do you mean?" I start to say, then stop talking when I realize that Lisa's disappearance has probably triggered traumatic memories of John's own family tragedy.

I understand his frustration with me but refuse to accept that nothing can be done. I return to the girls' dormitory to persuade Amy to help me find where Lisa's been taken.

She opens the door, and I can see her eyes are red and swollen from crying. She wipes her face with her sleeve as she shuffles back inside the empty room. I follow her and we sit on her bed.

"Mother*fuckers!*" she screams as she slams her fist down on her desk.

I recoil in surprise. I've never heard her raise her voice before, never mind use profanity. Then she drops her head on the table in exhaustion.

"You know how easy it would be for them to make *me* disappear? I could be arrested just for talking to you!"

"I know," I say, patting her back to comfort her.

"But what they did was so wrong," she reasons, to herself as much as to me.

We keep talking and Amy starts to calm down. Her mood then turns from fear to anger.

"*Tamade!* [Dammit!]" she exclaims and sits bolt upright. "These Communists are such cowardly bullies. They target the weak, and appoint themselves judge, jury, and executioner."

I fear she'll say or do something reckless, but I keep her talking. After venting her frustration, her normal even temper returns and she finally agrees to help me find out what happened to Lisa and where she's been taken.

Several days later, on my way to class, an anonymous woman bumps into me and slips a folded piece of paper into my hand. Without a word she disappears into the crowd. I look around to make sure no one's noticed, then unfold the note.

It's from Lisa, written in her elegant, unmistakable script.

> Because of our relationship, I've been transferred to a military academy in Linyi city, Shandong province. It's an army garrison 500 miles south of Beijing.

I know about this place from John. It's so militarily sensitive that it remains off-limits to foreigners. At the bottom of the note Lisa's written her address and drawn a map detailing directions to her dorm room. Part of me knows that visiting her would be insane. Any more reckless behavior on my part could cause her more harm. But I blame myself for Lisa's plight, and want to apologize to her in person and make sure she's all right. My motivation isn't purely selfless. I'm worried about her. Is she in trouble? I miss her. It's another painful loss, like Karen.

chapter seven

一不怕苦, 二不怕死

Yi bu pa ku, er bu pa si.
Fear neither hardship nor death.
—Chairman Mao

I wrestle with my conscience and change my mind several times, but finally decide to visit Lisa.

At the end of the work week I prepare to leave for Shandong. After my final class Friday afternoon I return to John's, pack my knapsack, and go to sleep early so I'll be well rested for the predawn train ride. I have a hard time sleeping. My mind races with visions of soldiers, spotlights, and gunshots.

I finally surrender to exhaustion. After what seems like less than an hour I peer at the bedside clock: 3 AM.

I quietly slip from under the quilt and dress quickly. I don't want to wake John. I haven't let him in on my plan to visit Lisa because I know he'll try to talk me out of it. He's used to me returning to my dorm or practicing *kung fu* before dawn and won't think anything of my getting up at this hour.

It's the middle of winter and the temperature is below zero. A gust of wind rattles the rickety windowpanes. I bundle myself in long wool underwear, a thick turtleneck, cashmere sweater, long green padded army coat, and cover my head with a fur-lined People's Liberation Army cap.

Then I pull on thick gloves and fit a white cloth surgical mask over my mouth and nose. Cotton gauze masks are ubiquitous here. People wear them both because of the pollution and whenever they feel a cold coming on. A glance in the mirror confirms that I don't stand out as a foreigner. I look like any other anonymous face in the sea of Chinese travelers.

I hop on my bike and set off on the ten-kilometer ride to the Beijing railway station. A headwind makes pedaling difficult. In spite of the cold, sweat drips down my back. By the time I reach the station I'm out of breath, but my blood is pumping and I feel wide awake. The huge station with its sprawling outdoor plaza occupies a city block. It was built by the Soviets in the 1950s, a classic example of Russian wedding cake architecture. Its arched entryway branches into two wings, with red and green fairy lights tracing the station's outline against the night sky.

A million migrant workers pass through here every day. Even at this predawn hour its plaza is filled with people.

I lock my bike in the station's parking shed and head for the ticket window. Several dozen people are lined up ahead of me. I take my place at the back of the line, and after a half hour arrive at the window. Fearful of being discovered purchasing a ticket to a closed military area, I cough and clear my throat, feigning illness, before mumbling a request for a third class, hard-berth seat. The saleswoman doesn't even look up from chatting with her workmate as she takes my money and hands me the cardboard ticket to Shandong.

I walk into the main hall of the station. It's packed with travelers sitting on canvas strap-lashed luggage. They're gnawing on roasted sunflower seeds, slurping tea from glass jars, playing Chinese poker and chess. Some are sleeping on the floor. The ceiling is obscured by a yellow cloud of cigarette smoke.

When I reach the train platform I take a seat on the wooden waitbench and pull out my dog-eared copy of *A Call to Arms* (*Nahan*), a short story collection by Lu Hsün, China's most popular early twentieth-century writer. Lu was one of Chairman Mao's favorite writers, in spite of his refusal to join the Communist Party.

It's a struggle to read this complicated literature without a dictionary, but because using one would expose my identity I have to make do. It's great practice.

At 5 AM the loudspeakers announce my train. I stuff the book into my backpack and climb up into the cabin.

I arrive in Linyi after dark and grab a pedicab. After a fifteen-minute ride we reach the military academy. I have the driver drop me a block from the gate. I smooth the wrinkles out of my army coat, look my disguise over once more, then say a silent prayer. Searchlights pierce the night sky and illuminate the entrance. Soldiers stand guard on both sides of the gate, the steel barrels of their AK-47 rifles glinting in the harsh white lights.

There's no turning back now.

I wonder if this is a moment that will change my life. Maybe I'll get arrested, or shot. I will fear out of my mind, stride forward, and fall into step with a group of students. We pass the guards without attracting so much as a sideward glance.

Once a safe distance from the gate I stop to check Lisa's directions again. This place resembles a boot camp. There are long lines of stark grey barracks and no trees. The ground is hard-packed dirt, probably from military marching drills.

I follow the black numbers stenciled on the otherwise identical buildings. After a few minutes I arrive at Lisa's dorm. I don't enter immediately for fear of encountering her roommates or neighbors. Instead I walk the perimeter of the building and size up the situation. I figure out which room is hers, tiptoe up to the ground-floor window, and peer inside.

Lisa is standing in the middle of the room, her back toward me. I wait a minute to make sure no one else is there and then tap on the glass. She stiffens with alarm, then comes to the window and shields her eyes. When her forehead touches the glass I put my face up close and pull off the surgical mask. She jumps back in shock, then realizes it's me. She quickly opens the window and helps me climb in.

"*Liumang!* [Scoundrel!]" she says, but I can tell she's happy to see me.

I'm relieved because I was afraid she would be angry at me for all the trouble I've caused. Then the smile I've missed so much lights up her face.

"I knew you'd come."

I'm surprised at my emotional response. I start to cry. To distract us both I grab Lisa in a bear hug and pick her up off the floor. She feigns a scream—I've never even touched her before, never mind hugged her—and admonishes me under her breath: "Stupid foreigner, you'll get us both arrested."

She puts her finger to her lips and whispers: "I'm on probation and forbidden guests. My roommates will report me, so you have to stay hidden. And we have to be totally silent while you're here."

I nod my head.

As part of her punishment Lisa isn't allowed her own room. She sleeps in the living room of a two-room suite shared with four other female teachers. She's created a degree of privacy by rigging a tent in the corner from bedsheets suspended from the ceiling.

I duck inside and we talk in whispers on her bed. She warns me that I can't even put my feet on the floor or her roommates will see that someone is visiting. These women are all in the army and will win political points by informing on her. They're at a political study session now, but could return at any time.

While Lisa fills a kettle to prepare tea on her electric hotplate, I can't stop staring at her. There's something so familiar about her, as if we've known each our whole lives. Her delicate, angular features and long braided hair remind me of Native American women in old photographs I've seen.

Sitting cross-legged on her bed, she tells me what happened since we last saw each other.

"I was sleeping when the police burst in. They started shouting accusations: *You supplied the foreign devil teacher information harmful to China!* I didn't deny it because I had nothing to hide. The Cultural Revolution is officially recognized as a tragedy, why shouldn't I talk about my experiences?

"They accused me of a counterrevolutionary act, harming the reputation of the motherland, and having an inappropriate relationship with a foreigner. Then they took me to the station and put me on a train here. I'm under house arrest, teaching English at this military academy hundreds of miles from my life and friends in Beijing and . . ." she sniffs back tears.

I reach out to comfort her and begin massaging her shoulders. We lean back against the wall, her body pressed against mine. She gradually stops crying and I wipe away her tears. Lisa leans forward to light a candle on her nightstand and sinks back into my arms. We sit this way for several minutes, holding each other silently, rocking back and forth. Her hair smells like sandalwood incense.

I've wanted to be alone with her like this for a long time. The feeling started in Beijing, but her roommate Amy was always there. Now I know Lisa shares this desire too. But I've never allowed myself to imagine this scenario, never mind act on it.

"Is this a good idea?" I hear her say, and then the final barrier between us falls. I kiss her, first softly, then with passion we've both long suppressed. Our hands reach for each other, pausing so she can put on classical music to mask our sounds. Then without words we take off our clothes and crawl under the cotton quilt. We make love silently, barely moving, afraid that any sound will reveal my presence and get us arrested.

Never in my life have I felt such powerful passion and grief simultaneously. It brings back painful memories of Karen. I'm trying to make sense of these confusing emotions when we fall asleep in each other's arms.

I open my eyes in complete darkness and am gripped by fear. *Where am I?* Then the reality rushes back to me. This isn't a nightmare I can wake up from. Lisa stirs beside me. We're both naked under the covers. The night air is freezing and our breath condenses in white steam.[42] We shiver and squeeze each other for warmth. We make love again, this time more slowly, savoring the precious intimacy. Lisa whispers that I have to leave before it gets light, but I'm already reaching for my clothes.

We kiss each other one last time and say good-bye. Then I slip out the window, disguised in my military clothes and surgical mask again.

---

42. This area south of the Yellow River gets limited indoor heating.

I hurry past the soldiers at the gate who stand unmoving. It's only their job to monitor who enters. The only sign they're alive is the vapor trail their breath leaves in the icy night air.

The streets are deserted. I walk to the station and recall every detail of the surreal night. Karen was a virgin when she died. Lisa is only the second person I've ever slept with. I've learned from painful experience to seize life's pleasures when they're available. You never know when they might suddenly be snatched away from you.

chapter eight

衣冠不整
Yiguan buzheng
UNORTHODOX IN DRESS AND MANNER

Back in Beijing, I seriously consider leaving China. There's too much baggage for this place to ever feel normal. Living here is a constant struggle.

But I'm unwilling to give up.

I feel an obligation to my students, John, and his music-playing friends—not to mention my complex new state of affairs with Lisa.

I confide my feelings to John, concealing the details about visiting Lisa. He tells me what I now expect to hear, and what will be repeated regularly to me in China: "How does your situation compare to my father being killed or my sister being crippled and brain damaged? Or to Lisa losing both her parents and spending a decade working on a pig farm in the countryside? *Hao shi duo mo*—all worthwhile undertakings are difficult."

"Another life lesson reduced to a four-syllable cliché," I mutter under my breath.

If these people are the repository of such ancient wisdom, then why is this place so fucked up?

I refrain from voicing this thought for fear of hurting John's feelings. Then he makes a quiet observation that interrupts my reverie.

"This is the most receptive China has been to outside influence in history. If people like you don't stay and help, we could fall back into our endless cycle of chaos, violence, and war. This is the best chance for progress in centuries, and you have an important role to play in that. How can you turn your back on us just because of one small setback?"

"*Yin xiao shi da*—don't miss the forest for the trees," he adds with a roguish smile.

"Fuck you and your goddamn proverbs," I say and we both burst out laughing. Then we reach for our guitars to lighten the mood with music.

I spend a quiet lunar New Year's Eve with John and his family. We prepare *jiaozi*—traditional pork and cabbage dumplings[43]—considered good luck because they're shaped like traditional gold ingots and augur good fortune for the coming year. John's mom tries to teach me how to roll the dough into silver-dollar-shaped circles, then wrap the delicate dumplings by adding just the right amount of filling and sealing them with a squeeze of the hands. I'm hopeless at both tasks. They joke that my dumplings are the ones that *liuchan* (abort) in the cauldron of boiling water.

We stay up all night eating, playing music, and singing. At midnight we go outside and light off fireworks to exorcise the ghosts of the old year and welcome in the New Year with a clean slate. It's the Year of the Tiger, believed by Chinese astrology to usher in dramatic change. We talk about our plans for the coming year, tell jokes, sing Chinese and American songs, gnaw on roasted sunflower and watermelon seeds, and play cards until dawn. No television, telephone, or cars to rush around in—just good friends and family enjoying a quiet holiday together.

After John's ego-boosting pep talk about my relevance, however small, to the historic drama unfolding around us, I resume teaching in the spring semester with renewed commitment. My students are making impressive progress and I'm proud of their improvement.

---

43. My vegetarianism has fallen by the wayside. It's too hard to maintain in this society of scarcity where just getting enough food to eat is a daily struggle.

I suppress my anger at the school authorities for their cruel treatment of Lisa. Her disappearance isn't broached by either side. I keep wondering if I'll be punished for our relationship, but no one says anything. Instead it's left to fester as just one more injustice in this already-brimming cauldron of resentment. This is how more than one billion people who have persecuted each other for the past several decades continue to live and work side by side. There's not enough space to indulge in anything more than stubborn, silent grudges.

I've learned a bitter lesson and with it several prerequisites on how to survive here:

Be on guard constantly. Trust no one. A single mistake—like leaving interview notes lying around—can ruin lives.

These weren't the survival skills I learned growing up in the States. I resign myself to this misfortune I can't fix, and settle back into the routine of a new semester and begin planning my next trip to see Lisa.

I'm sitting in John's apartment preparing my lesson plans for the coming week when I hear a soft knock on the door. It's Lisa's ex-roommate Amy.

"*Qüshile*," she says.

"What?!" I blurt.

"*Qüshile*. She passed away."

"Who passed away?"

"Lisa."

"No!" I shout.

"The university police came this morning and told me that she hung herself."

This can't be happening. I stagger and fall onto John's bed. Was it my fault? Did my visit cause this? I'm such an idiot! Of course I'm to blame for her death.

I hold my head in my hands in stunned silence, realizing that I have no way of learning the truth. Was my visit detected and Lisa punished, leading her to take her own life? Or is she rotting in a cell somewhere, and the authorities want me to forget about her so have staged this lie?

I beg Amy to assist me in finding out more, but she refuses.

"Don't you think you've caused enough trouble?"

I know she's right. Her words cut me like a knife.

When John gets home I confess everything to him: my train trip to see Lisa, every detail of our one-night romance, and the final news about her alleged death.

John just shakes his head in dismay.

When I'm done talking, he says: "There's nothing you can do."

"What do you mean, there's nothing I can do. . . ."

"Will you shut your big American mouth and listen to me for once?"

I stay silent.

"If the news is true then there's nothing you can do, right?"

"Right."

"And if it's not true, whether she's being held against her will or tortured, or she's initiated this herself because she knows your relationship can only lead to suffering for both of you, then this is the only way she knows to end it. You sticking your big American nose in can only make matters worse. *Jiachou bu ke waiyang.* Don't air dirty laundry in public. There are matters that must stay within the family. You're not, and won't ever be, part of *dajia*—the big Chinese family."

I know his words are true. I'll always be an outsider here.

Then John sees my look of despair and adds: "Without knowing for certain whether this news is true, you can harbor hope she's still alive and that you might hear from her again."

This gives me something to hold on to. There's a part of me that knows Lisa had problems from her past I could never understand, traumas she never shared with me. Perhaps she is capable of orchestrating this.

I initiate some effort through her English-department colleagues to locate surviving members of Lisa's family to confirm the suicide or at least find out what really happened, but all my inquiries meet dead ends. People aren't willing to stick their neck out for strangers who aren't members of their family or social network, never mind a foreigner nosing around.

I never find out what happened to Lisa and never hear from her again.

Despite this shock, I throw myself back into teaching with renewed commitment. When the school year ends, I collapse from the stress and exhaustion of the previous months and lie in bed with a high fever. The temptation to escape back to the States and visit my family and friends is stronger than ever, but I know that if I leave there's a good chance I won't come back. John reminds me repeatedly that if I quit now, just when I'm beginning to make real inroads, I'll fail myself and Lisa. It would be conceding defeat to her persecutors.

"*You shi bi you de*—with every loss comes opportunity," John says, teaching me another new proverb.

chapter nine

Rock and Roll on the New Long March

Rock-and-roll provokes the nerves . . . one may find one's body moving to the music against one's will.
—*How to Recognize Pornographic Music,* 1986 Communist Party Propaganda Department booklet

I'm sitting on John's bed reading the *Beijing Evening News* when he rushes in clutching a cassette tape.

"I've just discovered China's Bob Dylan!"

"Take it easy, you look like you're going to have a heart attack."

John catches his breath, then continues: "His name is Cui Jian.[44] He's a twenty-four-year-old trumpet player in the Beijing Symphony Orchestra. He writes and sings his own songs. His homemade recording 'Nothing to My Name (*Yiwusuoyou*)' is spreading around Beijing like wildfire."

John hands me the cassette. On the cover is a mimeographed black-and-white photo of Cui cradling his guitar like a rifle.

He does look like a Chinese Bob Dylan. Whip-thin, with chiseled

---

44. Pronounced *Tsway Jee-ehn.*

cheekbones and a defiant stare, he's got the rebellious look of a rock star. He's of Korean ethnic descent, adding to his exoticism. The liner notes say that his parents are professional military musicians and that he grew up in Beijing studying classical Western and traditional Chinese music. But like John and his friends, he became obsessed with banned Western folk, blues, jazz, and rock and roll, and has assimilated all these influences into a uniquely Chinese style.

John inserts the tape into his boom box and as the first song starts I understand his excitement. The guitar playing is deceptively simple, like on Dylan's early albums. But the lyrics—especially those of the title song—are compelling, not just for young Chinese but also for me.

*Nothing to My Name (*Yiwusuoyou*)*

I can't stop asking you
When will you come away with me?
But all you do is laugh at me
And say I have nothing to my name.
I want to give you my hope
And help set you free
But all you do is laugh at me
And say I have nothing to my name.
Oh . . . when will you come away with me?[45]

The rhyming couplets don't translate smoothly into English. But the slangy lyrics and subtle ensemble playing display real artistry.

---

45. The earth moves under our feet, the waters of life flow free.
But all you do is laugh at me, and say I have nothing to my name.
Why do you keep laughing at me? Why do I keep longing for you?
Could it be that in your eyes, I'll always have nothing to my name?
Oh . . . when will you come away with me?
I've waited too long, this is my final plea.
I want to take your hands in mine, and lead you away with me.
Your hands are trembling, your tears are flowing.
Do you really mean to tell me, that you love me as I am?
Oh . . . when will you come away with me? Oh . . . now you will come away with me.

"I get the Bob Dylan comparison," I tell John. "It's powerful art and protest."[46]

"And Cui has a better singing voice than Dylan," John adds with a laugh.

I have to agree. This sense of discovery must be akin to sitting in a New York City coffeehouse in the early 1960s and seeing a skinny teenager with a name borrowed from a drunken Welsh poet belting out instant masterpieces like "Blowin' in the Wind" and "The Times They Are A-Changin'." Dylan was the oracle for his generation of disaffected American students, and I have a hunch Cui Jian may play a similar role for his Chinese peers.

John and I learn all Cui's songs, and play them in our jam sessions. They're inspired anthems, comparable to the best compositions of our heroes Guthrie, Dylan, Lennon, and Marley. Cui sings with a defiant growl, and every word expresses the collective angst of China's youth.

One Friday night while John and I are playing one of Cui's songs at our school's soccer field, a guy in the crowd tells us Cui often jams in a park nearby.

John and I resolve to go meet him.

The next morning we rise early, strap our guitars across our backs, and pedal to the nearby Deep Jade Pool Park (*Yuyuantan*). We enter through a winding path of cherry trees, then a clear blue lake comes into view. Along the banks old men and women go through slow-motion *t'ai chi* routines, and families with kids sunbathe and swim. Under a Buddhist-style pagoda a jam session is underway. A group of guys with Beatles-style haircuts—itself a risky, rebellious gesture because long hair is still considered grounds for the criminal charge of "hooliganism"—are playing guitars and singing. All eyes are focused on the skinny guy in a white tank top in the middle. I recognize Cui Jian from the photo on his album cover.

We walk up and introduce ourselves, then I say: "I love your music."

46. The term "Nothing to My Name" comes from "The Internationale," the de facto anthem of the Communist Party. By saying he has nothing to his name, Cui is stating through subtle allusion that the Communist revolution hasn't succeeded in its promise to liberate all Chinese from oppression.

"Thanks, that means a lot coming from a young American," Cui replies in surprisingly good English.

I arch my eyebrows, and in anticipation of my question he adds, "I learned English in school, and from listening to so much Western music."

We smile at the irony of this statement, in an environment where popular Western music is still forbidden.

He's soft-spoken and friendly, not self-absorbed like most talented musicians I know.

He invites John and me to sit in. We strap on our guitars and tune up. Cui asks us to play something. John and I make eye contact, count out a four beat, and launch into our best rendition of Cui's "Nothing to My Name."

Like British rockers concealing their accents when they perform black American blues songs, I mimic Cui's guttural Beijing growl. As our final note fades, his eyes light up and a smile crosses his lips.

"You guys are great!" he says.

John and I look at each other and smile with relief. We passed the audition.

We jam for hours, taking turns playing rhythm and lead, and passing around my big-sounding American Guild guitar that sounds like a Stradivarius compared to their cheap, Chinese-made pinewood knock-offs. I teach them a couple of old American folk songs and Cui plays a few originals he hasn't recorded yet. I'm amazed at how prolific he is.

"How do you write so many songs?" I ask.

"Writing in Chinese is easy, everything rhymes," he jokes, and we all laugh at his self-deprecating humor.

We take a break and share a few warm beers John and I brought. Cui takes the opportunity to ask me a few questions.

"What's 'American Pie' about?"

"That's a great question. Every American knows the song, but few know the backstory. It's about the 1959 plane crash that killed Buddy Holly, Ritchie Valens, and the Big Bopper. That's the reason for the chorus, '*The day the music died.*'"

"How about '*The eagle flies on Friday, Saturday I go out to play*' in the blues standard 'Stormy Monday'?"

Wow, he really knows his American folk music.

"The eagle is the picture on the dollar bill. Friday is payday. After you get paid, you go out to play."

"I never would have thought of that!" he says with gratitude.

We continue to play until sunset. Then John and I have to head home.

"You're welcome anytime," Cui says, shaking our hands good-bye. "Really, come and jam again."

John and I attend a few more of Cui's jam sessions, but this routine is interrupted when he "blows up" as they say in the music business—becomes a hot commercial property. He wins a national songwriting contest, first prize of which is a previously unimaginable appearance on prime-time state-run television. Until now the only famous singers in China have been ageing revolutionary-era crooners and bubblegum pop stars from Taiwan and Hong Kong, promoted by the Communist Party for their anodyne, apolitical lyrics and music. I wonder if the government is aware of the subversive force they're unleashing by attempting to show tolerance of this budding youth counterculture and providing Cui a national television audience.

We watch his appearance on China Central Television (CCTV) in John's living room on a small black-and-white television set I've bought him. Cui is wearing his trademark green People's Liberation Army jacket—a subtle signal to his young audience that they're the true heirs to Mao's guerrilla revolution.

Everything about Cui Jian, his long hair and cool swagger, shouts hip rebellion.

He accompanies himself on acoustic guitar and sings "Nothing to My Name."

His performance is a time bomb. It has the same cathartic effect on this society as when Elvis, the Beatles, and Bob Dylan first appeared on the Ed Sullivan show in New York. The performance is rebroadcast on local television all over China, and kids start growing their hair long, buying guitars, and singing Cui's songs on street corners, in parks, and on school campuses nationwide.

On my work front, I've landed a coveted stringer position with *Asiaweek,* a Hong Kong–based newsweekly. It's not a full-time staff job, but it comes with a monthly stipend and my articles will be published in a major regional magazine. I file my first feature for *Asiaweek* on Cui Jian.

"We're running it on the cover," my editor tells me in our weekly phone conversation.[47] "And we'll continue to publish as much copy as you can provide on this new counterculture."

My first big scoop! But barely does this story gather steam than the Party extinguishes it. Chinese Vice President and retired People's Liberation Army general Wang Zhen, in response to Cui's television appearance, remarks: "What does he mean he has nothing to his name? He has socialism!"

This high-level denunciation, combined with Cui's irreverent inclusion of a revved-up rock-and-roll version of the revolutionary anthem *"Nanniwan"* ("Southern Muddy River Bend")[48] in his live performances, results in an official ban on his playing in public. He's also fired from his job in the Beijing Symphony Orchestra, for the offense of "indulging in popular music."

I'm shocked at this overreaction.

"Banning him from performing is bad enough," I say to John, "but firing him from his job?"

"*Shaji jinghou,* kill the chicken to frighten the monkeys," John says, drawing his finger across his throat for emphasis.

"Now you see why we're so paranoid," John adds. "The Party may be an ageing dragon, but it can still breathe fire."

"Sooner or later all these repressed emotions are going to erupt," I say.

John shakes his head at my naïveté.

Cui takes advantage of his enforced unemployment to put together a band, and compose new songs in preparation for recording. He's assembled a

---

47. I can now afford to make brief, work-related long-distance phone calls from the business centers of the five-star hotels sprouting up around Beijing.

48. *"Nanniwan"*—a propaganda song set to a popular folk melody during the revolution revived by Cui to conjure an image of a more idealistic, hopeful time for China but regarded by the Long Marchers as blasphemous.

supergroup, reflecting China's increasing cosmopolitanism. It features an African lead guitar player,[49] Hungarian bassist, Brazilian drummer, and cute Chinese chick on keyboards. They not only look great, but play a funky blend of blues, jazz, rock, reggae, and African-influenced music that, with Cui's original songwriting and singing style, is uniquely Chinese.[50]

It's China's version of World Music, long before that term has been coined.

Through a provincial government publishing deal[51] Cui goes into a studio with state-of-the-art equipment newly imported from Japan and records *Rock and Roll on the New Long March*—China's first homegrown rock album.

Tens of thousands of copies are sold through official bookstores and music shops—the only distribution channels the state monopoly permits—but corrupt cultural officials skim all the profits. The album is also pirated and sold by the hundreds of thousands on high school and college campuses, and in sidewalk bookstalls nationwide.

"Just like the music industry in the West," I joke to Cui as I conduct another interview for *Asiaweek*.

"Doesn't it bother you that if you'd sold this many albums in the West, you'd at least get rich, but here you still don't have two pennies to rub together?"

"*Geming bu shi qingke chifan,* a revolution is not a dinner party," he quips, quoting Chairman Mao.

"This isn't merely about money," he adds. "Of course I'd like to pay my band more and move out of my dorm room. But if I can help carve a space where Chinese artists can freely create, I'll have accomplished something much more significant than making money.

"And if my music reflects the aspirations and frustrations of my generation," he continues, draining a glass of beer, "then it will be supported."

---

49. Who grew up in Beijing attending school in the Cuban Embassy.

50. Reminiscent of traditional *shuochang* (說唱)—story-singing—a northern-Chinese-storytelling style accompanied by percussion and stringed instruments similar to modern rap.

51. Provincial publishers are willing to take risks their conservative counterparts in the capital aren't, in good 山高皇帝遠 (the mountains are high and the emperor is far away) fashion.

Cui's confidence proves well founded. His band is inundated with invitations to perform on college campuses, in newly opened nightclubs, and at parties in foreign embassies and luxury hotels. He's also booked to play in cities far from Beijing where central Communist Party censorship seems to be waning. I report on his legacy as he paves the way for a new generation of talented young musicians to establish thriving live music scenes from Shanghai to Xinjiang.[52] These bands perform regularly at unofficial parties where hundreds and sometimes thousands of young Chinese dance, drink, and engage in "bourgeois liberal" behavior—Communist Party code for sex, drugs, and rock and roll.

Renowned Chinese cultural critic Zhu Dake calls this phenomenon: "The birth of China's Woodstock generation."

French fashion designer Pierre Cardin's new nightclub Maxim's de Pékin is the fanciest live music venue in Beijing. It features a wraparound mahogany and black-leather bar, red velvet wallpaper, and a world-class sound system. Step inside and you feel like you've been transported to the Montmartre district of Paris.

Cui is invited to play a Halloween masquerade ball at Maxim's. On the day of the show John and I arrive early to help decorate.

We've recruited students from the nearby Central Art Academy to help with the preparations. With stage props borrowed from the school's design department, bolts of brightly colored silk, fluorescent paint, ultraviolet lights, and homemade lanterns, we transform Maxim's into a haunted house possessed by the ghosts and demons of Chinese legend.

After we finish decorating, John and I change into our costumes. He puts on my blue jeans, leather boots, flannel shirt, red neckerchief, and tops it off with a Stetson hat. He looks like an authentic Chinese cowboy. I borrow a red-and-green spandex suit from the art academy costume department, and a makeup artist paints an opera mask on my face. When she's finished I look in the mirror, and staring back at me

---

52. Pronounced *Sheen-jee-ang*, China's far northwest, Muslim-majority Central Asian region.

is the legendary Monkey King from the popular Ming Dynasty[53] novel *Journey to the West*. My costume wouldn't be out of place on a professional Beijing Opera stage.

Nights like this are why I love my life here. I stop every few minutes to jot details in my pocket notebook. I'm amazed by the diversity of the crowd. Ponytailed rockers mix with spiked, dyed-hair punks and model-gorgeous Chinese women in form-fitting silk and leather outfits. They're all defying the authority they've lived in fear of for so long. The pungent aroma of marijuana—another Western import—fills the air. Dry-ice smoke wafts around the bodies gyrating on the dance floor in front of the bandstand.

Cultural liberation that took decades for the West to achieve appears to be taking place overnight here.

A highlight of the evening is watching Cui Jian escort famous American actress Mira Sorvino backstage. I talk to her afterward and learn that she's studying at Beijing University on a Fulbright scholarship from Harvard. She'll go on to win an Oscar for her starring role in Woody Allen's *Mighty Aphrodite. Hollywood meets Beijing,* I scribble in my notebook.

Cui and his band play an inspired All Hallows Eve show. The music keeps the standing-room-only crowd dancing until dawn. They play hits from *Rock and Roll on the New Long March*, as well as crowd-pleasing covers of Rolling Stones, Beatles, Bob Dylan, and Dire Straits songs. Plainclothes Beijing police—beefy men in black leather jackets who remind me of Mafia thugs back in New Haven—smoke cigarettes and talk into brick-sized cellular telephones on the club's periphery.

One cop reveals to me that their orders are to monitor the event but not intervene. The younger officers can't help tapping their feet to the music, enjoying the spectacle. Mao must be rolling over in his coffin, with this brazen display of bourgeois liberalism taking place a stone's throw from his resting place in Tiananmen Square.

As the final sweet note of music fades, the crowd pours out into Beijing's early morning streets. An art student in a worn leather jacket with

---

53. Sixteenth century.

his hair pulled back in a ponytail provides me the best quote of the evening. In a voice reduced to a hoarse whisper from a long night's shouting, he says: "Rock 'n' roll will bring democracy to China."

Then his girlfriend straddles the bike behind him and they pedal off into the dawn.

chapter ten

Democracy is not a favor bestowed from above. It must be won through people's own efforts.
    —Astrophysicist and political activist Fang Lizhi, 1986

I'm having Sunday dinner with John and his family when he tells me he's heard exciting news: students at the University of Science and Technology are preparing to participate in local people's congress elections. China's recently revised constitution allows this, but no one's tested the Party's willingness to permit it in practice yet.

The University of Science and Technology is China's most elite technological institution. It's located in the provincial capital of Anhui province, 600 miles south of Beijing, near Lisa's military academy.

I propose to my editors to go to Anhui to cover the story. My angle is that the most aggressive challenging of the political status quo seems to be taking place in the provinces most distant from Beijing. *Asiaweek* approves my trip.

After my last class of the week, I hurry to John's apartment. I put on my military clothing and surgical mask disguise, bike downtown, and catch an overnight train south. I arrive in the sooty provincial capital of Hefei at dawn.

After my visit to Lisa's military academy, I'm confident in passing as a local. And I'm very excited about working on my first big breaking political news story.

The capital of Anhui isn't closed to foreigners, but few Westerners come here. My undisguised face would attract immediate attention, so I keep the surgical mask on.

The University of Science and Technology is located here because during the Cultural Revolution Mao exiled the entire faculty and student body from Beijing to be reeducated by the peasants. These intellectuals had to mine their own stones and build this university by hand. Two decades later this community of Beijing scholars is still here in backwater Anhui.

I arrive at the campus just as the bell rings for the start of morning classes. I mingle with a group of students and make it through the guarded entrance unnoticed. I double-check my directions, then find my way to the faculty compound where the university's vice chancellor Fang Lizhi lives.[54]

I'm nervous about meeting this renowned scholar and dissident. Fang's students cite him as the inspiration for their political activism. Professor Fang isn't expecting me, but I have a letter of introduction from a mutual friend in Beijing. Eager to make a good impression, I smooth my hair, straighten my clothes, and knock on the door.

I hear footsteps, and then the metal security grille opens. Professor Fang is bigger than I expected, but thick tortoiseshell glasses soften his appearance. He's surprised to see a foreigner standing in his doorway, never mind one who speaks Beijing-accented Mandarin. He scans my letter.

"*Hao, hao, hao* [good, good, good]," he says and invites me in.

He takes my hat, scarf, and jacket, and hangs them on a coat rack behind the door. Then he leads me to his book-lined living room and seats me on a comfortable old cotton couch. He prepares tea and places a cup on the table in front of me.

I can't help thinking that this large, affable man doesn't fit my preconception of a firebrand activist. His most distinctive features are his lively eyes and warm smile.

Decades of life-and-death struggle have produced unlikely leaders of dissent here. Fang's personal circumstances illustrate well the paradox of

---

54. Pronounced *Fahng Lee-jih*.

political activism in contemporary China. Not only is he a Communist Party member and National Academy of Sciences official, he's the vice chancellor of this prestigious university.

But he's also the nation's most outspoken dissident. He's criticized the privilege and corrupt cronyism of the Communist Party since his student days, and paid a heavy price, sacrificing career, family, and years of freedom.

Eager to learn more about how he became such a strong human rights advocate before inquiring about his students' campaigns, I ask Professor Fang to tell me his story.

"I was born in Beijing in 1936. My father was a railway worker and mother a schoolteacher. Then the war with Japan started. Beijing was occupied, and my earliest memories are of Japanese soldiers patrolling the streets with attack dogs. I saw them feed on corpses," he recounts calmly.

"Witnessing this cruelty at such a young age is probably why I so strongly advocate for the oppressed and speak out against injustice now."

He slurps a mouthful of tea, then continues: "I joined the Communist Party as a high school student and helped organize labor unions. Then at sixteen I entered Peking University (*Beida*) as a physics major. I met my future wife Li Shuxian there. We were the top students in our class. Upon graduating I was chosen to work on the country's top-secret nuclear weapons program. She stayed on at Peking University as a faculty member."

I'm mesmerized by his story and record every word in my notebook.

He refills my teacup, then continues: "But before we could begin our future together, politics intervened. In the summer of 1956 Chairman Mao encouraged intellectuals to criticize the Party. He called this the Hundred Flowers movement—'*baihuaqifang, baijiazhengming*, let one hundred flowers bloom and one hundred schools of thought contend' was its slogan. The longer the Communist Party stayed in power, the more bureaucratic and corrupt it became. Li and I wrote a critique of the education system, suggesting its emphasis on rote learning was a relic of the feudal Confucian past, and it should be modernized with more critical thought and debate. Our letter was never published, but the flood of criticism in response to Mao's campaign alarmed the Chairman, and he declared the movement a success in its ulterior motive of 'attracting vipers from their lairs' (*yin she chu dong*). He launched the Anti-Rightist campaign to silence his critics. More than half a million of China's best educated were targeted, including me and Li. No one knew about our letter, but out of loyalty to the Party we confessed to it," he says, shaking his head at their tragic innocence.

"It was the worst mistake of our lives," he adds, his voice cracking with still-raw emotion.

"We were labeled 'enemies of the people,' fired from our jobs, and then arrested.

"What a lot of people don't realize," Fang continues, thumping the table for emphasis, "is that Chairman Mao worked in the Beijing University library when he was a teenager. He couldn't afford tuition, and the faculty treated him badly. He resented intellectuals for the rest of his life, especially those from Beijing University.

"But I didn't learn all this until too late," he says with a deep sigh.

I'm amazed that he can relate this tragedy with such equanimity. *What strength of character*, I think.

I'm captivated by his story, and scribble notes as fast as I can. Hearing his tale reminds me of sitting as a child listening to my grandfather recount his experiences as a U.S. Marine fighting the Japanese during World War II.

"My wife and I spent the following two decades in and out of labor camps," Fang resumes. "We had to wait until Mao's death in 1976 and Deng's return to power to be rehabilitated. Hu Yaobang, Deng's chosen successor as Communist Party leader, reversed the verdicts on tens of thousands of us 'Rightists.'

"My wife resumed teaching at *Beida* (Beijing University), and I was assigned to the University of Science and Technology. But we're still not trusted to live in the same city."

Undaunted by their 600-mile separation, Fang and his wife are working to make up for their lost years, he explains. They're well-respected teachers, and have trained many outstanding young colleagues and students in their respective fields. They've coauthored books on Newtonian physics and Einstein's special theory of relativity[55] that have become standards in their fields. They also were the first PRC scientists to write popular books on complex astrophysics subjects like black holes, and Fang's groundbreaking book *Creation of the Universe*[56] introduced basic cosmological theories and has had a profound influence on science students nationwide.

But Fang feels that it's important to supplement his academic work with social activism.

"I also write political essays for popular magazines, and lecture at universities around the country on the social responsibility of intellectuals," he explains. "I recently wrote to a group of fellow well-known Rightists suggesting we gather to memorialize the martyrs of the 1957 Anti-Rightist campaign."

This act of courage astounds me.

"After all the time you spent locked up, you've gone right back to political activism?"

"Yes, I feel a sense of urgency. I've initiated democratic reforms on this campus, including open-ballot student government elections and public reviews of administrative decisions. And I've urged the designation of all universities as special democracy zones, where free speech and electoral politics can be experimented with."[57]

I'm moved by this man's lifelong commitment to participatory, accountable, and transparent government.

Fang's students have embraced his ideals, and are now putting them into action.

As he describes these developments to me, I'm struck by the similarity to the Free Speech Movement on U.S. campuses in the 1960s.[58]

---

55. Fang Lizhi and Li Shuxian, *Introduction to Mechanics*, World Scientific, Singapore, 1989.

56. *Yuzhou de Chuangsheng* (Fang Lizhi and Li Shuxian, *Creation of the Universe*).

57. His proposal was modeled on the special economic zones of the early 1980s, tax-free areas in cities along China's east coast that attracted foreign investment and successfully jump-started China's economic boom.

58. That gave rise to the antiwar and civil rights movements.

"This is why our leadership fears independent political activity," Fang explains. "'A single spark can start a prairie fire,' Mao said. My students are just carrying out Deng's dictate to put theory into practice *(cong lilun dao shijian)*. I'm leading China's top scientific institution and have a heavy responsibility. Am I training students to be unquestioning servants of dictators, or preparing them to lead a modern, democratic, and hopefully more-humane China in the future?

"Scientists shouldn't just blindly follow orders. Einstein was a role model in this regard. He called for banning the nuclear weapons his theoretical breakthroughs made possible. Chinese intellectuals should learn from his example. Those privileged enough to receive higher education should take the lead in speaking out on pressing social, economic, and political issues.

"China doesn't require more silent obedience," Fang continues, his voice rising with conviction. "That's what brought us decades of tragedy. Each new generation's idealism is exploited by selfish politicians. What China needs now is for educated members of society to set an example of rational debate and tolerance, and replace our authoritarian system with democratic institutions and rule of law."

The professor's words move me deeply. Now I understand why his students are so inspired by him and are pressing to participate in political change.

I'm so absorbed by our conversation that I barely notice the hours pass. It's dark by the time we finish talking. As my thoughts turn to where I'm going to spend the night, I hear a knock on the door. Fang opens it, and after a whispered conversation introduces me to an earnest graduate student named Xiao (Little) Li.[59] During a break in our hours-long conversation, Professor Fang quietly delivered a message through trusted neighbors and made arrangements for me to stay with his grad students. I thank him, say good-bye, and follow Little Li back to his dormitory.

Once we're inside, Little Li introduces me to his five roommates. They're all my age, twenty-two. They're eager to talk to the first American they've ever met. But first Little Li plugs in an electric hotplate and prepares

---

59. Xiao—pronounced *She-ow*, meaning *young* or *little*—is a diminutive commonly used as a familiar address for youth in China.

me a bowl of soup noodles with cabbage and homemade chili sauce. After I wolf down the simple but delicious meal, he fills an enamel washbasin with boiled water and hands me a clean face towel. I wash my hands in the bowl, brush my teeth, and we turn off the lights just before the 10 PM lights-out curfew. Following Little Li's instruction, I take the bunk bed farthest from the door, which two of his roommates have made available by bunking together above me—to reduce the risk of detection by a dorm monitor or informant.

Little Li takes the added precaution of turning on classical music to prevent our conversation being overheard. Then, in response to my inquiry, they fill me in on the latest political developments on campus.

"Right after our student leaders announced their intention to participate in the elections," Little Li says in an excited whisper, "a sympathetic official revealed that the provincial Communist Party committee had already selected the winners of the election in advance.

"We were being tricked into participating in a *gewu shengping* [false show of peace and prosperity], a fake election," scoffs the student in the bunk above me.

"After learning this," Little Li continues, "our student association decided to stage a public protest."

I ask when the protest is scheduled to take place. They answer in unison: "Tomorrow."

I'm shocked by this news. They assumed I was here to report on the protest. But long-distance communication in China is still restricted to privileged-access telephones, and sensitive, timely political information is hard to come by. By the time foreign reporters in Beijing learn about breaking news in the provinces, it's certain that the state security apparatus is in the process of crushing it.

"I came here to cover the elections," I tell them. "That's a big news story, but your protesting is much bigger."

I have a thousand questions, but Little Li tells me that we have to stop talking now or risk attracting the attention of the dorm guards. I'll have to wait until morning.

Little Li, his roommates, and I rise before dawn. We share a quick meal of *doujiang* and *youtiao*, fresh soy milk and fried dough sticks, at a restaurant by the school gate. Then we head toward the central campus plaza where the students are already gathering.

I can see my breath in the frigid morning air. But the sky is clear, and as the sun crests the horizon it starts to warm up. By 8 AM more than 3,000 students have gathered on the central square. I leave Little Li and his roommates and, in my surgical mask disguise, blend into the crowd.

At a prearranged signal the student protesters line up in rows, as they've been trained to do through years of participation in Communist Youth League activities, and march toward the campus gate.

I'm struck by the historical significance of this event. The only spontaneous student-led protests in four decades of Communist Party rule happened a decade ago, on April 5, 1976. John, then a teenaged participant, described to me in detail how tens of thousands poured into Tiananmen Square on the traditional day of ancestor worship to eulogize the recently deceased popular prime minister, Chou En-lai. What started as a show of grief for the death of a leader turned into an outpouring of anger against the extreme policies of the ailing Mao and his wife Jiang Qing and leftist allies, the Gang of Four. They ordered the Beijing security forces to suppress the gathering, injuring many and killing several. There was a harsh police crackdown on participants afterward, and many of John's friends were imprisoned.

It later emerged that the real target of the crackdown was Deng Xiaoping. With Chairman Mao's health deteriorating, Deng was seen as a threat to the Gang of Four's power. He was publicly blamed for inciting the uprising, and removed from his post as acting prime minister—the third time he'd been purged. When Mao's wife and her henchmen were overthrown in a coup orchestrated by Deng less than six months later, the official verdict on the April 5 protests was overturned, and demonstrators who'd been branded counterrevolutionaries—including many of John's friends—were released from jail and celebrated as patriotic heroes.

The student protesters I'm with now were still in primary school in 1976. They have, at most, a vague childhood memory of the events.

Political ignorance confers a mixed blessing here: Each new generation is unaware of its predecessors' sacrifices, but also not afraid to repeat their acts of resistance.

As the crowd of protesters approaches the university's main gate, Professor Fang steps into their path and urges them to reconsider taking to the streets.

"As long as you stay on campus," he says to the crowd, "I can protect you. But once you pass through these gates, forces beyond my control will be unleashed."

I can see how much these students respect Fang. They take his words of warning very seriously. They consult among themselves for several minutes, but reaffirm their commitment to proceed with the demonstration. Fang steps aside as they stride through the gates, loudly singing the national anthem "March of the Volunteers,"[60] their voices rising in unison for the final chorus: "Our million hearts beating as one, brave the enemy's fire, march forward!"

I trail behind the students as they march the several miles to the provincial government headquarters, singing patriotic songs, chanting slogans, and brandishing signs and banners declaring:

> WE WANT GOVERNMENT OF THE PEOPLE,
> BY THE PEOPLE AND FOR THE PEOPLE.
> EVERY DAY THE NEWSPAPERS TALK ABOUT 'PEOPLE'S DEMOCRACY.'
> BUT WHERE CAN WE FIND ANY?
> WE WANT DEMOCRACY, LIBERTY AND FREEDOM OF THE PRESS.
> NO DEMOCRATIZATION, NO MODERNIZATION!

Upon arrival at the heavily guarded provincial government compound, the protesters continue to voice their demand that independent candidates be allowed to participate in the upcoming elections, and

---

60. Arise! All those who don't want to be slaves! Let our flesh and blood forge a new Great Wall! The Chinese nation has arrived at its most perilous time. Every person is forced to expel their very last roar. Arise! Arise! Arise! Our million hearts beating as one, Brave the enemy's fire, March forward! Brave the enemy's fire, March forward! March forward! March forward! Forward!

that the contest be fair and free from Communist Party interference. Their numbers have swollen into the thousands, with students from other local universities and curious onlookers joining the crowd. Officials peek nervously at the throng from behind curtained windows in the government building, but the armed guards at the gate continue to stand at attention, their AK-47 rifles cradled across their chests. After a tense hour's standoff in which the students begin to debate whether they'll be required to take more extreme action for their message to be heard, a government representative comes out to receive their written petition. The protest leaders huddle and decide not to press their advantage. They declare the march a success, and request that the large crowd of onlookers disperse and return to campus to await an official response. The drained but elated crowd breaks up and the protesters start their long walk home.

I fall into step beside Little Li. A group of his classmates are debating the day's events and I eavesdrop on their conversation, furtively scribbling notes in my pocket notepad.

"The May Fourth Movement[61] declared that China needed to import 'Mister Democracy' and 'Mister Science'[62] from the West in order to escape our feudal past," exclaims a tall, thin student in a green Mao jacket. "How tragic it is that seventy years later we're still struggling for the same goals!"

"I have no faith in the government. It's impossible to believe they'll act on our proposals," a young woman in a quilted blue cotton coat adds. "If they really allowed free elections, the Communist Party would lose!"

Her classmates respond with shouts of approval.

A bespectacled young woman notices me hovering at the edge of the crowd and strikes up a conversation. She tells me her name is Su, and when I pull away my surgical mask and reveal I'm a foreign reporter

61. May 4, 1919, antigovernment protests widely seen as giving rise to China's revolutionary movement. The Communist Party of China was founded less than two years later by May 4 Movement student activists.

62. The use of the imported term "mister" making clear they're Western ideas.

documenting the events, she recoils in surprise and then composes herself and says, "Please tell the world what's happening here. We have no free press and our rights are meaningless. The only law that matters is what the Communist Party boss dictates. Now that no one believes in Communism, everyone's struggling to get rich by any means necessary!"

She stops to catch her breath, and then continues: "The core contradiction in our society is that a privileged Party elite pursues its own self-interest. China's revolution was fought to redress poverty and illiteracy, inequality, the rights of women and ethnic minorities, and arbitrary rule by unelected dictators instead of the rule of law. These problems are all worse now than when the Party came to power forty years ago!"

I'm impressed by her idealism and insight, as I am by all of Professor Fang's students. The sincerity they embody will not be easily silenced. This pent-up yearning to govern themselves and openly debate matters of pressing social concern by China's new generation must be given vent or it will surely boil over.

I spend the rest of the week observing and documenting the campus rallies that have now spread to other universities in Hefei. Fortunately for me, the powers that be have much more pressing concerns than a prying foreign reporter. Their lack of response to the students' demands betrays paralysis at the highest levels of local government and only serves to fuel the students' frustration.

Finally the provincial government, acting on orders from Beijing, announces that the elections have been postponed indefinitely. This compromise resolves nothing, but it achieves the objective of getting the students off the streets and back into their classrooms.

At significant personal risk, Professor Fang allows me to use his office telephone to place long-distance calls to my editors in Hong Kong.

Despite a strict ban on the reporting of these demonstrations in the state-run media, international radio broadcasts—including my eyewitness reports—have spread news about the protests to cities across China. Students in Beijing, Shanghai, and in provincial capitals nationwide have begun displaying wall posters detailing their own grievances and declaring that if they're not permitted to participate in local elections they too will take to the streets.

I consult with my editors on how best to proceed with reporting on this breaking story. We agree that developments in China's largest city, Shanghai, are the most newsworthy, and that I should travel the 500 kilometers east to the financial capital.

I return to the student dormitory to pack my backpack and thank Little Li and his roommates for their hospitality. Then I return to Professor Fang's apartment to say good-bye. His face is pale and drawn and there are dark circles under his eyes. He looks exhausted. He sees my alarm and explains, "I just spent the whole day mediating between the provincial and central authorities and my students to try to protect them from official backlash."

I'm struck by the gravity of these momentous events.

"Thank you for all that you've done for me," I say, then to inject humor into the tense situation, add: "*Jianchi daodi*—keep up the fight!"

This example of the revolutionary terminology I've learned from both John and now Fang's students over the past week makes Professor Fang laugh, and I'm happy to give him some comic relief.

We say good-bye, then I rush to the train station to catch the overnight express to Shanghai.

chapter eleven

不是我不明白，這世界變化快

Bu shi wo bu mingbai, zhei shijie bianhua kuai.
It's not that I don't understand, it's that the world is changing
too fast.

—Cui Jian, "It's Not That I Don't Understand"

I emerge from the downtown Shanghai railway station during morning rush hour and take a bicycle rickshaw to the old French Concession area of the city.

It's good to be back in Shanghai. I visited here a few times as a student, and have been back on recent teaching breaks. Shanghai—literally, "City on the Sea"—is often regarded as Beijing's alter ego. Beijing is China's tradition-bound, intrigue-laden political capital, and Shanghai is the country's brash, freewheeling commercial center. Washington D.C. versus New York City. Little more than a century ago Shanghai was a sleepy fishing village. Following the defeat to Britain in the Opium Wars in the mid–nineteenth century, it opened up to foreign occupation and trade.

European powers and the United States carved Shanghai into foreign concessions they governed according to extraterritoriality—foreigners exempt from Chinese law—generating tremendous local resentment. By the time of the 1949 Communist takeover, Shanghai was the largest Asian metropolis. When Mao's Red Army marched in they expelled all foreigners and shuttered the dance halls, gambling parlors, brothels, and opium dens that earned the city its moniker "Paris of the East." Shanghai remained China's international trade and investment center until Mao extinguished all vestiges of capitalism. But since the initiation of Deng's Open Door policy, the city has quickly recovered its former entrepreneurial spirit.

In the early–mid-1980s, while Beijing residents feared that Deng's new reforms might be reversed and private business was limited to marginal members of society like school dropouts and ex-cons who couldn't secure salaried work in state-owned enterprises, Shanghai natives embraced entrepreneurial activity and charged ahead with the new gold rush. The city night lit up with bustling outdoor food, clothing, and consumer electronics markets. Newly opened nightclubs were simply labeled *Ba*, a transliteration of the English word *bar*. Private mom-and-pop restaurants—usually a few tables and chairs in a family's living room—served delicious Shanghai cuisine typified by fresh seafood (river and sea fish, fresh and saltwater shrimp, and the famed *maoxie*, hairy lake crabs), a wide variety of local vegetables, assorted *dim sum* (steamed, baked, and fried dumplings), and China's best green tea.

The city's famous waterfront, the Bund,[63] is lined with neoclassical skyscrapers. Its skyline resembles a European capital or prewar New York, a sharp contrast to the hodgepodge of traditional sloping eaves and somber Soviet-style architecture typical of Beijing and most other Chinese cities.

My pedicab pulls up to the Shanghai Conservatory of Music. I hand the driver ¥5 (US$.75) and tell him to keep the change. It's a little-known perk that with a university ID a dorm room in the colonial-era conservatory can be had for less than US$1 a night. The stately, European-style buildings and quiet, tree-lined campus provide a pleasant respite from the frenetic pace of the big city. As I enter I hear the soothing sound of classical piano being practiced.

I arrive just in time for the day's one hour of hot water, and take my first shower in a week. Revived, I change into clean clothes and stroll out the arched, wrought-iron conservatory gates.

---

63. Anglo-Indian slang term for "muddy embankment."

The French influence in the neighborhood is still evident in the arching parasol trees and elegant saffron-colored villas lining the narrow streets. The district is dotted with coffee shops, another vestige of its French colonial past, and the air is fragrant with roasting coffee beans and fresh-baked baguettes. I fill my thermos with the best coffee to be had outside of China's southern coffee-growing region on the border with Vietnam, grab a fresh French roll, and walk toward Shanghai's university district sipping the coffee and munching on the piping-hot bread.

After a fifteen-minute hike I arrive at the gates of Jiaotong University,[64] Shanghai's leading science and technology institute. I head for the bulletin board area at the center of campus. A crowd of students is gathered around a colorful array of posters written in bold calligraphy.[65] They're reading, photographing, transcribing, and discussing the incendiary political content. This open debate and political ferment on a Chinese campus is so unusual, it reminds me of a politically active campus back home.

I stand at the edge of the crowd. In cosmopolitan Shanghai there's no need to disguise myself, and a curious male student notices my presence and strikes up a conversation. When I reveal that I've just come from the protests in Hefei, a crowd forms around me. I recount all that I witnessed—the origin of the protests, the tense standoff at the Communist Party headquarters, the subsequent week's rallies, and the Party's final postponement of the elections.

Expressions of approval and excited chatter from the crowd remind me of how serious an undertaking civil disobedience is here. It's a far cry from the risk-free demonstrating I took part in on campus in the States—apartheid, U.S. policy in Central America, and environmental protection protests. Back home I was little more than an armchair activist. These students are protesting about things that affect their lives directly and taking significant political and personal risk with their participation.

The demonstrators take turns detailing their grievances: rapid price rises as government subsidies for food and daily necessities are

---

64. Pronounced *Jeeow-tong.*

65. Known as *dazibao*—big-character posters—in Chinese.

phased out, corrupt and incompetent local government officials and university bureaucrats, run-down campus facilities, and dangerously overcrowded student dorms. But what's really focused their anger and brought them out in large numbers is a police beating of a Jiaotong University student for dancing during a recent rock concert. The young man remains hospitalized, and his classmates have demanded local authorities denounce the excessive use of force by the police and punish those responsible.

They tell me that Shanghai Communist Party leader Jiang Zemin[66] will address the student body at his alma mater this evening. *What a scoop! It's very unusual for Party officials to make unscheduled public appearances.* They say that Jiang's fellow Party officials are concerned his populist gesture may backfire and exacerbate the unrest. But Jiang has reassured his fellow cadres that due to his own background as a student leader in the 1940s, he'll have no trouble establishing rapport with this new generation of student protesters and defuse the campus tension.

As night falls I stand outside the reception hall on the Jiaotong University campus and watch Jiang's entourage arrive in a sea of flashing lights and sirens. The rotund party secretary enters the overflowing hall to polite applause, but it quickly becomes apparent that he's here to lecture, not listen. Rather than express any sympathy with the students, Jiang chastises them for their selfish demands and contrasts this with the glorious sacrifices of his own revolutionary wartime generation.

"Without political and social stability, China's modernization effort will be imperiled and the country's very survival threatened," Jiang intones, pounding the lectern for emphasis.

He then orders the students to end their protests, address their concerns through the official student union controlled by the Communist Youth League, and focus on their schoolwork.

I look around the hall and see idealistic young faces contorted in frustration and anger. But instead of being intimidated, they shock Jiang by aggressively challenging him.

---

66. Pronounced *Jee-ang Zuh-meen*.

One young man stands up and says, "Our Constitution protects the rights of free speech, press, assembly, and demonstration. Why do you, Communist Party Secretary Jiang, seek to deprive us of these basic civil rights?"

His statement is met with thunderous applause. Then a female student raises the issue of their injured classmate, to which the flustered Jiang replies with a defense of the police, and urges the students to respect the socialist justice system.

As the event goes on the defiant mood escalates, and Jiang eventually loses his cool and bellows at one outspoken student: "Do you dare to tell me your name?" To which the student calmly responds with his full name, academic department, and student ID number.

Far from pacifying the crowd, Jiang's intensified their anger and is unceremoniously hooted out of the hall.

As the outraged students pour into the night, they head for the campus commons. There, after brief deliberation, they decide that this official display of contempt for their concerns demands they take to the streets right away. Slogans are hastily scrawled on bedsheet banners, battery-powered bullhorns procured, and the crowd marches out the campus gates. Word of the demonstration spreads quickly to neighboring campuses, and thousands more join in the march. The students exult in this unprecedented opportunity to express their discontent publicly, and head for People's Square, Shanghai's equivalent of Beijing's Tiananmen and the symbolic heart of the city.

I hurry to keep up with the crowd while scribbling in my notebook some of the phrases scrawled in large black characters on the white banners:

10,000 YEARS IS TOO LONG TO WAIT, WE WANT DEMOCRACY NOW.

JIANG ZEMIN, WHO ELECTED YOU TO OFFICE?

IF YOU WANT TO KNOW ABOUT FREEDOM OF EXPRESSION,

JUST ASK IMPRISONED DISSIDENT WEI JINGSHENG.[67]

---

67. Beijing Democracy Wall activist sentenced to fifteen years in prison in the late 1970s.

Fascinating to me is a sign held aloft by a pair of students clearly alluding to Martin Luther King's famous *I Have a Dream* speech: I HAVE A DREAM, A DREAM OF FREEDOM. I HAVE A DREAM OF DEMOCRACY. I HAVE A DREAM OF A LIFE ENDOWED WITH HUMAN RIGHTS. MAY THE DAY COME WHEN ALL THESE ARE MORE THAN JUST DREAMS. MARXISM-LENINISM AND MAO ZEDONG THOUGHT, GO TO HELL!

Thousands of local citizens join the march as it floods through Shanghai's narrow streets on its way to the main east–west thoroughfare Nanjing Road. Some just gawk at the spectacle, but others are emboldened to join in and express their own dissatisfaction with China's rulers. The atmosphere is celebratory. This reveals an important truth to me: in spite of the risk, people feel a huge emotional release when they confront repression and express their feelings openly rather than continue to suppress them.

I linger with the protesters in People's Square until well after midnight, commiserating over the frustratingly slow pace of reforms, discussing protest strategies, and debating how China can escape its historical cycle of tyranny and chaos. As the night sky gives way to dawn, the demonstrators return to their campuses to discuss how best to proceed with this unplanned political movement.

The next day more than 30,000 students join an estimated 100,000 workers and city residents in a mass gathering in People's Square. The crowd marches in an unbroken column that stretches as far as the eye can see to the Shanghai municipal government headquarters three miles away. Downtown traffic comes to a halt. But the atmosphere is festive. People are giddy with the sudden sense of freedom and absence of fear.

I walk beside the marchers to gain the broadest possible perspective and photo angles. I always carry a pocket-sized camera to photograph breaking news.

Upon arriving at the riverfront government headquarters, the crowd shouts for Communist Party boss Jiang Zemin to come out and address them. A line of police with arms interlocked guards the European-style walled compound, but when the swelling crowd appears on the verge of overwhelming them, Party Secretary Jiang emerges on a balcony and speaks through a bullhorn:

"We all desire the deepening of socialist democracy," Jiang says in stilted Party-speak. "And I recognize that your motives are patriotic.

"But this mass gathering disrupts public order and social stability," he adds ominously. "The political process should be carried out in the halls of Congress, not in the streets."

The crowd is angered by his patronizing tone. Scattered catcalls coalesce into a loud chorus of "Jiang Zemin is a coward!" as the Party leader scurries back into City Hall.

I'm shocked that such a high-ranking politician would treat China's politically savvy students and citizens so condescendingly. It's clear to me that the skills needed to rise in the Communist Party are very different from those that enable a politician to gain office in the West. Despite the clear outrage of the crowd, Jiang stubbornly hews to the Party line. In the States, any politician who successfully ran an election campaign would know how to better finesse a volatile public gathering. Jiang is, through lack of a common touch, intensifying the conflict.

Huge demonstrations continue throughout the week, paralyzing downtown Shanghai's business and shopping districts. I accompany the protesters and interview students and workers. The demonstrators are emboldened by rumors that moderate city officials are sympathetic to their cause.

Signs appear expressing discontent with Jiang Zemin's performance over the past several days. Their sentiments are summed up in the banner: DOWN WITH TWO-FACED BUREAUCRATS.

I'm looking for signals that the government's patience is running out like it did in Hefei. State-run radio, television, and newspapers broadcast police warnings that the ongoing demonstrations are illegal, and that participants in further protests will be arrested. Luckily for Party boss Jiang and his cronies, people from all walks of life are now taking to the streets objecting to everything from China's draconian one-child birth control policy to inadequate retirement benefits. These diverse voices drown each other out. The students who launched the campaign are concerned their original message is getting lost in the general clamor.

University final exams are also pending, and the students don't want to jeopardize promising careers for unattainable goals. They've expressed their dissatisfaction, and believe that the administration should be given time to respond.

A planned afternoon rally in People's Square is canceled when riot police with steel helmets, batons, and shields confront the gathering crowd and force it to disperse. The movement in Shanghai seems to have reached a stalemate.

In a call to my Hong Kong editors, I learn that the Shanghai protests have given rise to demonstrations in more than a dozen other cities. Most significantly, students in Beijing—the traditional pioneers of political protest in China—are preparing to take to the streets. My editors decide I should return to Beijing right away.

I check out of the Music Conservatory, grab a pedicab to the train station, and catch an overnight express back to the capital.

chapter twelve

誰都不怕誰

Shui dou bu pa shui.
No one is afraid of anyone anymore.
　　　　—Professor Fang Lizhi, 1986 Beijing University speech

It's after midnight by the time my train pulls into the downtown Beijing railway station. There are no cabs, so I decide to walk the ten kilometers back to John's apartment. It's a clear night, and I can use the hike to reflect on the events of the past three weeks. The streets are deserted, and a crescent moon illuminates a layer of freshly fallen snow.

I leave a trail of footprints across the empty expanse of Tiananmen Square, and pass beneath the floodlit portrait of Chairman Mao perched above the Gate of Heavenly Peace. The Great Helmsman's suspicious eyes—*xiaoxinyan'r*, Beijing natives call them—seem to follow me.

I pass through the arched moon gate and come to the padlocked Forbidden City[68] entrance. I turn left and continue along the path between the moat and towering vermilion walls of the emperor's former residence. Looking up at the ornate corner watchtower, I think I see a shadow moving.

I shake my head.

"*Jiangui* [seeing ghosts]," I mutter. There can't be anyone here at this hour.

---

68. Former imperial palace.

This is the heart of not just the capital but the Chinese empire. Why do I feel so desolate?

My friends and family back home are preparing for the winter holidays. If I were there I'd be skiing in Vermont right now. No one here celebrates our Western holidays, and Chinese New Year doesn't come until spring. A wave of sadness washes over me. But I will thoughts of home away, and pick up my walking pace.

By the time I arrive at John's, the sky is lightening. His family is already up and preparing breakfast. Their warm welcome lifts my spirits. My exhaustion disappears as I fill them in on what I've seen and done the past three weeks. John describes the tense atmosphere in Beijing as students are threatening to take to the streets here too. After wolfing down a bowl of oatmeal and gulping mugs of strong black tea, we set out on the fifteen-minute bike ride to Beijing University to see what's happening on the nation's most politically active campus.

We arrive at the foreign student entrance and ride straight to the dirt bulletin board area in front of the student dormitories known as *Sanjiaodi*, The Triangle. Hundreds of students are reading posters and discussing the protests in Hefei and Shanghai I just witnessed. One popular post calls for Beijing University to be designated a special free speech and democracy zone, echoing the ideas of Professor Fang. John tells some students where I've been, and a crowd forms around me. I answer their questions about what I saw in south China. The students are electrified by the news, seeing themselves as part of a nationwide movement.

Out of the corner of my eye I see a pained expression on John's face.

"*Zenmele?* What's up?" I ask.

"Nothing," he responds with a shake of his head.

I don't press him, and after a couple of seconds he says, "I can't help feeling excited but also afraid. I know this will have a bad ending."

I'm heartbroken by the fact that a person as gifted and generous as John can be so pessimistic about his country's future.

By midafternoon the crowd has swollen to several thousand. They take turns addressing the gathering from a dormitory balcony with a bullhorn. The speakers criticize the lack of long-promised reforms, and demand to be allowed to participate in local congress elections like their counterparts in Hefei and Shanghai.

Then a menacing voice breaks in over the school's public-address system: "This student gathering is illegal and must disperse. Violators will face severe consequences."

This scare tactic, far from intimidating the students, fuels their anger. They decide to take to the streets right away. They march out the main gate and turn toward neighboring Tsinghua[69] University, China's top science and engineering school. Advance word has reached Tsinghua and a crowd of students waits as the Beijing University students arrive.

The combined group decides to head for the highly symbolic destination of Tiananmen Square, the center of the capital and the traditional site for petitioning China's rulers.

As the crowd turns onto White Stone Bridge Road[70]—the main thoroughfare of the university district—a line of baton-wielding police blocks their path. A ripple of fear passes through the crowd, but the momentum of their numbers propels them forward. As the front row of students approaches, the uniformed barricade unexpectedly parts and lets them through.

This restraint shocks me. Cops usually crack heads at the slightest provocation here. These officers withdraw to the march's periphery, limiting their activity to rerouting traffic and photographing and videotaping the demonstrators. I strike up a conversation with one young cop.

"*Nin shouleile* [what a headache]."

He's startled by a foreigner speaking with a Beijing accent.

"Just obeying orders," he replies, hinting at private sympathy with the students.

I chat with him for a few minutes, and learn that the cops have been instructed to monitor the activity, but not use violence or disrupt the march.

This tolerant approach is uncharacteristic of the hardline Beijing

---

69. Pronounced *Ching-hwa*.

70. Baishiqiao.

regime. Just as in Shanghai, forces for moderation appear to have the upper hand in the central leadership, at least for now. The government's strategy appears to be to let these idealistic students blow off some steam, then persuade them to return to campus.

On this initial march, no arrests are made. The Beijing students reach Tiananmen, shout pro-democracy slogans like their peers in Hefei and Shanghai, and disperse after a few hours. Predictably, state-run media doesn't report the event. Propaganda broadcast on public loudspeakers echoes the Party line and warns that without social stability all that has been achieved in the past decade of reform will be lost.

John and I spend the following days trying to discern which way the political wind is blowing. The signaling of factional shifts is a highly ritualized drama here, and John, like all educated Chinese his age, is skilled at deciphering the code.

"When a *People's Daily* editorial says there are *contradictions among the people*," John explains, "there's still hope of a moderate approach. But when the Cultural Revolution is mentioned or the term *enemies of the people* is used, then you know that a crackdown is imminent."

The state-run press begins publishing denunciations of the protests and its student leaders, recounting the long years of social unrest and terrible suffering during the Cultural Revolution from which the country has only recently emerged. Finally there's an official pronouncement: *Student-penned political posters at Beijing University launched the Cultural Revolution*, reads the front-page state media editorial. This is a tactic to smear the movement by associating it with that disastrous decade, omitting the critical distinction that these students are acting on their own initiative, while their 1960s counterparts were manipulated by Mao and his wife.

"The words *counterrevolutionary, running dog,* and *puppets of imperialism* are a bad sign," John continues. "They're serious charges that haven't been seen since the Cultural Revolution. I thought they'd been relegated to the past, but I guess we can't escape our painful past so easily."

He blows on his teacup, then takes a sip.

"Hardliners in the leadership must be pushing for a Maoist-style political campaign and purge. This is a clear indication that the gloves are off inside *Zhongnanhai,* Communist Party headquarters."[71]

Conservative elders[72] believe that Deng's market-oriented reforms have gone too far, and are convinced that China's students are being corrupted by Western influences. They think that patriotic ideological education on campuses has been neglected and must be reemphasized.

An additional factor is that the conservative Old Guard distrusts Deng's handpicked successor, Party general secretary Hu Yaobang. They think he's too liberal, and that his sweeping economic and political reforms—never mind rehabilitation of progressive intellectuals like Professor Fang and his wife—threaten to undermine Mao's legacy and their own entrenched interests. They control the old state-planned infrastructure industries of manufacturing, energy, transportation, raw materials, and agriculture in China's still highly centralized economy. Because Deng's position as paramount leader is inviolable, these reactionaries have targeted his heir-apparent Hu Yaobang.

The hardliners escalate their offensive over the final week of 1986. The Beijing city government issues a ban on all protests in the capital— the same measure taken in Shanghai in advance of decisive police action to end the demonstrations there. Beijing University authorities tear down all *dazibao* (big-character posters)[73] on campus and outlaw the displaying of new ones.

I'm standing in The Triangle at Beijing University. Previously brimming with posters, it's now stripped bare. A passing student offers me a copy of the *People's Daily,* highlighting the unusual, full front-page, bold-red-headlined editorial. It announces the launch of a Maoist-style ideological campaign against "Bourgeois Liberalization" (Party code for Western democratic political and cultural values). It will be carried out nation-

---

71. The walled compound next to the Forbidden City where the Party leadership works and meets.

72. Those named in the media include Long March and Red Army veterans Wang Zhen and Bo Yibo, National People's Congress chairman Peng Zhen, and propaganda czar Hu Qiaomu.

73. Hand-calligraphed posters written on white rice paper scrolls and publicly displayed.

wide through mandatory study sessions in schools and workplaces. "We must wake up," the angry commentary warns, "Bourgeois Liberalization is poisoning our children and must be ruthlessly exterminated."

To ring in the Western New Year, Beijing University students convene a New Year's Eve protest on campus. Several thousand students gather at The Triangle. The mood is jubilant as they take turns making speeches, sarcastically singing revolutionary songs like "Without the Communist Party, There Would Be No New China"[74] that satirize how far the Party has strayed from its populist roots, and denounce the official media's vilification of their movement.

As the crowd grows increasingly restless, a student twists a copy of the *People's Daily* into a torch and lights it. This leads to a bonfire, with copies of the offending government newspaper being fed into the roaring blaze along with strings of firecrackers. Students looking on from dormitory windows and local residents perched on the campus walls greet the explosions with loud cheers.

"The *People's Daily* fabricates lies about our actions," a male law student tells me as his classmates dance around the fire. "Maybe this response is immature," he adds, gesturing at the revelers, "but we're so frustrated that our 'People's Government' won't even address our most modest proposals that we feel this is our only choice."

As the campus clock strikes midnight, more than 1,000 students decide to set off on a final New Year's Eve march to Tiananmen. The broad streets of the capital are windswept and bitter cold. We huddle together for warmth as we set off on the ten-kilometer hike. It's a somber scene after the euphoric campus rally. As we pass the crumbling old

---

74. "Without the Communist Party, There Would Be No New China."
The Communist Party of one mind saved China.
It pointed to the road of liberation for the people.
It led China towards the light.
It supported the War of Resistance for more than eight years.
It has improved people's lives.
It built a base behind enemy lines.
It practiced democracy, bringing many advantages.
Without the Communist Party, there would be no new China.

imperial gates—this is the same route that the Emperor used to take between his winter and summer palaces—I can't help thinking about a similar procession in another walled capital nearly 2,000 years ago. All that's missing is a martyr on a cross. But perhaps I'll see something like that before this movement ends.

When we finally reach Tiananmen at 4 AM, police in padded blue overcoats cinched with leather gun belts surround the square. A tense standoff ensues, but they finally give way and we surge onto the empty plaza.

Suddenly everyone starts slipping and falling.

"They flooded the square with water after sunset," a night watchman tells me, nodding at the police. Predictably, the subzero temperatures have transformed the hundred-acre square into a solid sheet of ice. Traversing the slippery surface is like walking on a hockey rink.

"*Liumang zhengfu* [Criminal government]*!*" a tall student behind me yells. "Can't even play fair at this," he adds, summing up our collective frustration.

Undeterred, the students make their way to the center of the square and huddle around the Monument to Revolutionary Martyrs. There they strike up one last refrain of the national anthem, shouting the chorus: "China faces its greatest danger. We must join our voices as one. Rise up! Rise up! Rise up!"

As the last defiant voice fades, the protesters decide that their exercise in civil disobedience has reached its conclusion, and they can claim at least a symbolic victory and return to campus with their heads held high.

As the new day dawns, I follow the students out of the square. They pass the line of police who are heading back to their barracks. I'm struck by the similarity between this scene and antiwar rallies back home: privileged students on one side, working-class cops and demobilized soldiers on the other.

A couple of students call out: "*Jingcha tongzhimen xinkule!* [Police comrades are hardworking!]"

It's a gesture of respect to fellow youth they see as victims of the system too. Several cops nod in appreciation, but most look frustrated at the extra work these pampered college kids have caused them.

chapter thirteen

We cannot do without dictatorship. We must not only affirm the need for it, but also exercise it when necessary. Of course we must be cautious about resorting to dictatorial means and make as few arrests as possible. But if some people attempt to provoke disorder, what are we going to do about it? We should first expose their plot and then remove the ringleaders. . . . If we back down, we will only have more trouble down the road.
—Deng Xiaoping, addressing the Communist
Party Politburo, January 1987

With final exams finished and students heading home for the Chinese New Year holiday, I'm watching the evening news with John. China Central Television's (CCTV) primetime newscast shows mug shots of three men: Liu Binyan, Wang Ruowang, and Fang Lizhi. These are writers-scholars I've been spending time, interviewing, and becoming friends with the past year.

What kind of system charges, tries, and convicts—on prime-time television—three law-abiding, patriotic scholars just because a few conservative leaders don't like their ideas?

An ominous voiceover announces that for their treasonous activities Professor Fang Lizhi, *People's Daily* investigative journalist Liu Binyan, and muckraking Shanghai-based writer and activist Wang Ruowang have been stripped of their Communist Party posts, fired from their government jobs, and banned from publishing or public speaking. It's akin to the McCarthy-era Communist witch hunts.

Professor Fang has been identified as the "black hand"[75] behind the protests. The government accuses him of planting seeds of dissent in his students' heads through his subversive teaching, critical articles, and rabble-rousing campus speeches nationwide since the inception of reforms. Liu Binyan is famed for his daring investigative reports on abuses of power by corrupt Communist officials.[76] And the final scape-goat[77] Wang Ruowang's dissident credentials date back to being jailed by both the ruling Nationalists before World War II and the Communists after the revolution.

As the shocking news of these purges sinks in, my anger turns to fear for Professor Fang's safety. John, in his typically clearheaded manner, reassures me that it's still early in the campaign.

"We need to wait and see how this plays out," he says as he pours me tea.

The regime follows up the public denunciation with a massive propaganda blitz against the three writers. I grow accustomed to seeing the slogan: "Resolutely Oppose Bourgeois Liberalism,"[78] together with the three men's names, in newspaper headlines and on propaganda broadcasts blaring from public loudspeakers.

So this is what a Maoist political campaign looks like.

I begin to have a better idea of what it was like for John's father and his university colleagues to be paraded through the streets by Red Guards, denounced in public struggle sessions, and beaten by students, neighbors, and, not uncommonly, one's own children.

An encouraging sign is that none of the three victims have been arrested, at least not yet. Perhaps China has moved on from the extreme ruthlessness of Mao's days.

From my daily forays around the city observing and interviewing citizens, documenting the progress of the campaign, and nightly conversations with John, I see that the democracy protests have presented

---

75. *Heishou.*

76. Most published in the Party's mouthpiece newspaper the *People's Daily,* where Liu is a veteran reporter.

77. *Tzuiyang.*

78. *Jianjuedi Fandui Zichanjieji Ziyouhua.*

leader Deng Xiaoping with a dilemma. He remains firm in his conviction that market economic reforms are the best path forward for China. The success of his Open Door policy is evident by China's rapid development, and Deng is convinced that he has the strong support of China's people.

But he's a product of his times.

For most of his eighty-three years this has consisted of chaos: Western colonial occupation, two world wars, Japan's brutal invasion, the civil war with the Nationalists (who rule Taiwan in exile and still claim sovereignty over all of China), the Communist revolution, followed by Mao's decades of despotic rule. The only prolonged peace China has known in more than two centuries has been during Deng's resolute—albeit benign compared to Mao's—dictatorship. It's understandable for a man with his background to fear political upheaval.

"Let China have fifty years of uninterrupted economic development then we can talk about democracy," Deng says.[79]

He understands this requires a delicate balancing act—advance reforms or risk China's fragile economic development. Simultaneously he must fight a rear guard action against fellow revolutionary elders who've appointed themselves arbiters of political correctness. These conservative veterans see ideology as Deng's Achilles heel and seize every opportunity to pressure him. Through control of China's propaganda organs and the official media, they impose a rigid code of Marxist puritanism on society, thereby preserving an important political role for themselves.

But Deng didn't become paramount leader without a few political moves of his own.

He adopts a brilliant counterstrategy to combat these ideologues, derived straight from Sun Tzu's 2,500-year-old Chinese classic *Art of War*: "A leader must be prepared to sacrifice pawns."

Deng's pawns are selected from the same expendable pool that emperors have used for millennia—obsequious officials and loyal scholars. The enduring relevance of this Machiavellian approach to China's politics becomes increasingly clear to me in the days ahead.

---

79. Related to me in a conversation with his son Deng Zhifang.

Economic freedom has changed Chinese citizens' values in the decade since the end of the Cultural Revolution. People are too preoccupied with improving their standard of living to take much interest in a Cold War–style political campaign. Opinions regarding these dissidents and the general political atmosphere range from apathy—the safest public stance—to principled opposition.

Through his conversations with well-informed friends John learns that moderate forces in the leadership[80] are seizing upon this public indifference to turn the political tide and resist the hardliners. This limits the crackdown's scope, a welcome development, but creates the potential for a dangerous split in the leadership that could escalate into open conflict. During the Cultural Revolution armed street battles resulted from such power vacuums.

"*Chengmen shihuo, yangji chiyu*, when the city gate is on fire it brings disaster to innocent people," John comments, describing what happens when a no-holds-barred leadership power struggle tramples everything in its path.

So much wisdom from so much suffering.

A week later, I'm hanging out in John's room waiting for him to get off work when he rushes in out of breath and turns on the radio. I start to talk but he puts his finger to his lips, silencing me.

"After an emergency expanded meeting of the Politburo, Communist Party General Secretary Hu Yaobang has resigned," the radio announcer intones.

"*Tamade*, motherfucker," John curses.

"What does it mean?" I ask.

"Hu Yaobang is the protector of educated families like ours. This could mean that the hardliners have gained the upper hand."

Over dinner and then our usual pot of tea, John and his mom explain to me that they see Hu as the protector of open-minded, educated Chinese like them, and wonder if the bad old days of public denunciations and torture-induced confessions will return.

---

80. Most notably, Communist Party chief Hu Yaobang and Prime Minister Zhao Ziyang.

While we're drinking tea, there's a break in the broadcast for another special announcement:

Hu's replacement as Communist Party chief is Prime Minister Zhao Ziyang. Zhao's another liberal proponent of economic and social reform, so the hardliners have succeeded in eliminating one political enemy, but they aren't sufficiently powerful to handpick his successor.

"Deng's maintained his balancing act," John explains. "Just like the *Art of War* counsels, he's sacrificed a pawn to keep his economic reforms on track."

Particularly auspicious is the fact that the purged Hu is permitted to keep his Politburo seat. This is a Communist Party–infighting first, John tells me, and a break from the *You die I live*,[81] cutthroat past.

In a further conciliatory gesture to the hardliners, Deng appoints Soviet-trained central economic planner Li Peng, already the most powerful conservative member of the Politburo Standing Committee, to replace Zhao as prime minister. So the precarious balance between pro-reform and conservative forces in the Party hierarchy is maintained.

"This sets the stage for the next round of struggle," John explains, describing what sounds like a murder mystery plot.

As the weather turns warm the Anti-Bourgeois Liberalization propaganda campaign dies down as quickly as it started. The shrill political tone gives way to the familiar refrain of stern-faced news anchors extolling record foreign investment, soaring trade surpluses, climbing income, and shiny, happy ethnic minorities looking ahead to bigger and brighter futures for themselves and the PRC.

But there is an unavoidable backlash on campuses. High-profile student-protest leaders are expelled from their schools. Military training and rigorous political indoctrination is reinstated in colleges and high schools nationwide. And the recently discontinued policy of requiring university graduates to work in underdeveloped rural areas after graduation prior to receiving coveted state job assignments is revived. This is

---

81. *Ni si wo huo,* a sad summation of the political ethos of the time.

a significant hardship to less privileged students, usually from the provinces, who've borrowed money to attend university and now must defer the start of their professional careers and ability to repay loans for at least a year after graduation.

Professor Fang, I discover, has been transferred from the University of Science and Technology to the Central Astronomical Observatory in Beijing where conservatives can keep a closer watch on him. This punishment is a blessing in disguise. It reunites Fang with his family. It also frees him to pursue his passion for theoretical research and writing.

But hardline officials aren't satisfied with merely firing him from his job, stripping him of his Chinese Academy of Sciences leadership post and Party membership, and forcibly relocating him halfway across the country. They're determined to publicly humiliate him, to set a lasting example for anyone who dares to defy Party orthodoxy and sing out of political tune.[82]

All workplaces are required to carry out political study sessions to reinforce the lessons of the Anti–Bourgeois Liberalization campaign. The reading material contains a collection of Fang's speeches. Conservative elders are convinced that average citizens will find Fang's views as dangerously liberal as they do, and understand why he must be silenced.

John's mother tells me that these reactionary ideologues are mired in the past, and their thinking is out of tune with the times.

"Most people agree with Fang's ideas," she tells me. "And they're not afraid to say so. Social change is giving rise to competing interests, and to keep pace the government has to become more responsive and transparent or risk discontent."

I'm impressed by the political sophistication of a woman who serves on her neighborhood watch committee and washes and recycles glass milk bottles for a living. Once again the old guard has badly misjudged the popular mood.

"Fang also addresses the problem of official corruption," John's mom adds. "He witnessed Party cadres with no qualifications accompany scientific delegations abroad to sightsee, shop, and wine-and-dine at public

82. *Chang fandiao* in Chinese.

expense. The government's attack on Fang portrays his words as dangerous defiance of Party discipline and sowing social discord, but it's the squandering of public funds that most infuriates average Chinese," she concludes, adding an uncharacteristic curse: "*Qù tamade!* They can all go to Hell!"

I can't help laughing at this straitlaced woman's profanity.

Then I ask John's mom to show me the political study documents, and she gives me her copy. With my dog-eared Chinese-English dictionary and John's help I pore over the speeches. It's hard for me to see why Fang's commentary on topics ranging from reform of China's education system to innovations like eliminating mandatory political study sessions in schools and workplaces is perceived as threatening by the government. But China's aging leaders are so insecure that they see Fang's criticism—regardless of how constructive—as an existential threat.

The publicizing of Fang's speeches backfires. It disseminates his practical ideas about a more open society to tens of millions of average Chinese nationwide who would never have seen them otherwise. The influence of this miscalculation is immense. It turns him into a revered symbol of resistance, and makes the Party appear fearful and out of touch.

Fang is hailed as China's Sakharov[83] by the foreign media and international human rights organizations. The notoriety and support this status confers on him, and the resulting political pressure it exerts on Beijing, intensifies the ideological impasse among the Party leadership and propels the conservatives and moderates toward open conflict.

---

83. Andrei Sakharov was the Soviet nuclear physicist, dissident, and human rights activist who won the Nobel Peace Prize in 1975. Russian Communist Party leader Mikhail Gorbachev, initiator of political and economic reforms in the 1980s, brought Sakharov back from internal exile to enhance his reformist credentials.

chapter fourteen

I only regret that, due to my Chinese birth, I can't be the U.S.
ambassador to China myself.
—Bette Bao Lord, wife of U.S. Ambassador Winston Lord,
addressing students at Beijing University, spring 1987

After delivering my résumé and copies of my published articles to all the
foreign news bureaus, I receive a call from the *Los Angeles Times* Beijing
bureau chief David Holley. He's a veteran foreign correspondent who
started his career covering the Vietnam War. He invites me for an interview the following morning in the *Times*' downtown office.

I get to the bureau early and knock on the door. A tall, thin man with
a brown goatee and wire-rimmed glasses opens the door. He introduces
himself and I follow him into the office. We sit on a brown leather couch
and he pours me coffee.

We chat for more than an hour as he reviews my clips[84] and quizzes
me on my Chinese ability. He's just begun studying Mandarin himself.
He asks about my reporting experience and political views, and we seem
to hit it off.

We're both liberal—David studied at Berkeley in the '60s—and laid-
back. And we share a passion for reporting on the dramatic changes taking place here.

It's clear to me that we would work well together. The telephone

---

84. Journalism slang for copies of published articles.

rings, and David says he has to take the call. It's his wife Fumiyo, a Japanese photojournalist. I sit back sipping coffee and look out the office window. It's on the tenth floor of the Jianguomenwai Diplomatic Compound building, overlooking the Avenue of Eternal Peace traffic.

After David gets off the phone, he picks up my résumé and clips, but appears to have made a decision.

"How would you like to work together?"

"Great!" I say, almost too loudly.

He extends his big, bony hand and we shake on the offer. Just like that, I'm closer to fulfilling my dream of becoming an accredited foreign correspondent for a major American newspaper, my lifelong goal.

Chinese astrology divides the human lifetime into twelve-year cycles, with each year symbolized by a different animal. The start of each new cycle, in Chinese *benmingnian* or zodiac year, is decisive in influencing one's *yuanfen*—fate. This summer marks the start of my third cycle.

I'm thrilled by this stroke of good luck, and can't help reflecting on the accuracy of the old monk's palm-reading prediction when he told me my career would take off in my twenty-fourth year.

The few foreign newspaper bureaus in Beijing are permitted only one accredited correspondent by the Chinese government, to limit the number of reporters requiring full-time surveillance. So I have to work unaccredited—illegally—and get paid under the table. I don't mind, I'm getting used to skirting the rules here.

"*Xianzhan houzou, zhaner buzou* [Act first then seek permission, or act and don't seek permission]," Chairman Mao counseled regarding bureaucracy.

I'm starting to see how life here works: *kaizhiyan, bizhiyan* [one eye open, one eye closed]. All the foreign newspaper bureaus fill research assistant positions with hungry young would-be foreign correspondents like me.

My duties include maintaining the office's Chinese- and English-language research files, translating newspaper articles and government press releases, and interpreting for my boss's interviews. David's Mandarin isn't good enough to conduct interviews by himself. But what really excites me is that now I have an opportunity to write for the prestigious *Los Angeles Times*, in addition to continuing to freelance for *Asiaweek*.

To celebrate, John and I take a night off from our usual *zaoshui zaoqi* (early-to-bed, early-to-rise) routine, and attend a dance party at Beijing University. We approach the foreign student dormitory—*Shaoyuan* (Soup Spoon Garden) was its traditional name during the Qing Dynasty. Rainbow-colored Christmas lights drape the evergreen trees in the dorm courtyard, adding to the festive air as foreign and Chinese students chat, sip drinks, and sway to the music.

"*Say it loud, I'm black and I'm proud!*" godfather of soul James Brown shouts from loudspeakers in a dorm window.

John and I make eye contact and smile at the ironic choice of music.

We see some friends and walk over to say hello. Standing in the group is a young Chinese woman wearing a tight, sleeveless, black silk dress.

"*Nin hao?* How are you?" I say in careful Mandarin.

"You don't have to speak Chinese, I'm American too."

I flush with embarrassment.

"How did you know I was American?"

She answers with her eyes, scanning my attire: half-tucked-in flannel shirt, faded Levi's jeans, and Timberland hiking boots.

"Everything but the Yankees cap, eh?" I say, and we both laugh.

"Where are you from?"

"New York City."

That explains it. She radiates the cool confidence of a native New Yorker.

"How about getting away from this loud music and taking a walk?"

She raises her eyebrows at my directness, but it's clear we'll have to shout over the music to hear each other. So I lead the way to *Weiminghu*—No-Name Lake—the body of water at the center of campus.

We stroll in silence, the music giving way to the soothing sound of crickets chirping. As we reach the willow trees surrounding the lake, I ask about her background.

"My name's Deirdre Huang. Huang De-li in Chinese. But my family and friends call me Dede."

"Little brother?" *Didi* means little brother in Chinese.

"No, *Dede*'s short for *Deirdre*. But that was the joke in my family, that I became a tomboy because of my name."

We both laugh.

"*Hen rongxing renshi ni* [Honored to meet you]," I say as I take her hand and shake it.

Dede's a head shorter than my five feet eleven inches", has intelligent brown eyes and a kind smile. I can see that she has an athletic physique. We discover that we share a lot in common: love of the outdoors, sports, reading and writing, and a passion for traditional Chinese culture and the exciting changes underway here.

"So, you're a Twinkie—yellow on the outside, white on the inside—and I'm an egg—white on the outside, yellow on the inside," I joke and she rolls her eyes.

"Very funny. I'm sick of being teased because my Chinese isn't fluent."

"I get complimented just for saying hello and being able to use chopsticks."

We shake our heads at the disparate treatment of ethnic Chinese foreigners and "white" people like me. Prejudice against other Chinese is deeply ingrained here.

Dede continues: "I went to Exeter Academy and then Harvard, every immigrant parents' dream," "After graduating I needed to get away from my parents' pressure—my dad's a big investment banker in Manhattan—so I came to Beijing University to study and delay life decisions."

"*Hun rizi*, slacking like me," I joke, and she playfully punches my arm.

"My family's from Shanghai and never spoke Mandarin at home, they thought it was more important for me to be all-American. So after I finished a year of language study, I decided to stay on in Beijing and look for a job. I applied to be executive assistant to the wife of the U.S. ambassador, Bette Bao Lord. I just found out that I got the job."

"*Zhongxin zhuhe!* Congratulations!"

"Thanks. I'm really relieved. This is my first job after college, and it'll get my parents off my back. I guess I'm celebrating."

"I'm celebrating too." I tell her about my new *L.A. Times* job. We realize that the ambassador's residence where she'll be working is half a block from the *L.A. Times* office.

"So I guess we'll be seeing a lot of each other," I joke and she narrows her eyes in mock annoyance before smiling.

Dede's landed a dream job. Mrs. Lord is a celebrity here. She was born in Shanghai, but exiled as a child with her Nationalist government official parents following the Communist takeover, and grew up in Brooklyn. She became a professional dancer and then attended Tufts University where she met her husband, the Pillsbury dough-heir Winston Lord. Now she's a best-selling author and a cultural ambassador between China and the U.S. She's better known here than her ambassador husband.

But Ambassador Lord's China credentials are impeccable too. He was Top aide to National Security Adviser Henry Kissinger in the Nixon administration, he helped arrange his boss's secret trip to China in 1971, which laid the groundwork for President Nixon meeting Chairman Mao the following year, starting the normalization process between Washington and Beijing. Just thinking about Dede's privileged insider's view on the U.S.–China relationship gives me a thrill—both personally, and, I have to admit, professionally as an ambitious young reporter.

Dede and I start spending an increasing amount of time together. We go for long bike rides, run and swim in nearby Deep Jade Pool Park, picnic in the hills west of the city, and take moonlight walks. Arriving back at John's house late one night, he jokes that he's getting jealous. But I can see he's happy for me. He likes Dede. He knows it's healthy for me to be starting a new relationship, and accompanies us on our excursions as often as he can. But his band is getting more popular and securing bigger gigs, and he's meeting lots of women too.

"When are you going to get a girlfriend?" I ask teasingly.

He flushes with embarrassment.

"What do you think I am, a loose American?"

I know he's waiting to meet the right woman to get serious. It's acceptable for two Americans to casually date, but John retains the traditional Chinese view that this would be dishonorable, and that two filial young Chinese will know when they meet that they're meant to spend the rest of their lives together.

Summer ends and Dede and I start our new jobs downtown. Every morning we bike the six miles to work and home again. We soon tire of the commute and decide to move closer to our jobs and look for an apartment. Moving in together might be considered rash back in the States—we've only known each other a few weeks—but here it makes sense. Beijing feels less foreign and lonely living as a couple. And what her conservative Chinese investment banker father doesn't know won't hurt him, Dede reasons.

Neither of us can afford to rent a place by ourselves. Foreigners are forbidden to live in local Chinese housing, and the only apartments legally available are in luxury, gated compounds for foreign business executives or serviced hotel apartments where rents average several thousand U.S. dollars a month, far beyond our means.

After putting out word that we're looking for a place, Dede's friend and my new foreign correspondent colleague Nina McPherson, a Yale University graduate and reporter for Agence France-Presse, offers us a room in her large diplomatic compound apartment. In addition to foreign reporters, all foreign diplomats are required to live in this tightly-guarded apartment block where my *L.A. Times* office—and all the foreign news bureaus—are located. The two, three, and four-bedroom flats have high ceilings, spacious kitchens, balconies with views, and a previously unimaginable luxury: hot water at the turn of a kitchen and bathroom tap.

The compound is located in Beijing's tree-lined downtown embassy district, where most of the capital's foreign legations are. Dede's job in the ambassador's residence is a block away. My commute consists of walking across a playground to the building next door.

Dede and Mrs. Lord begin to develop a mother-daughter relationship, and before long I'm adopted as well. The Ambassador's residence becomes our second home. We're invited to share meals, drink tea, and discuss the dramatic changes going on here with them. Mrs. Lord is a former fashion model as well as professional dancer. She's still strikingly beautiful. Ambassador Lord is an Andover prep school and Yale University graduate, and a member of the infamous Skull and Bones secret society.[85] And due to the Ambassador's long tenure in government, they are consummate Washington insiders.

Our primary topic of conversation is the growing economic interdependence between Beijing and Washington with simultaneous still-strong Cold War hostilities. At my urging, Ambassador Lord regales us with accounts of the role he played in the U.S.'s opening to China, details of the invasion of Cambodia while Kissinger's aide, and other fascinating aspects of the Nixon White House. But politics is the Ambassador's full-time job, and he understandably tires of the topic. He's much happier talking about his beloved New York Giants, Yankees, Knicks, and Rangers. I'm only too happy to oblige, as I share his sports fanaticism.

The Lords are always eager to hear about my experiences on reporting trips outside Beijing, and ask Dede and me about our Chinese friends and social activities. We bring John to the embassy to meet them, and he predictably charms the Lords, although he's intimidated by their opulent lifestyle, never having seen the similar privileged circumstances China's Communist Party leaders live in.

I initially ascribe the Lords' interest in our lives to politeness, but over time realize they feel trapped in their gilded cage. Their existence consists of an endless string of cocktail parties, high-pressure political events, and meet-and-greets with VIPs. They never get to walk out of the embassy into the streets unrecognized. Dede and I have the freedom of anonymity, which facilitates our deepening understanding of this country. So the Lords try to experience Beijing vicariously through our eyes, and we're more than happy to reciprocate their kindness with our stories and observations.

---

85. The Yale University secret society that's produced a disproportionate number of U.S. presidents—including George Bush Sr. and Jr.—and C.I.A. directors.

The Lords' ivy-covered villa is also becoming a sanctuary where high-ranking government officials, People's Liberation Army officers, and dissident intellectuals and artists can come together and share ideas. China's increasing political ferment is reflected in the nonstop buzz of activity in the ambassador's residence. With a white Steinway grand piano in the parlor and an impressive collection of modern American art on the walls—Jackson Pollock, Georgia O'Keeffe, Willem de Kooning, Andrew Wyeth, and Jasper Johns, to name a few—the residence has the air of an old-fashioned European cultural salon. In a nation that's known nothing but war, revolution, and grinding poverty for nearly two centuries, the opportunity to mingle, sip cocktails, and debate ideas in a relaxed and open environment is liberating.

Mrs. Lord hosts these gatherings with consummate skill. Her unique bilingual charm allows her to engineer lively conversations while steering discussions around sensitive shoals of controversy. Frequent guests at the embassy include Minister of Culture and famed Chinese actor Ying Ruocheng,[86] revered octogenarian playwright Cao Yu,[87] PLA General Zhang Zhen, famous novelist Bing Xin and her People's Congress representative daughter Wu Qing, film director Zhang Yimou, environmental activist Liang Congjie,[88] female investigative reporter Dai Qing, and contemporary art scholar Li Xianting.

Mrs. Lord doesn't let any potential resource go to waste. She recruits me to play guitar and sing in Chinese to jump-start the festivities. At a special gathering to celebrate the birthday of famous revolutionary-era folk singer Wang Kun, Mrs. Lord signals me and I stand up with my guitar and lead the crowd in singing "Happy Birthday" to the black-dyed-bouffant-haired woman. After the final chorus, wishes of *shoubi nanshan furu donghai*—may you live longer than the Southern mountains and be richer than the Eastern sea—and hearty cheers of *ganbei*—bottoms up—I sit back on the white leather sofa in the living room.

---

86. He played the prison warden in Bernardo Bertolucci's Oscar-winning film *The Last Emperor*.

87. His revolutionary-era play *Thunderstorm* is considered China's most popular modern drama. Zhang Yimou's 2006 film *Curse of the Golden Flower* is a remake of the play set in the Tang Dynasty.

88. Grandson of Qing Dynasty political reformer Liang Qichao and son of China's most famous architect Liang Sicheng.

Next to me is the charismatic Minister of Culture Ying Ruocheng, cradling a glass of Scotch in his thick, ruddy hands. Old Ying, as he likes to be called, compliments me on my singing and playing.

"*Bu gan dang*, I'm unworthy," I say in self-deprecating Chinese.

Then, perhaps due to the rush of adrenaline from singing or the beer I just guzzled, I add: "You know, in the United States I would never perform in public because I'm not that good. But here I'm such a novelty that anything I do gets praised."

The moment the words leave my mouth I regret my bluntness. People my age are supposed to speak only when spoken to here, especially in such esteemed company. Those gathered around me arch their eyebrows in surprise at my cheekiness.

But Minister Ying, loosened up by whisky and more open-minded than his conservative colleagues, is intrigued.

"*You yisi*, very interesting," he says. "You're the youngest person here, but you've lived in both China and the United States. What do you think the biggest difference between our two countries is?"

Now I'm in trouble. There's no avoiding this question. So I take another swig of beer, sit up, and clear my throat. Then I gesture at the venerable playwright Cao Yu.

"The difference between China and the United States is like the difference between Master Cao[89] and me. I'm young, energetic, and ambitious. But I lack refinement and tread on toes."

The listeners laugh at this acknowledgement of my faux pas.

"Master Cao has experienced more in his lifetime than I can imagine. Civil war, revolution, famine, he's seen all the major events of the twentieth century and is well-versed in thousands of years of Chinese culture. My country's history is shorter than one of your dynasties."

I take another sip of beer and let my words sink in.

"Us Americans see ourselves as a new chosen people. This self-centeredness offends many, but is also the source of our optimism. It's the reason the world admires and seeks to emulate America's culture and

---

89. Cao Laoshi in Chinese. "Master" or "Teacher" is a common honorific used when referring to one's elders.

lifestyle. But it's also the reason China—the world's oldest civilization—and the United States—the youngest—find it hard to see eye-to-eye."

I scan the crowd, and then conclude: "And why it's so important for our two countries to better understand and learn from each other."

I let out a sigh of relief, bow my head in the traditional Chinese gesture of respect, then sit back on the sofa and drain my beer.

Most of the guests have drifted over to listen to this unusual exchange between the youngest person in the room—a foreigner to boot—and the oldest and most revered. They whisper among themselves, but keep a close eye on Cao Yu, waiting for his response.

After a minute's pause, the venerated playwright says, "Your words are insightful. But there's another point to consider. Our People's Republic is less than four decades old, a child by nation-state standards. We desire democracy, but because of our cultural and historical circumstances, and traumatic recent past, we have to be careful how we pursue this. Our solution must work for a population of more than one billion—five times that of the United States—so any political change will at best be 'democracy with Chinese characteristics.'

"So in this sense," he claps his hands together for emphasis, "we're the child, and you're the revered elder."

Then he does something that surprises and moves me. He shifts his weight onto his carved wooden cane, pushes his thin, erect frame up off the couch, and begins to recite, in English: "Four score and seven years ago, our fathers brought forth on this continent a new nation, conceived in Liberty, and dedicated to the proposition that all men are created equal. . . ."

An eighty-year-old Chinese man reciting the Gettysburg Address from memory. How many American politicians can do that?

This inspiring performance is why China never ceases to amaze me. Just when I'm on the verge of losing hope that it will ever become a more diverse, tolerant, open society, something like this happens to revive my faith.

Mrs. Lord hurries over to help Master Cao sit back down. Then she proposes a toast: "*Zhong-Mei youyi wanshou wujiang*—long live U.S.-China friendship."

Everyone raises their glass and adds: "*Ganbei*, bottoms up."

Then, at Mrs. Lord's urging, I grab my guitar and launch into a rousing rendition of the folk song "*Nanniwan* (Southern Muddy River Bend)"[90] that the guest of honor Wang Kun was famous for singing during the civil war. Everyone in the tipsy crowd sings along.

I shake my head at this surreal scene. I'm glad that, rather than maintaining deferential Chinese silence, I spoke my mind. It's so tricky to know where the invisible line between honesty and overstep lies here. After the crowd leaves and Dede and I help Mrs. Lord and the embassy staff clean up, we walk back to our apartment and reflect on the evening.

"We're really lucky to witness all this," Dede says as she slips her hand in mine.

"I know," I agree. "How often do you get to see history in the making?"

Then we resume our silence, savoring the glow of the starlit night and the special evening we enjoyed.

---

90. A propaganda song set to a popular folk melody during the revolution.

chapter fifteen

I don't mind being a wandering artist. China needs more of this spirit of freedom, independence, and rebellion.
—Photographer Gao Bo, from the underground documentary film *Bumming in Beijing*

Dede and I work long hours at our new jobs, but most weekends we bike out to the university district to hang out with John and his friends. One chilly autumn evening we arrive at John's place after dark, and he tells us about a special outing he's planned for the next morning.

"It's as big as us discovering the rock star Cui Jian," he reveals, but won't say more because he wants to surprise us.

I'm so excited about what we're going to see that I have a hard time falling asleep.

The next morning we rise at dawn and pedal our bikes toward the Western Hills that fringe Beijing. It's a crisp, sunny Saturday, and golden-leaved gingko trees sway against the cloudless blue sky. The fan-shaped gingko leaves rustle in the breeze, creating a soothing rhythm. We ride on a dirt path that runs along the old Imperial canal to the Summer Palace, now a popular park.

As the trail steepens we veer onto the grounds of *Yuanmingyuan* (Garden of Pure Brightness). This run-down public park once served as a holiday retreat for Qing Dynasty emperors.[91] The site has been intentionally left in ruins as a symbol of China's humiliation at the hands of foreign

---

91. Before it was ransacked by French and British troops in 1860 during the second Opium War.

occupiers, and as a reminder to young Chinese of the tragic consequences of a nation's inability to defend itself. Resentment over this indignity still runs so deep that new Communist Youth League members swear their oath of allegiance here.

Behind a lake on the park grounds is a farming village. It's lined with small shops and single-story red brick huts. At the far end is a six-foot-high wrought-iron gate. John knocks loudly, and a voice calls out "*Lailo!* [Coming!]"

The door swings open and a guy our age greets us. He's whip-thin, with piercing brown eyes and a thick mane of wavy black hair pulled back in a ponytail. His bohemian appearance is completed by a wispy beard. He shakes my hand, and with a big grin says in accented but clearly understandable English: "Hello, my name is Gabriel."

He leads us inside a dirt-floored shack that appears to serve as both his living quarters and art studio. There's no indoor plumbing. He tells us he shares a cold-water tap in the courtyard with his neighbors, also artists, and uses a chamber pot that he empties in a public toilet. Despite the primitive conditions, the space resonates with creative energy. Vibrantly-colored oil paintings and subtle Chinese-style ink washes cover the white walls.

"Some of those are mine, but most are by my art school classmate Zhang Dali," he says, following my gaze. "But I want to show you some other work."

"*Qing bangge mang* [please help me]," he says to John as he walks to the back of the room.

They carry a heavy wooden crate to where we're sitting, and Gabriel carefully lifts off the top.

It's a stack of framed black-and-white large format photographs Gabriel took traveling across Tibet in the past year. The pictures are mesmerizing. They're three by four feet, matte-finished images of Tibetan nomads living in the harsh environment of the highest-altitude landscape on the planet. These photos could be exhibited in any art gallery in the world. They capture the rugged spirit of Tibet, and reflect the grace, dignity, and pride of its people trying to maintain their traditional lifestyle in the face of relentless "modernization."

John, Dede, and I remark on the intimacy of the shots. It astounds us that the subjects would let a Han Chinese photographer get close enough to capture a nomadic Tibetan woman breast-feeding her child, given the complex and troubled history between the two peoples.

"I earn the confidence of the people I photograph by living with them, helping with their daily chores, and showing respect for their life-style and religion," Gabriel explains. "It's the only way to get close enough to honestly document their lives."

Now I understand why he wears his hair so long. If not for his Beijing-accented Mandarin, he could easily pass for a *Khampa*—a long-haired eastern Tibetan cowboy.

"Your photographs remind me of the work of the nineteenth-century American photographer Edward S. Curtis," Dede says, sharing her knowl-edge of art history—her college major. "He documented the Native Amer-ican Plains Indians before they were confined to reservations, earned the trust of tribal leaders, and was permitted access to rituals and ceremo-nies—including the sacred Sun Dance—forbidden to most outsiders."

Gabriel lights up at Dede's comparison. "Curtis's *North American Indian* project inspired my decision to travel to Tibet and document the traditional culture before it's gone."

While Dede, John, and I continue to pore over the photographs, Gabriel prepares tea on an electric hotplate. Every new photo aston-ishes us with its insight and sensitivity. We're impressed that someone so young has the courage to undertake such an ambitious project. It occurs to me that Gabriel may be the perfect photographer to work with me on my story assignments.

The kettle whistles, and as Gabriel fills our teacups he continues describing his background and artistic vision.

"I'm from Sichuan province, and the hot climate and spicy peppers give us a *huoqi* [fiery temperament]," he says with a laugh. "That fuels my artistic vision."

Then a shadow seems to cross his face.

"My earliest memories are of watching political struggle sessions and executions during the Cultural Revolution. I thought that it was all a big game until I saw my grandfather paraded before the village and beaten by Red Guards for being a university professor."

I glance at John and see him wince at this familiar story.

"Even though I was labeled a 'bad political element' because of my grandfather's class background," Gabriel continues, "I showed talent for drawing and painting in school and the government used me to produce propaganda posters.

"I practiced my art nonstop; it was a welcome relief from the political chaos in the streets. Then I tested into the high school attached to the Sichuan Fine Arts Academy. We trained in Soviet-style social realism. All those heroic male model workers and their comely female comrades chiseled from stone," he says, striking a revolutionary raised-fist pose.

"After graduating from high school, I was admitted by the National Academy of Art and Design in Beijing. It was the first time I ever left home."

Gabriel refills our teacups and continues.

"I loved going to art school in the capital, meeting new classmates from all over the country, visiting art galleries, museums, and bookstores. The Mao era was over and the cultural atmosphere was just opening up. I was assigned to the graphic design department, but my passion was oil painting and I pursued it obsessively, until I was exposed to the black-and-white photojournalism of Magnum photo agency founders Capa, Cartier-Bresson, Kertész, and Brassaï. They confronted the most monumental events of their time—world war, revolution, endemic poverty, famine—and documented it so powerfully that their work remains cutting edge a half-century later.

"While in school I lived extremely frugally, working odd jobs and saving all my money so I could buy a used Nikon camera. I began traveling on local buses and trains to rural China, documenting traditional folk culture, art, music, religious rituals, and holiday festivals fast disappearing under the pressures of modern life.

"In my senior year of college in 1986, I entered my pictures in a national photography contest and won. First prize was a large-format, four-by-five-inch negative Hasselblad camera. That's what I took to Tibet and used to take these pictures."

Dede, John, and I nod in amazed appreciation. Gabriel explains that after his college graduation, rather than accept a government-assigned job working for the provincial propaganda bureau in Sichuan, he chose to remain unemployed and homeless in Beijing. Without a *hukou*—the residence permit all Chinese need to be assigned an apartment, receive ration coupons for food and clothing, even purchase a bicycle—he's an illegal migrant subject to arrest and forced relocation at any time, not to mention all the daily difficulties of living outside China's still predominantly state-planned economy. The rationing of food and household goods is being discontinued, so with extra money it's possible to purchase food and shelter. But without a residence permit it's impossible to obtain housing in the city. Gabriel and his fellow provincial artists—many also graduates of the nation's top art schools—have pooled their resources and rented these rooms from local farmers in Beijing's outskirts. Technically outside the city limits, these villages aren't subjected to the same police supervision as the capital's neighborhoods.

His photographs and the beauty they preserve disappear back into the wooden box. The sun is setting and we have a long bike ride home so we say good-bye and pedal away.

As we ride, John, Dede, and I remark on the fact that these artists are the first group of Chinese since the revolution to live outside the Communist Party's pervasive system of social control. This has not only profound cultural but also political implications. These artists are pioneering role models for creative youth nationwide. They're symbols of the fact that after thirty-five years, the Party's totalitarian grip is starting to loosen and can be successfully circumvented. A legend has started to grow up around this community, and Gabriel and his buddies are labeled *liulang yishujia*—outsider artists—and the rural huts they've colonized the Artists' Village (*yishucun*), a nod to the artists' enclave in New York City's Greenwich Village they're trying to emulate.

During a subsequent visit, Gabriel introduces John, Dede, and me to his neighbor Wu Wenguang, a fellow outsider artist from China's far Yunnan province. Wu has procured a video camera and is chronicling the itinerant life of Gabriel and four of his fellow artists for a documentary film entitled *Bumming in Beijing (Liulang Beijing)*.[92] Wu subsequently films some scenes in our downtown apartment. Through this experience, Gabriel and I begin to form a strong friendship. He often shows up at our apartment and my *L.A. Times* office unannounced. With his long hair and beard he passes as a foreigner; only a handful of Chinese artists dare to adopt this bohemian appearance. He confidently strolls past the Chinese soldiers standing guard at the entrance to our compound. Gabriel always seems to show up at mealtimes. The Chinese call this *cengfan*, freeloading meals. It's a necessary survival trait for these impoverished artists.

We're happy to feed him and hear his crazy stories of dodging the police while living on the edge of society. As our bond deepens, I decide to ask Gabriel to become my regular photographer and join me on reporting trips. He eagerly accepts. Bylines in the *Los Angeles Times* will give him the professional credentials he needs to jump-start his own career.

To showcase Gabriel's talent and raise funds for him to continue his photography projects, Dede and I organize an exhibit of his work at our apartment. We invite our new work colleagues and neighbors— international diplomats, business executives, and foreign correspondents from all over the world. They're enthralled by Gabriel's work and buy more than a dozen of his prints, funding film and camera equipment purchases for his next trip to Tibet.

One guest is particularly intrigued by not just the photographs, but the story of the artist behind them. David Tinnin, a tall, silver-haired former *Time* magazine foreign correspondent based in Germany during and after the war, is in town scouting investment opportunities for the Swiss publishing company Ringier. He invites Gabriel and me to dinner at his hotel the following evening.

Over a fancy French meal at the newly opened downtown Jianguo Hotel that costs more than an average Chinese worker's annual salary (US$300), Tinnin asks Gabriel about his approach to photography, artistic vision, and future plans. He also regales us with stories of his adventures

---

92. Bumming in Beijing (流浪北京 Liulang Beijing in Chinese), produced and directed by Wu Wenguang, won critical acclaim at international film festivals upon its eventual release in 1991. It is generally recognized as China's first underground documentary film.

as a spy in Berlin during and after the war. He sees in us a reflection of his own daredevil youth and welcomes the opportunity to vicariously relive it by supporting our work.

Over after-dinner coffee, Tinnin pulls out a roll of bills and peels off US$1,000. This is more money than Gabriel has ever seen. The publisher hands the cash to Gabriel and tells him to buy new equipment and film, and travel to take pictures of China's ethnic minority areas for a book he intends to produce. He wants me to write the text.[93] I'm ecstatic, but Gabriel keeps cool.

After we finish and thank Tinnin for everything, we bike home.

"*Niubi* [Cow's vagina]*!*" I shout (dirty Beijing slang for "that's awesome!"). But Gabriel remains silent.

"You're not excited?"

"I am, but not surprised," he says quietly. "I know my work is valuable, and will be recognized and rewarded as long as I stray true to my vision."

His words will prove more prescient than either of us can imagine.

---

93. *Life in the Middle Kingdom* is published in 1990 by Bücher, a German publishing house.

chapter sixteen

Why did the spark go out of Chinese civilization after the seven-teenth century? How did a nation that set the pace for the world for thousands of years suddenly become so weak and vulner-able? What did we possess yesterday that we have lost today? China is pondering. Her children are questioning history.
—from the June 1988 television documentary *River Elegy*

Chinese New Year, 1988 (Year of the Dragon)

Chinese astrology ascribes special significance to Dragon years, believing they're a time of major adverse events. The tragedies of the previous Dragon year, 1976, bore this out. The year began with the death of popular Prime Minister Chou En-lai, sparking a public outpouring of grief in Tiananmen Square that turned into the largest antigovernment protests ever in contemporary China. In July an earthquake in the Beijing suburb of Tangshan killed more than 500,000 people, the deadliest earthquake in human history. And the September death of Chairman Mao led to Deng Xiaoping launching a coup and arresting Mao's wife and her henchmen, the Gang of Four, before the Dragon year was done.

As I consider New Year's resolutions, I reflect that if 1988 is remotely as eventful as 1976, I'd better be prepared. Dede and I spend a quiet New Year's Eve with John and his family, preparing and eating *jiaozi* (steamed dumplings) and then going outside after midnight to watch the fireworks and exorcise the ghosts of the old year.

On New Year's Day, Dede works at a reception Ambassador and Mrs. Lord host at the embassy for leading Chinese cultural figures. I tag along, and at the event run into my old friend Su Xiaokang.[94] He's a thirty-nine-year-old lecturer at the Beijing Broadcasting Institute, the nation's premier training ground for radio and television journalists, and one of China's leading investigative reporters. His newspaper and magazine exposés and best-selling books based upon them investigate taboo subjects previously deemed too politically sensitive to be aired in public. At great professional and personal risk he's reported on endemic poverty, official corruption, and the Party's relentless power struggles and purges, both in the past and, much more sensitively, in the present.

Su looks the part of the intrepid investigative reporter. He's five foot eight, shorter than most northern Chinese, but he's built like a pit bull with a barrel chest, thick neck, and bulging biceps and forearms. Whenever he greets me he grips my hand so tightly he leaves it throbbing and numb.

"*Lao Su*, Old Su," I say as I slap him on the back in greeting. "What muck have you been raking up lately?"

"*Jimi*, top secret," he says, then drapes his arm over my shoulders and steers me to the edge of the room. Out of earshot of the other guests, he whispers: "I'm putting the final touches to a documentary film that's going to whip up a storm of controversy."

His words stun me. If spoken by almost anyone else, I would treat it as typical Beijing *dahua*—big talk or hyperbole—a trait the capital's residents are renowned for. But coming from a writer with Su's track record, I take his claim seriously.

"Some progressive-minded officials at China Central Television [CCTV] have decided that, due to *wenhuare*—the cultural reflection fever sweeping the country[95]—the time is ripe for some political risk. They commissioned me to produce a film critically examining China's tragic modern history, viewed through the lens of the nation's conservative Confucian past."

Su guzzles the rest of his beer, wipes his mouth with his sleeve, and continues: "This script is the culmination of all my investigative reporting.

---

94. Pronounced *Sue Shao-Kahng*.

95. In concert with increasing economic prosperity, the public is paying growing attention to cultural and social concerns.

Because TV is such a popular medium, it'll reach far more people than all my books and articles combined. And when it airs on primetime state-run television this summer and is seen by hundreds of millions nationwide, it has a good chance of spurring the debate about these critical issues that's long overdue."

I stay silent, letting Su's words sink in. If what he says is true, and nothing derails the project, the film will likely have the profound impact he predicts. Seeing a scoop, I ask if I can observe him producing the program. He agrees, on the condition that I delay publishing until after the film is broadcast so as not to further jeopardize its already-sensitive status.

A few days later I leave work at the *L.A. Times* early, swing by the embassy to pick up Dede, and we bike to Su's house in the university district. We walk our bikes past the guard at the residence compound gate. A foreigner visiting a Chinese professor is no longer a rare sight in Beijing. We appear to be a typical pair of students visiting their teacher, not a foreign reporter and his embassy-employed Chinese-American girlfriend, and pass undisturbed.

"Hello'r!" he greets us in his thickly Beijing-accented English. "Please come in," he adds, laughing at his own poor pronunciation.

We follow Su into his study, and he seats us at his writing desk and hands us each a copy of the documentary script. Then he retreats into the kitchen to prepare tea. Dede and I dive right into reading the handwritten manuscript.

As we turn the pages, we realize why Su is so enthusiastic but also anxious about the fate of this film. Its daring is evident in the title alone. *River Elegy*[96] *(He Shang)* is a clear reference to the classical Chinese poem *Ruler Elegy (Guo Shang)*, a famous epic[97] lamenting the early state's[98] downfall due to its leader's hubris. The river in the film's title is the Yellow River, revered as the birthplace of Chinese civilization. And the term *shang*, in

---

96. *Elegy* means "funeral song or lament for the dead."

97. Composed by court historian Chu Yuan in the third century BC. The poem expresses his deep concern at his country's downfall, and his anger at the self-indulgent ruler who'd allowed this tragedy to occur.

98. Zhanguo/Warring States is the general term used to describe the belligerent state of affairs prior to China's unification under the first Qin emperor in 221 BC.

addition to funeral song or elegy, has the added meaning "to die young." So Su and his colleagues[99] are saying, in typically coded Chinese fashion, that the Middle Kingdom's insular, Yellow River–based, conservative traditional culture has stagnated and that fresh, seaborne (international), modern cultural influences are necessary for its revitalization.

The film's irreverence extends far beyond the title. It harshly criticizes China's most cherished cultural symbols: the Great Wall, Imperial Dragon, and the Yellow River itself. Rather than rhapsodize about the past glories these emblems represent—the theme of Communist Party propaganda since Mao's death and the bankruptcy of his revolutionary ideology—the film mercilessly skewers them, arguing that through excessive glorification of the past, China has become self-absorbed, internationally isolated, and incapable of the self-criticism necessary to become a truly modern nation.

The Great Wall, depicted in school textbooks and state media as a symbol of strength, self-assurance, and technological prowess, is condemned in *River Elegy* as epitomizing extreme conservatism and debilitating xenophobia. The documentary maintains that these faults have enabled China to slavishly copy the West, but not succeed in developing its own innovative culture. The script emphasizes that the actual Great Wall has fallen into disrepair, with peasants pilfering the centuries-old stones to build new homes all along its length. Only a few select sites receive state subsidies, and this not to preserve the old wall but to tear it down and rebuild Disney-fied versions for foreign and domestic tourists.

The dragon, traditionally worshipped as the god of life-giving water and believed personified by the emperor—hence the traditional Chinese belief in the "Mandate of Heaven" and a supreme leader's divine sanction to rule—is disparaged in *River Elegy* as an example of the nation's tragic willingness to submit to tyrannical rule. This has been the case for millennia and continues today.

And the Yellow River, revered throughout the Middle Kingdom's history as the cradle of Chinese civilization, is portrayed in the script

---

99. Coauthor Wang Luxiang and director Xia Jun.

as the source of a singular destructiveness that justifies its traditional moniker "China's Sorrow." The film portrays the Yellow River as an embodiment of the Chinese people's resignation to cyclical chaos and upheaval—natural and man-made—that has afflicted the country throughout its 3,000-year history.

There's nothing new about any of these assertions. Chinese writers have been making them for more than a century, dating back to the failed late nineteenth-century "Self-Strengthening Movement" to reform the corrupt Qing Dynasty with military, political, cultural, and economic modernization.

This effort continued through the May Fourth "New Culture Movement" of the 1920s. That national revival called for an overhaul of China's outmoded Confucian tradition and gave birth to the Communist Party.

Chairman Mao paid lip service to democracy as a means of modernization, but once he seized power he proved no better than his dynastic predecessors and perpetuated absolute dictatorship. And once Mao died, his ideology of fomenting Third World revolution was abandoned and the Party had to bolster its legitimacy through inculcation of extreme nationalism and a martyr complex among China's people.[100] The Party leadership recast itself as savior of the nation, defender of its sovereignty, and guardian of its ancient cultural heritage the same cultural heritage it had sought to destroy a decade earlier.[101]

This abrupt about-face could be expected to confuse China's people, but the masses were so accustomed to frequent, dramatic shifts in policy that they accepted this new dogma without question. It reminds me of the

---

100. 國恥 *Guo Chi* in Chinese—literally "national humiliation"—which refers to the official narrative that the majority of China's present problems are rooted in the exploitation it has suffered at the hands of foreign imperialist invaders for the past several centuries.

101. Going so far as to portray itself as the proud protector of Confucian tradition, in spite of Mao's vitriolic attacks on the old sage and his conservative legacy, labeled the "Four Olds"—Old Custom, Old Culture, Old Habits, Old Ideas—and targeted for eradication during the Cultural Revolution. Mao's attacks on Confucius are epitomized in a poem he wrote in 1973: *"I urge you to scold Emperor Qin Shihuang [the revered first unifier of China] less, his burning of books and burying of scholars, we should reassess. Our ancestral dragon, though dead, lives on in our minds, Confucianism, though renowned, is really worthless. Qin's political model of extreme authoritarianism has been practiced through all time."*

rise of fascism and its attendant extreme nationalism in Europe before World War II.

Dede and I comment to each other as we read, ensuring that we fully understand the content and its context in Chinese history. We confirm each other's conviction that in this present hair-trigger political environment, the mere suggestion that core aspects of China's tradition aren't only unworthy of glorifying and defending but are obstructing the nation's progress will be seen by the Communist Party as dangerous heresy.

After a few hours of reading, we take a break to stretch our legs. We step out onto Su's balcony just in time to watch the sun set over the Western Hills.

"This film, if it's ever broadcast, will surely rile up the old fogeys in Zhongnanhai,"[102] Dede says under her breath, to spare Su her pessimism. Her words reflect my thoughts exactly.

As the sky darkens, we step back inside and Su leads us to his living room sofa and inserts a preliminary cut of the film into the video player. Any doubt we retain about its controversial nature is immediately dispelled. My first response is to fear for Su's safety, not just professional but personal. The film attacks China's most sacred icons from the opening frame. The first episode, "Searching for Dreams," commences with an aerial shot of the Yellow River flowing into the sea. As the camera pans back over the barren yellow earth plateau where the river originates, the narrator's voice intones: "There is a blind spot in our national psyche. We dismiss our humiliations in the past several centuries as a break in our glorious tradition. Since 1840, the year of China's humiliating defeat to the British in the first Opium War, there has been no lack of sycophantic individuals seeking to use the greatness and splendor of the past to cover up China's present weak and backward state. After suffering through more than a century of painful reality, we seem to be in constant need of timeworn panaceas. We derive great solace from every headline-grabbing archaeological discovery. But the fact remains that at present our civiliza-

---

102. Pronounced *Jong-nahn-high,* literally: south central lakes, the Communist Party headquarters in the old western pleasure grounds of the Forbidden City.

tion is moribund." This pronouncement is crowned by the solemn quote: "History has proven time and again that the root cause of cultural decline is not attack by some outside force, but rather internal degeneration."[103]

With this scathing opening, *River Elegy* cuts to the core of China's deep-seated contemporary cultural insecurity and social malaise. And it confronts the nation's Communist rulers in a way that average Chinese couldn't imagine seeing in the nation's strictly censored press, never mind on prime-time state-run television. Although the content of the film is extremely bold, *River Elegy*'s visual style is uninspiring. The production values are low by Western standards, with amateurishly-edited historical footage interspersed with staid, talking-head interviews with progressive Party officials, liberal intellectuals, and the film's creators underscoring China's pressing need for far-reaching reforms.

But as a whole the film packs a visceral punch. It's presented in an engaging, anecdotal style that will be easily understood by the nation's 600 million television viewers. And Su and his crew have taken care to connect the complex historical examples to pressing present-day realities to maximize the film's relevance for its mainstream audience.

We continue to watch transfixed for several hours, barely stirring so as not to break the spell of the artistic work and its critical but hopeful vision for China's future. We're finally roused from our reverie when Su's wife calls us to dinner. As we pass around the plates of simple stir-fried rice and sautéed greens, Su elaborates on his vision for the film.

"I wrote *River Elegy* because Chinese intellectuals have been too timid," he says as he serves us, his guests, first. "This isn't a new problem. Scholars and artists have pandered to officials for millennia to secure patronage and power. But after the revolution, when we had the chance to break from this slavish past, we struck a Faustian deal with Mao. We forfeited our duty to speak out on pressing social and political issues and became willing propaganda tools. Both we and the country have paid a tremendous price for our compromise."

---

103. By British historian Arnold Toynbee (1889–1975).

Su takes a long sip of beer, then continues: "We have no tradition of intellectual independence. Educated people should serve as the conscience of society. Instead we've been used by the politically powerful for half a century and watched as their injustices and abuses mount, threatening to eradicate traditional civilization and the collective welfare of society."

He drains his beer, slaps the empty glass down on the table, and concludes: "China needs a civil rights movement like you had in the U.S. in the 1960s. I really admire Martin Luther King. China needs courageous activists like him. The Communist Party will oppose this with all the means at its disposal, and the process probably won't be peaceful. But this is a price worth paying for us to finally straighten our backs and reclaim our independence."

Then he amazes us by quoting Reverend King from memory: "*The measure of a man is not where he stands in moments of comfort and convenience, but where he stands at times of challenge and controversy.*"

I look over at Dede and she arches her eyebrows, showing that she's as impressed by Su's words as I am.

We finish and try to help clean up, but they refuse our assistance. So we thank them for their hospitality and tell them we have to get home. It's after midnight and the residential compound is deserted. Dede and I ride home in silence, letting the inspiring experience sink in.

I spend as much time as possible with Su in the following weeks. His daily routine consists of shuttling back and forth to the CCTV production studios to edit the film, while seizing every spare moment to make last-minute revisions to the script. Throughout this process he continually reassures station officials that the critical tone of the program will not cause them trouble with China's conservative cultural czars. Su is hopeful that *River Elegy*'s thought-provoking content will generate critical and commercial support, and this will protect it from the censors' knives.

The documentary is completed in late May 1988. There's nothing more for Su to do but wait for its broadcast, and pray that the popular response he expects will protect his work from political backlash.

When the film begins airing on Saturday June 11, it's broadcast with little advance publicity. But the capital's political grapevine is so efficient that by the second night's broadcast everyone I know, from Party officials to average workers, is glued to their television sets after the 7 PM evening news broadcast for the start of the daily *River Elegy* episode.

As Su predicted, the program becomes the leading topic of conversation in Beijing and nationwide. Its presentation of critical and unpopular views leaves people wondering how the Party is going to react to such a direct challenge to its self-appointed right to dictate political orthodoxy. The feared backlash is not long in coming. Conservative commentators writing in state media, most prominently the Communist Party mouthpiece the *People's Daily*, accuse the film of "cultural nihilism," "denying the accomplishments of socialism," "evaluating China according to foreign criteria," and the crowning condemnation "advocating total Westernization."

"*River Elegy* distorts Chinese history, entirely negates the fine traditions of Chinese culture, and vilifies the Chinese people," the *People's Daily* declares in a front-page editorial.

But Su and his co-creators aren't alarmed by this harsh criticism because they expected and prepared for it. As he says to me over lunch after the film's initial airing: "Whether all of *River Elegy*'s assertions are legitimate is less important than society's ability to debate these issues. A discussion of this type is evidence that the problems the documentary identifies aren't insurmountable, and may be on their way to being relegated to the past."

Popular response to the documentary is overwhelmingly positive. But the film has offended powerful Communist Party elders.[104] This poses a dilemma for Su's CCTV patrons. The film has created such a powerful buzz, from opinion columns in newspapers to conversations around dinner tables throughout the capital and country, that refusal to rebroadcast the series in the face of mounting calls for another primetime airing could arouse public unrest. But a repeat showing risks the ire and retaliation of conservative Party elders.

---

104. Collectively known as the "Eight Immortals"—Communist leaders who fought alongside Mao during the revolution and still wield disproportionate weight on vital matters of state and especially cultural issues.

After weeks of indecision and back-channel negotiations, CCTV authorities inform Su and his *River Elegy* colleagues that the Bureau of Radio, Film, and Television—the central government bureaucracy in charge of approving television content—has green-lighted the series for rebroadcast, pending minor revisions. Aware that a principled refusal to alter the work will preclude its rebroadcast for a potentially much larger audience—Su and his colleagues agree to the dictated changes.

The amended version still constitutes a strong indictment of the negative aspects of conservative traditional culture, but the explicit references to highly sensitive current political issues are toned down or deleted. In the midst of this controversy I visit Su at CCTV's editing studio and he's surprisingly upbeat about this outcome, in spite of the censorship.

"This is the kind of conflict that Chinese intellectuals should welcome," he says with a dismissive wave of his hand. "We finally have the opportunity to speak out without being shot or arrested. This is when it's most important to take a principled stand. Censorship is regrettable, but a few changes won't undermine the impact of the work."

As usual, I'm inspired and impressed by his courage. But I'm not the one who's going to pay the price for the protest. The sanitized new version omits a positive analysis of the 1986–87 student demonstrations. Also cut are passages deploring the paltry remuneration, poor working conditions, and low social status of China's intellectuals. And the re-edited film removes the angry condemnation contained in the original's voiceover, and comments by leading intellectuals and liberal officials on Communist Party corruption and its harmful effects on both the nation's economy and public morale. Also excised is a prediction that growing dissatisfaction with increasing wealth disparity will eventually give rise to large-scale social unrest.

In spite of these deletions, the second airing of *River Elegy* on August 15, 1988, causes a bigger stir than the original broadcast. Due to the controversy surrounding the program and the enormous advance publicity it's generated, the streets of the capital and other major cities are empty when the show goes to air each evening for a weeklong run. National newspapers feature daily commentaries, interviews with the authors, and letters from readers debating the strengths and shortcomings of the film. Conferences and seminars are convened nationwide to discuss the documentary's ideas and their implication for China's future. I report on the film and its social impact for *Asiaweek*, calling it "the most daring and important documentary ever broadcast on Chinese television."

China's media dubs this wave of publicity the "*River Elegy Phenomenon.*" Tens if not hundreds of millions of viewers watch the film's episodes in installments every night for a week. Abridged versions of the script are published in newspapers and magazines, and a flood of books and articles—both favorable and critical—are produced in its wake. The full, uncensored script, published in standalone book form, sells out several printings totaling more than a million copies. And videotapes of the original, uncensored broadcast sell out as fast as they can be stocked in bookstores and at sidewalk bookstalls across the country.

But soon the inevitable occurs, and the discussion shifts from focusing on the film's content to the extremely sensitive topic of how free intellectuals should be to question the Communist Party's policies. Liberal commentator's assert that China's reforms can only succeed in an atmosphere of open debate.

But as John, Dede, and I worry aloud to Su over tea at his house one summer evening after the second airing of the documentary, he could be in personal danger.

"The Party leadership sees itself as the sole arbiter of political truth," John reflects. "They'll never relinquish the right to dictate social, political, and cultural correctness."

"That's true," Su says. "But my CCTV sponsors assure me that there are people in high places supporting us."

The top Party leadership does remain impartial throughout the early rounds of the debate. They appear to be upholding a new internal policy, implemented in the aftermath of the Anti–Bourgeois Liberalization campaign, to refrain from interfering in cultural affairs, a damaging practice that has resulted in so much loss of popular legitimacy for the Party in the past.

But as media rhetoric heats up, it becomes increasingly difficult for Party leaders to preserve their pretense of unity. The façade is shattered by a pronouncement by PLA general and state vice president Wang Zhen that appears in all major newspapers:[105] "There's a television series called *River Elegy* that negates our great Chinese nation in its entirety. This television program curses the Yellow River and the Great Wall. It vilifies our great Chinese nation and the descendants of the Yellow Emperor."[106]

This single published statement transforms the debate over *River Elegy* from a cultural issue to a grave political one. In the past, a single remark by a leader of Wang's stature was sufficient for a work to be banned and its creators blacklisted, if not imprisoned. By publicly expressing his opposition to the program, the revolutionary elder forces the central leadership—in particular newly appointed reformist Communist Party chief Zhao Ziyang—to take a public stand. The leadership must either uphold the policy of non-intervention in a cultural matter and expose itself to accusations of supporting the film's liberal views, or accede to General Wang's wishes and take action against the program. In the midst of this conflict I ask John: "Don't these people realize they're fighting about a television documentary?"

John frowns at me. "That's the difference between you and us (America and China)," he says in the tone of a scolding parent. "Mao knew that challenges to the Communist Party would come in the form of cultural ideas.[107] That's what he meant when he said that political power comes from two barrels: the barrel of the pen and the barrel of the gun. Why do you think he kept such a tight leash on China's intellectuals?"

I again marvel at John's ability to sum up complex political matters with a few telling words. It's tragic that this wisdom had to be gained at the price of so much suffering.

---

105. The same conservative elder who banned rock guitarist Cui Jian from performing publicly.

106. It is traditionally believed that all Chinese are *yanhuang zisun*, the descendants of the same mythical Yellow Emperor of antiquity.

107. In September 1962, at the Communist Party's tenth plenum, Mao warned his comrades to "Never forget the class struggle. Some people are using the writing of novels to carry on anti-party activities and creating a public opinion for the restoration of capitalism." This is generally seen as one of the first salvoes in the launch of the Cultural Revolution.

The outcome of the dispute becomes clear in November 1988. Following a Communist Party Central Committee plenum, *River Elegy* is officially banned. It can no longer be broadcast, further distribution of the videotape is outlawed, and printed copies of the text are removed from bookstore shelves and burned in public denunciation campaigns.

On the internal circular informing central authorities of the decision, Party Leader Zhao curtly notes: "It is necessary to respect the views of the veteran cadres."

Thus ends the short life of *River Elegy*, the most creative and controversial television program ever produced in China. But contrary to historic precedent, the creators aren't arrested or otherwise punished. By the time they learn of the film's blacklisting, they've already moved on to new cutting-edge projects.

Su is writing the script for a CCTV documentary to commemorate the seventieth anniversary of the 1919 May Fourth "New Culture Movement," set to air in the spring of 1989. And he tells me over lunch at the Beijing Broadcasting Institute that his *River Elegy* coauthor Wang Luxiang and producer Xia Jun are working on a retrospective of the past decade of reforms.

"Do you want to hear the proverb that sums up this whole episode?" Su asks with a wry smile. "*Yugai mizhang,* the more you forbid something the more people want it."

chapter seventeen

外來和尚會念經
Wailai heshang hui nianjing
FOREIGN THINGS SEEM EXOTIC

It's my twenty-fifth birthday, and I have a big interview for the accredited foreign correspondent position I've been pursuing.

I arrive at the United Press International (UPI) office a few minutes before the 9 AM meeting. Telex machines clatter, churning out UPI's international wire copy as well as the Xinhua News Service's official propaganda. These machines are the lifeline to the outside world for these foreign news bureaus.

The office is huge. It takes up the entire ground floor of the *Qijiayuan* Diplomatic Compound building—one of the oldest Russian-built structures in the city. It's a historic landmark with wedding-cake architecture and spacious apartments appointed with teakwood floors, carved wooding moldings, and expensive copper plumbing. The main office consists of two big rooms with picture windows looking out over the Avenue of Eternal Peace. It resembles a wartime spy movie set.

A large two-bedroom apartment abuts the office. This rent-free flat comes with the position I'm applying for. The bureau chief lives in a palatial four-bedroom, three-bathroom suite at the building's next entrance.

I walk down the office hallway, stepping around rolls of telex paper, old-fashioned wooden cases of Coca-Cola in green glass bottles, and broken-down telex machines cannibalized for replacement parts. In the main newsroom five people are hard at work. Three are foreign reporters, hunched over their computer terminals staring at glowing green text pulsing on black background screens. Two Chinese staff members are busy translating a Foreign Ministry press release. Filing cabinets, stuffed to overflowing with research clips, line the walls.

A stocky guy with a bushy red beard looks up from the far corner and grunts: "Grab a seat, I'll be with you in a minute."

He's bureau chief David Schweisberg, a former Detroit police beat reporter. He finishes what he's writing, rapidly hunt-and-peck typing with his index fingers, then hits the *send* button on his computer and the file is transmitted via satellite to UPI headquarters in Washington, D.C., where it will be final edited and then circulated to clients all over the world. He tells the other staff members we'll be in the spare apartment then signals for me to follow him out.

He leads me through the double French doors in the hallway. We sit at a long oak dining table. I notice that the apartment is fully furnished. *I really want this job.*

Dave opens a manila folder containing my résumé and clips.

"You graduated from Duke, eh?" he says. "So what are you, smart or rich?"

"Neither," I reply, eliciting an amused snort.

He's done his homework. He knows about my connection to Dede, that she works for Ambassador Lord's wife, and that I'm fluent in Mandarin. He doesn't speak Chinese, and language skills are essential for this job. Dave then turns toward the office and yells out, "Yale!"

A Chinese guy my age, the office translator, comes in and Dave tells him to sit down. Then he turns to me and says: "Let's hear your Mandarin."

I roll my eyes, and say in my best gutter slang: "*Wo cao! Ta tama xiang rang wo liao shenme?* [Fuck, what the hell does he expect me to say?]"

Yale laughs out loud. We chat for a minute in Chinese, then Dave asks Yale what he thinks and he gives the thumbs-up. Dave nods and tells Yale to go back to work.

We talk some more, discovering that Dave grew up on Long Island, a ferry ride from my house in New Haven. I expect to be dismissed with a promise that he'll get back to me. But instead he says, "When can you start?"

I'm thrilled. "Right away," I tell him, and we shake on the offer.

I run out the door and bike as fast as I can to the embassy to share the good news with Dede. She and Mrs. Lord are planning tonight's dinner party. I burst in and blurt out: "I got the job!"

"*Taibangle!* That's great!" they say in unison.

"This calls for a toast." Mrs. Lord says, and she goes into the kitchen and pours us all a glass of vintage Burgundy.

"To Scoop[108] and many big scoops," Dede says, and we clink glasses. "I'm so proud of you," she adds and kisses me on the cheek. Mrs. Lord clucks her tongue in mock disapproval, but looks as pleased as if we were her own children.

I give the *L.A. Times* notice that I'm taking the new job, and find and train my replacement Nick Driver. Then I start spending all my spare time in the UPI office learning the specialized language, shorthand codes, and conventions of wire service reporting.

I've written plenty of newspaper and magazine feature stories, but writing twice-daily 1,500-word news dispatches on fixed deadlines is a brand-new challenge for me. Wire service reporting is often referred to as the trench warfare of print journalism. Foreign correspondents for newspapers like the *L.A. Times* and *The New York Times* pick and choose the stories they cover, and rarely file more than once a week. But we're expected to write twice that much every day. Our articles are picked up by thousands of newspaper, radio, and television stations, as well as investment banks, brokerages, and corporate and government clients all over the world. My reporting heroes Martha Gellhorn, Lucien Carr, Seymour Hersh, and Neil Sheehan all started their careers at UPI.

My new life as an accredited foreign correspondent shifts into high gear. My boss is a celebrity on the Beijing nightlife circuit. He sings in a rock-and-roll band called the Back Door Band (*Houmen Yuedui*)—an

---

108. Her half-joking new nickname for me.

ironic reference to how things really get done in China—and has even penned a hit song: "R & B [Rhythm and Blues] in the PRC." He drinks and parties until the wee hours every night, and chain-smokes Marlboro Reds all day. He's also my first professional mentor. I've watched him come back to the office in the middle of the night stumbling drunk, sit down at a computer, take a slug of strong black coffee, and crank out pages of crystal-clear prose. It mystifies me how he does this. I pray I can learn to do it too.

Dave and my other new colleagues are gratified when I volunteer to open the bureau every morning at 7 AM because they're all night owls.

The first task of the day is reporting the Beijing weather to our D.C. home office. Then I rip the overnight wire copy from the telex machine to see if Xinhua—the official New China News Agency—has reported anything newsworthy. Most of it is Chinese government propaganda. But it's necessary to review it carefully in case there's some real news buried in the fluff.

At 8 AM I listen to the Radio Beijing newscast. Then I scan the newspapers—*People's Daily, Beijing Daily, PLA Daily, Legal Daily Beijing,* and *Shanghai Evening News*—in search of "pickup" material, information that we can follow up on and turn into our own news stories.

All the major U.S. newspapers and news magazines—*The New York Times, L.A. Times, Washington Post, Wall Street Journal, Chicago Tribune, Baltimore Sun, Philadelphia Inquirer, Time,* and *Newsweek*—have one foreign correspondent accredited by the Chinese government. But the wire services—Associated Press (AP), UPI, Reuters, and Agence France-Presse (AFP)—have three accredited reporter positions, as well as still and video photographers. In addition to my bureau chief, the deputy bureau chief is Mark DelVecchio, a veteran UPI reporter who's married to a Beijing native. I'll be the third member of the writing team. We use freelance instead of staff photographers because UPI's budget is stretched so thin.

Our direct competition, AP, occupies a similarly large office in the building next door. They have an all-star lineup: veteran Vietnam War-era reporter and bureau chief Jim Abrams, experienced Asia hand Kathy

Wilhelm, and the hotshot new recruit John Pomfret. He's my direct competition, also specializing in street reporting. We also compete with the
British news service Reuters and to a lesser extent AFP for international
story placements, but our Washington bosses base our evaluations on
how we compete head-to-head with AP.

Every evening we receive a scorecard showing how many international outlets pick up our stories versus AP and the other wire services.
I love this competition. Pomfret and I are neighbors and pass each other
on our way to work every day. We nod with respect, but both know we're
competing for scoops, professional recognition, and career advance-
ment. Pomfret makes no secret of his ambition for a Pulitzer Prize. Both
AP and Reuters are far better funded than UPI,[109] but with Schweisberg's strong embassy contacts—the U.S. Embassy military attaché Larry
Wortzel is his close friend—and my daily access to Ambassador and Mrs.
Lord, we more than hold our own in the competition for exclusive news
stories and international headlines.

There's a US$10,000 per month dedicated satellite dish on our roof.
All the wire services have one. Our computers are directly connected to
every UPI bureau in the world—Tokyo, Delhi, Nairobi, Jerusalem, Paris,
London, Rio, New York, D.C. As I sit at my desk sending instant messages across the globe I think: *If a network like this ever became available
to the general public it would change the world.*

One of the first things I do with my new US$4,000 monthly salary is buy
a flame-red 500cc Honda motorcycle. One of John's friends purchased it
on a business trip to Tokyo and had it shipped back to Beijing, unaware
that it's almost impossible for a local to register a private motor vehicle.
As an accredited foreign correspondent I'm automatically issued a coveted black license plate, and I slap it on the back of the bike.

It's like legal carte blanche on the Beijing streets, almost as untouch-
able as a white People's Liberation Army military plate. Beijing beat cops

---

109. There's an old joke that goes: you can't spell cheap without AP but you can't spell stupid
without UPI.

don't dare stop a military vehicle for fear it could contain a high-ranking officer. Cops likewise don't want to stop a foreigner who probably can't speak Chinese anyway. So traffic police just look the other way as I speed past. They don't even have walkie-talkies to call ahead for a traffic stop. I don't like exploiting the privilege accorded expatriates here, but I'm not doing this for fun. My work requires that I get to the scene of a story as fast as possible.

The Honda is the biggest, fastest bike on Beijing's roads. Because I head out on high-speed forays after work most nights in pursuit of news stories, my colleagues start jokingly referring to me as the Night Stalker.

I'm the youngest accredited foreign correspondent in China, but have been living and working in Beijing longer than most of my colleagues and know the streets like a local. Schweisberg jokes that the government will regret they ever accredited me.

chapter eighteen

We believe pluralism to be a necessary nutrient for society's normal growth. Two centuries ago, this conviction led the people of France to storm the Bastille. Seventy years ago, it spurred China's youth to rise up in nationwide protests against authoritarian rule in the [1919] May Fourth Movement. And the pursuit of this ideal still inspires our efforts today.
—Student activist Wang Dan, *New May 4 Manifesto,*
Beijing University student newspaper

I decide to combine work with pleasure and going for an afternoon run with John at Beijing University. Then I'll check out what's happening on the nation's most politically active campus. Telephones are still rare, so the only way to find out what the students are up to is to go see them in person.

I leave the UPI office after lunch and weave the Honda through the *hutong* back alleys to avoid the traffic-congested main streets. Then I open the throttle on the Ring Road and get to John's in fifteen minutes. He hears me pull up, bounds down the steps, and hops on the back. We ride the mile north to the entrance of Beijing University. He leans into my back and turns his face away from the guards as we coast through the gate. John doesn't want to get off and register—a requirement for all locals since the student protests here two years ago. He could get in trouble just for visiting the campus, so he has to avoid getting caught. We make it through undetected and I park my bike in front of the foreign students' dorm.

We change into our running gear and store our clothes in a dorm bathroom locker. We'll return to shower and change after our run. Then we head out to the path around No-Name Lake (*WeimingHu*).

We start out jogging to warm up. Our breath condenses in white clouds behind us. The sky is clear and the cold air stings our cheeks. A breeze shakes the last brown leaves from the willow trees, and sunlight shimmers on the water.

"*Qiugao qishuang*—high autumn, exhilarating air," John says between breaths as we pick up our pace. "That's what we call this weather; it's Beijing's best season."

"I know. It's one of the first things you taught me. I think you're going senile."

He punches my arm playfully, and then we lower our heads and start running in earnest. We set a fast, six-minute-mile pace. Our clothes soak with sweat as we push each other around the two-kilometer path five times for a sub-forty-minute, ten-kilometer run. We race the final hundred meters to the moon arch bridge at the lake's inlet. John stretches his upper body like a sprinter and beats me by a head. We high five and compliment each other on a good hard run. Then we walk the few hundred meters back to the dormitory to cool down.

Around the last lakeside curve we come upon the famed statue of Cervantes.[110] A group of students is gathered around it, engaging in a heated debate.

"University professors earn one-tenth of what an ex-convict does selling smuggled goods at street stalls!" exclaims a male student in a jacket with frayed cuffs.

"Communist Party officials get rich selling government licenses and scarce raw materials on the black market!" adds a ponytailed woman in a blue army coat.

"*Qiong de xiang jiaoshou, sha de xiang boshi* [as poor as a professor, as foolish as a person with a PhD]," a man with a wispy beard declares,

---

110. Miguel de Cervantes (1547–1616) is the Spanish author of *Don Quixote*, considered the first modern novel. His role in popularizing literature is what made him a symbol of progressive social change and why he is revered at Beijing University, the pioneer of progressive social causes in China.

lamenting the low social status of intellectuals in a society that traditionally revered learning.

Then a petite woman in oversized glasses adds in a high-pitched voice: "*Na shoushudao de buru na guatoudao de, zuo daodan de buru mai chayedan de* [those who wield surgeons' scalpels earn less than those who wield barbers' razors. Those who produce guided missiles earn less than those who sell tea eggs]." The crowd laughs at the incongruity of such sharp criticism coming from such a small woman, and it breaks the tension.

"You Beijingers sure can *chuiniu* ['blow cow' or bloviate]," I say to John.

"Because that's all the Party allows, and it's free," he wisecracks, and we both grin.

We listen to the discussion a while longer, then I turn to John and whisper: "I didn't know this kind of sensitive political debate was taking place in public again." John knows I'm referring to the protests here two years ago and subsequent crackdown that forced all activism underground.

"It's brave but reckless to do this so soon after the protests," he whispers back.

What moves me most about these students is their deep passion and insight. It's clear they've given a lot of thought to their society's problems. In a culture dominated by censorship and conformity, critical thinking is a precious commodity.

Standing in the center of the circle is a slender, soft-spoken young man whose face is dominated by horn-rimmed glasses that he keeps pushing up the bridge of his nose. They lend him a wise, owl-like appearance. When the debate concludes, John and I approach him.

"I'm sorry to trouble you," I say in polite Mandarin. "That was an impressive exchange."

"*Nali, nali* [not at all]."

I extend my hand and introduce myself, and John does the same.

"My name's Wang Dan,"[111] he says in a voice hoarse from moderating the debate.

---

111. Pronounced *Wahng Dahn.*

He tells us he's twenty years old, a history major at *Beida*, and this is the semester's first meeting of a group he founded last spring called Democracy Salon (*Minzhu Shalong*).

"*Yi bu pa ku, er bu pa si* [fear neither bitterness nor death]," I say, giving him the thumbs up, and he laughs at the oddity of a foreigner quoting Chairman Mao on the virtue of revolutionary struggle to him, a *Beida* student.

John needs to get home to make dinner for his mom and sister, so I tell him I'm going to stay and talk some more and that I'll meet him back at his place.

Wang and I start strolling along the shaded path back toward his dorm, and he tells me more about himself.

"I'm a Shandong [province] native,[112] but grew up on the Beijing University campus. My mother and father are both *Beida* graduates. My dad is a geology professor here, and my mom works as a historian at the Museum of Revolutionary History."[113]

"*Guaibude* [no wonder]," I say. "That explains why a new undergraduate would dare to take such a risky leadership role in campus politics."

He nods in silent agreement.

We arrive at his dorm, and climb the cement steps to the second floor. He opens a padlocked door, revealing a cramped room lined with four bunk beds. *Eight students share this tiny room, and American college students complain about the size of their dorm rooms.* He leads me to the bunk closest to the window and pulls back the mosquito netting. A shelf on the wall is lined with books, much of it foreign literature in Chinese translation: Thoreau, Kafka, Hemingway, Woolf, Orwell, Havel.

Wang pours me a cup of tea, and continues:

"Last spring I saw the need for a political discussion group. First we called it the Wednesday Salon because we met every Wednesday afternoon. Then people started calling it the Democracy Salon and the name stuck."

---

112. All Chinese discern between their ancestral hometowns—where their family originated—and where they grew up, similar to an American stating their ethnic-national background versus where they grew up in the States.

113. Located in Tiananmen Square.

"Be careful, you know what happens when you call something 'Democracy' here," I joke, and he laughs uncomfortably.

"This semester our planned speakers are the veteran political activist Ren Wanding, the female investigative reporter Dai Qing, and then on the seventieth anniversary of the May Fourth movement Fang Lizhi and his wife—our faculty adviser—*Beida* physics professor Li Shuxian."

"Wow, that's ballsy."

"*Buru huxue, yande huzi* [you can't catch a tiger cub if you don't enter the tiger's den]," Wang says, his eyes set in steely resolve.

Such brave words from such a fragile-looking kid.

It's getting dark, so I thank Wang for his hospitality and we agree to meet again soon.

Back at John's over dinner, I describe the rest of my talk with Wang Dan.

"They're inviting every hardcore dissident to address Democracy Salon, including 'enemy of the people' Fang Lizhi on the May Fourth anniversary."

"*Wo cao! Shuyujing er fengbuzhi*—Fuck! Here we go again. The trees want to rest but the wind won't stop blowing," John exclaims.

"The weather's getting colder," he adds in English, "but the political atmosphere is heating up."

Democracy Wall cofounder Ren Wanding—an activist I've interviewed several times and really admire—speaks at November's Democracy Salon. He's so inspired by his interaction with the students that in early December he drafts a petition calling for the release of his imprisoned Democracy Wall cofounders Wei Jingsheng and Xu Wenli.[114] This is a direct challenge to paramount leader Deng Xiaoping, who personally ordered the imprisonment of these dissidents.

Ren asks me to organize a press conference for him at our UPI bureau. As the foreign press corps crowds into our office apartment, he holds up a copy of the petition he's addressed to the United Nations Commission on Human Rights (UNCHR), Amnesty International, and other international human rights organizations. The petition story

114. Ren himself had been released from prison in 1983.

runs on the front page of *The New York Times*, plays widely in the international press, and succeeds in refocusing attention on Beijing's problematic human rights record.

"The ball's in Deng's court now," I say to my boss Dave as we watch the media circus of television cameras, radio microphones, and photographers jostle for space in our living room.

"One thing about this place," he deadpans, "it's never boring."

In early January 1989 Fang Lizhi takes Ren's amnesty petition a step further and issues an open letter to Deng Xiaoping calling for the release of all political prisoners in China. He recommends May 4, 1989—the seventieth anniversary of the start of the "New Culture Movement"—as a suitably symbolic occasion for a general amnesty for all political prisoners. This carries much more weight than Ren's action—and is viewed as much more of a threat by the authorities—because Fang is now an internationally renowned dissident and a hero to students and intellectuals nationwide due to his leadership role in the pro-democracy protests two years ago.

I interview Fang at his home after he issues the appeal, and in an emotional voice he utters the incendiary phrase: "*Shui dou bu pa shui*—no one is afraid of anyone anymore."

Ren's petition could be seen as an isolated incident, but when Fang throws down the gauntlet and directly challenges the Party leadership less than two years after his expulsion from the University of Science and Technology vice presidency, the leadership takes it seriously.

"*Zhi baobuzhu huo*—paper can't conceal fire," John says, to sum up the situation.

Fang's willingness to speak out again so soon after being purged emboldens his fellow intellectuals to take public action.

In mid-February popular writers Bei Dao and Chen Jun draft, and thirty-three of China's most prominent authors sign, a petition supporting Fang's call for a general amnesty for all political prisoners. They add a demand for acceleration of political reform. The snowball effect accelerates.

In early March, forty-two of China's most revered scholars and scientists—including noted physicist Xu Liangying; political scientist and former head of the Leninism-Marxism-Mao Tse-tung Thought Institute of the Chinese Academy of Social Sciences Su Shaozhi; and ninety-year-old author and teacher Madame Bing Xin—send a letter to Communist Party leaders and the Standing Committee of the National People's Congress echoing Fang's call for the release of all political prisoners.

These incidents mark the first time since Mao's 1957 Hundred Flowers campaign that public intellectuals have dared to collectively oppose party policy on sensitive political issues.

After interviewing the petition organizers and hurrying back to the UPI bureau to write it up, I run into Dave, who nods, half-smiles, and says: "It looks like spring is coming early this year."

chapter nineteen

斩草不除根，春风吹又生
Zhancao bu chugen, chunfeng chui yousheng.

IF THE ROOTS ARE NOT REMOVED DURING
WEEDING, THE SEEDLINGS WILL GROW BACK
WHEN THE SPRING WIND BLOWS.

It is more dangerous to silence the people than to dam a river.[115]
—Chairman Mao, quoted by investigative journalist
Dai Qing in her spring 1989 address to
Beijing University's Democracy Salon

Saturday April 15, 1989

I arrive at the UPI bureau at 7 AM and put a kettle of water on the stove to make tea. Then I rip the Xinhua and Reuters teletype news copy piled up on the floor overnight to scan for stories or clips for our research files. As I'm reading, the heavy rotary phone on my desk rings.

---

115. 防民之口甚于防川 fangmin zhikou shenyu fangchuan.

"*Wei!* Hey!"

"*Gemen'r*, Buddy," John's familiar voice says.

I'm surprised he's calling because he has no home telephone. He must be ringing me from his mom's neighborhood committee office at the university. Something must be up.

"Have you heard the big news?"

"*What* big news?" I say warily.

I've been covering big news nonstop since starting this job last year. I just want to go home after work, have dinner with Dede, hang out with our friends, and enjoy a quiet life. But something in John's voice tells me this is going to be delayed a little longer.

"Hu Yaobang just died of a heart attack."

"*Wo cao.* Fuck me."

This is five-alarm news.

Hu was held responsible for the student protests two years ago and purged as Communist Party leader. But in contrast to past purges that resulted in the ousted leader being imprisoned or killed, Hu remains a Politburo member.[116] His unexpected passing at the age of seventy-three is sure to rekindle conflict among the leadership and restlessness in students whose nationwide protests in support of his progressive policies were suppressed two years ago.

"Students are gathering at Beijing University right now. They're wearing white paper mourning flowers,[117] laying funerary wreaths, pasting up political posters, and giving speeches praising Hu. The first banner I saw read: THOSE WHO SHOULD LIVE HAVE DIED, THOSE WHO SHOULD DIE STILL LIVE.

"*Tamade!* Motherfucker! Don't they know that's suicide?"

I know John shares my concern. We witnessed this vicious cycle in 1986–87. What started as well-intentioned student activism ended with organizers and participants being rounded up and punished, a

---

116. The Politburo (Political bureau) of the Communist Party Central Committee consists of China's twenty-five top leaders and oversees Communist Party policies.

117. A traditional sign of mourning.

black mark on their secret personnel files damaging future employment opportunities and tainting them as troublemakers for life.

"At least they're not arrested or killed like your sister and father during the Cultural Revolution," I say, trying to find a silver lining. "They're just kids exercising newfound political awareness. Why can't the government tolerate a little steam venting?"

"*Shabi Meiguo qingnian*, stupid young American. For you politics is a game. For us it's *shengsi cunwang*—a life-and-death, winner-take-all struggle."

I know he's right.

"I'll head over to *Beida* and meet you at the front gate," John says, knowing I need to cover the story.

I hang up and call my bureau chief Dave, and wake him from sleeping off his usual all-night bender.

"This better be good, Savitt."

"It is. Hu Yaobang just died."

"*What?*" he shouts, not welcoming the specter of more nonstop work any more than I do. I hear him try to shake the cobwebs from his hungover head.

"Students are gathering on the Beijing University campus, laying wreaths and making pro-democracy speeches."

"All right, I'll jump in the shower and head over to the office."

"I'm going to *Beida* to do interviews and take photos. I'll see you back at the bureau."

I hang up and hurry to the kitchen to take the whistling kettle off the stove.

Here we go again, another political shitstorm. Not even time for a morning cup of tea.

I grab my leather jacket, head out the door, hop on my bike, and speed off.

Light rain is falling. Traffic is sparse this early in the morning, and I make it to *Beida* in fifteen minutes.

John's waiting beyond the front gate, reading a newspaper to avoid attracting the guards' attention. He hops on, and we race along the wall to the foreign students' entrance where it's safer to enter.

We coast through the gate and speed to the Triangle, weaving around groups of students buzzing with the news.

"There were more than a hundred gathered before I left to call you," John shouts in my ear.

As we round the last corner, it's clear that the crowd has grown much larger. There are now thousands gathered at the bulletin boards reading posters, taking photographs, and transcribing the pasted-up essays, poems, and eulogies into notebooks.

I pull up in front of Wang Dan's dorm and park the bike. The atmosphere is electric. Some students are heatedly debating the significance of Hu's death, while others flock to the newest posters.

I recognize a female student from a Democracy Salon event and ask her about her reaction to Hu's death and her decision to come to the Triangle.

"My roommate woke me with news of the former Party leader's death," says Little Lu. "So I came outside and students were already here debating, pasting posters, and hanging homemade white paper flowers."[118]

I scan the wall poster titles as we talk: *A Great Loss of Democracy and Freedom. The Star of Hope Has Fallen. One Man Cared For All Under Heaven, For One Man All Under Heaven Mourn.*

"Hu genuinely cared about the welfare of the people," she continues. "He rehabilitated millions of intellectuals persecuted by Mao, and even tried to moderate policies toward ethnic minorities. We want to honor his memory even though we know it's politically risky and could harm our future."

I feel like I'm watching a rerun of early-twentieth-century Chinese history, and it's the May Fourth "New Culture Movement" all over again.

The students stay in the Triangle for several hours, but when the gathering starts to break up we leave too and I drop John at his house on my way back to the bureau.

This is how revolutions start, I think as I speed back to the UPI office to write up the story.

---

118. A sign of mourning in Chinese culture.

I hurry to file this groundbreaking news. My bureau chief Dave and assistant bureau chief Mark flesh out my lead story with background details on the deceased leader, and both write sidebar pieces on the likely consequences of this event to complement my main article.

Our editors in Washington—twelve hours behind Beijing—stay up all night to polish our reports and send them as urgent news bulletins to UPI's subscribers worldwide.

Sunday April 16, 1989

I grab a few hours' sleep in the office apartment while Dave and Mark keep working. It's hard for me to stop thinking, but I finally drift off and have anxiety dreams about racing around on my motorcycle chasing protesters like I was doing in real life all day.

My eyes pop open, and I'm wide awake before dawn. I hop out of bed, pull on jeans and a T-shirt, and head across the hall to the office.

Dave and Mark are still hard at work. Bleary-eyed, they're hunched over their computers hammering away. A thick cloud of cigarette smoke floats above their heads—they're both chain smokers. A pot of coffee is percolating on the stove. I open the office windows to let in some fresh air.

"Anything new?" I ask and they both shake their heads and keep typing.

I see they're topping up their stories with fresh quotes from campus interviews conducted by our office translator Yale, and adding background and historical details because student protests are so rare here. This is already a big international news story.

"Why don't I take a ride to Tiananmen?"

"Good idea," Dave and Mark say without looking up from their screens.

It makes sense for me to be the street reporter on this story. I have the best Mandarin, my souped-up bike can get to the scene faster than any car, and I'm friends with the student-protest leaders so will have unparalleled access to the newsmakers. I grab my camera bag and keys and run out the door.

There's little traffic on the Avenue of Eternal Peace, and I make it to the square in five minutes. As I veer off the main road, I'm stunned by what I see. Students and citizens are scaling the ten-foot-high base of the

Monument to Revolutionary Martyrs at the center of Tiananmen and laying memorial wreaths for the deceased popular leader.

Displaying funerary wreaths is a traditional act of political protest in China. The last time public memorializing of a deceased popular leader happened was in April 1976, when spontaneous mourning of Premier Chou En-lai turned into large-scale antigovernment rallies that were finally violently suppressed by Mao's police. This highly unpopular action, ordered by Chairman Mao's wife Jiang Qing, initiated the chain of events that led to her and her Gang of Four's purge later that year and the formal end to the Cultural Revolution.

Those laying wreaths now are probably risking a similar fate. There could be a police crackdown at any time. But if the authorities don't take action, the numbers in the Square will surely increase.

I interview the protesters and take photos. They're mostly students, but some are workers and ordinary Beijing residents taking advantage of this rare opportunity to express political views in public and honor the deceased leader while implicitly criticizing the hardliners who ousted Hu and are still in power.

The general sentiment—as it was among the pro-democracy protesters who gathered here two years ago—is that it's time for meaningful political liberalization to accompany China's economic reforms, and reactionaries in the leadership are blocking the country's democratic progress.

What's most striking is the lively public debate. Unremarkable back in the States, here it's extraordinary.

More and more citizens, emboldened by the growing crowd and spirited discussion, come to lay floral wreaths and join the spontaneous demonstration.

What started as a handful of people when I arrived has grown to a crowd of more than 1,000. This many protesters in Tiananmen Square is headline news by itself. I rush back to the bureau to report it.

"Thousands are gathered in Tiananmen!" I yell as I run into the office, pull the film out of my camera, and toss it to our staff assistant, then sit down and start typing.

Dave, next to me, copyedits over my shoulder.

I hammer out a thousand-word lead news story about the events I've just witnessed in Tiananmen. When I'm done, Dave sits in my seat, final-edits the piece, then sends it via satellite link to UPI's tens of thousands of clients worldwide.

I lean back, close my eyes, and take a big gulp of tea as the story transmits.

It's afternoon, and Dave and Mark have been working nonstop for more than twenty-four hours.

"You guys rest and I'll mind the bureau. I'll wake you if anything new happens."

They gladly accept my offer and wearily stumble off to their apartments to sleep.

I call Dede at the embassy and update her on the news. She already knows more than I do. Mrs. Lord has much better sources of information in the government and political activist communities than any of Beijing's foreign news bureaus.

"Why don't you come to my office for dinner?" I say to Dede because she knows I can't leave the bureau with these events going on.

She agrees and says she'll bring some good wine left over from today's embassy lunch. She arrives just as it's getting dark. I hear her let herself in and walk down the hallway to our main office. I get up from my desk, kiss her hello, and we head into the kitchen to prepare a simple meal of stir-fried rice and Chinese greens.

Over the simple meal and red wine we discuss the significance of the past two days' events.

"What do you think's going to happen?" I ask her.

"*Meiyou hao xiachang*—no good outcome," Dede says, shaking her head.

I nod in agreement, and reflect how sad it is that at the ripe old age of twenty-five we're both so jaded. But all we've seen is constant political struggle and repression since we arrived here. It's difficult to be optimistic about anything.

We finish the food and drain our wine. Then, exhausted, we climb into bed and cling to each other for warmth and comfort and fall asleep.

Monday April 17, 1989

I wake before dawn as usual. Dede doesn't get up this early so I'm careful not to wake her. I slip out of bed, throw on my clothes, and head over to the office. The wire copy piled on the floor tells me that Dave and Mark haven't been back to the office since last night. There's no new protest information on the Reuters or Xinhua news feeds, so I do what I normally do, file a description of the Beijing weather to our Washington D.C. headquarters:

> *Monday April 17, 1989. Beijing. 6 am. Overcast. Light precipitation. Wind from the west, 55 degrees Fahrenheit (12.77 Centigrade).*

With nothing else to do in the office, I ride back to Tiananmen. It's just getting light as I arrive at the empty square. I'm shocked at what I see—overnight all the funerary wreaths and memorial posters have been removed from the Monument.

People begin arriving shortly after I do.

"I live across the street, in Suzhou Alley," says a thirty-year-old crew-cut man with a strong Beijing accent. "Around 2 AM the police came and removed the memorials."

The crowd is furious at this news. They immediately go and get new flowers and resolve to stay on the square to protect their displays until the authorities acknowledge their discontent.

This is an important new development and I rush back to the office to report on the overnight police action and the public's angry response. As I start typing Dave and Mark walk in.

"The cops took down all the wreaths overnight, and the students and citizens are so pissed off they've started a sit-in in the square," I tell them and then return to typing.

Dave and Mark sit down next to me and read over my shoulder and edit my words as I write. Then Dede walks in, her hair still wet from showering. She looks at us huddled over the computer screen, shakes her head, and says: "There goes the quiet spring I was hoping for."

Dede has to get to work, so I get up and walk outside with her. I give her a peck on the cheek and watch her straddle her bike and ride off to the embassy. Then I head back inside and finish my story.

After I file my report to Washington, Dave, Mark, and I spend the rest of the day making phone calls and shuttling to Tiananmen, trying to figure out where these events are headed. Between John, Dede, and local sources of Dave and Mark's, we learn that the Beijing leadership is divided on how to respond to these protests. The hardliners want to crack down immediately, but the moderates—led by progressive Communist Party leader Zhao Ziyang—argue for letting the students blow off some steam before coaxing them back to campus.

The day flies by, and as it begins to get dark outside I get a call from Dede at the embassy.

"Get out to Beijing University," she shouts. "Thousands of students are marching to Tiananmen."

"Thanks," I say as I grab for my work gear.

I tell Dave and Mark about the new protests, shoulder my backpack and camera, run out to my motorcycle, and take off.

As I arrive at *Baishiqiao* (White Stone Bridge) intersection—near the Beijing University entrance—several thousand *Beida* students are converging with another crowd of at least a thousand coming from Qinghua University next door.

They're carrying banners and shouting slogans including: LONG LIVE DEMOCRACY AND FREEDOM, and DOWN WITH BUREAUCRACY AND CORRUPTION.

I see Wang Dan at the head of the crowd. We make eye contact and nod in silent greeting. I ride ahead of the marchers and park my bike in the nearby Friendship Hotel parking lot. Then I run back and fall into step beside Wang.

"*Dan'r zhen tamada!* Some balls!" I say and clap him on the back.

"I had no choice," he responds. "We formed an independent student union and I got elected leader."

"*Zhongxin zhuhe,* congratulations," I say facetiously, shaking my head at him.

"I know it's reckless," Wang Dan continues. "But Confucius said: '*ershi ruogan,* at twenty-one is ready to assume adult responsibilities.'"

We both laugh at the irony of him quoting Confucius during a student protest.

When Wang and his classmates get to the square, they gather at the base of the monument and post a list of demands for the Party leadership:

- Rehabilitate Hu Yaobang and affirm as correct his views in support of democracy and freedom.
- Repeal the "anti–bourgeois liberalization" and "anti–spiritual pollution" campaigns against Western and capitalistic influences that were launched in response to the student protests of 1986–87.
- Release income reports of high government officials.
- Allow privately run newspapers and stop media censorship.
- Increase funding for education and intellectuals' pay.
- End restriction on demonstrations in Beijing.
- Provide objective coverage of the protests in official media.

I get quotes from Wang Dan and his classmates and rush back to the office to file this story update.

Then Dave, Mark, and I sit down and discuss how we're going to continue covering these protests. They're clearly just getting started, and we're understaffed and under-resourced.

"Savitt, you're lead street reporter," Schweisberg says, and we all agree this makes the most sense.

"Mark and I will man the bureau. We'll stagger our hours so the office is occupied all the time. I'll also ask Washington to send more reporters."

D.C. decides it's a big enough story to send us more manpower. They dispatch Jonathan Landay from Delhi and Denholm Barnetson from Islamabad to help us cover the story in Beijing.

Tuesday April 18, 1989

I'm up before light. I open the office and make a mug of strong black tea. Then I tear the overnight wires and see that there's been no breaking news. So I report the Beijing weather.

> *Tuesday April 18, 1989. Overcast. Intermittent drizzle. Light wind from the east. 58 degrees Fahrenheit (14.4 Celsius).*

Then I ride down to the square. A few thousand students remain huddled around the Monument to the People's Heroes in the center of Tiananmen. They've been here all night. They're clinging to each other for warmth and dozing under quilted army jackets.

As day breaks thousands more students march into the square. They walked the ten kilometers from the university district from the other major campuses there: People's University (*Renda*), Beijing Normal University (*Beishida*), China University of Politics and Law (*Zhengfa Daxue*), Central Nationalities Institute (*Minzu Xueyuan*), and China Sports College. They heard about the *Beida* and Qinghua march last night and decided to show their solidarity.

They're carrying portraits of Hu Yaobang and banners reading: THE SOUL OF CHINA, DEMOCRATIC YAOBANG, and NOW THAT HE'S GONE, WHO CAN WE LOOK UP TO? They join the ongoing sit-in at the center of the square.

I sit down next to a student protester who appears to be my age, twenty-five. He tells me he's a graduate student at the China University of Politics and Law and his name is Little Zhou.[119]

"Last night got violent. People started posting aggressive messages like: *Overthrow the Dictators*. There were also lots of speeches calling for political reform and democratic participation in government decisions by the citizens. Then everyone started smashing glass bottles."

---

119. Pronounced *Joe*.

This is an ominous development.

Small Bottle is a homonym in Mandarin for Deng Xiaoping's first name. This symbolic protest against Deng began during the 1986–87 protests. Now it's back. The danger is in calling for the overthrow of the Communist Party. It's taboo, and will always be responded to with force.

I scribble it all down in my notepad as fast as I can.

All morning students keep arriving, adding to the numbers occupying the square.

At noon I head back to the bureau to file on the morning's events. Then I grab a nap before heading back to the square in the afternoon.

By nightfall there are more than 100,000 students and ordinary Beijing residents gathered in the square. It's like a carnival. People revel in this opportunity to debate politics openly. They passionately debate, give speeches, and sing the revolutionary worker's anthem, "The Internationale":[120]

---

120. Stand up all victims of oppression
For the tyrants fear your might
Don't cling so hard to your possessions
For you have nothing if you have no rights
Let racist ignorance be ended
For respect makes the empires fall
Freedom is merely privilege extended
Unless enjoyed by one and all
So come brothers and sisters
For the struggle carries on
The internationale
Unites the world in song
So comrades come rally
For this is the time and place
The international ideal
Unites the human race
Let no one build walls to divide us
Walls of hatred nor walls of stone
Come greet the dawn and stand beside us
We'll live together or we'll die alone
In our world poisoned by exploitation
Those who have taken now they must give
And end the vanity of nations
We've but one earth on which to live
And so begins the final drama
In the streets and in the fields
We stand unbowed before their armor
We defy their guns and shields
When we fight provoked by their aggression
Let us be inspired by like and love
For though they offer us concessions
Change will not come from above.

Stand up all victims of oppression
For the tyrants fear your might
Don't cling so hard to your possessions
For you have nothing if you have no rights
Let racist ignorance be ended
For respect makes the empires fall
Freedom is merely privilege extended
Unless enjoyed by one and all.

Wednesday April 19, 1989

I spend the night in the square. A festive mood prevails. This atmosphere provides a glimpse of what this society might look like with the weight of repression and censorship lifted. This crowd is full of intelligent, engaged, idealistic young people who care deeply about the fate of their country.

I return to the office and turn on the TV. The U.S. networks and CNN are using sound bites like "freedom" and "democracy" to label the movement, but savvy Chinese like John can see a much more complex shadow play unfolding.

"Why no crackdown by the police?" I wonder out loud. "Are politicians seeking to use this opportunity for selfish ends?"

The answer isn't long in coming. Hardline Prime Minister Li Peng, seeing an opportunity to usurp his rival moderate Party leader Zhao, whispers in half-senile, octogenarian Deng Xiaoping's ear that the protesters resemble the Cultural Revolution Red Guards that tormented his family and crippled his eldest son. The paramount leader is alarmed enough to run a front-page editorial[121] in the *People's Daily* that defines

---

121. Titled "We Must Take a Clear-cut Stand against Disturbances" (simplified Chinese: 必须旗帜鲜明地反对动乱; traditional Chinese: 必須旗幟鮮明地反對動亂; pinyin: Bìxū Qízhì Xiānmíngde Fǎnduì Dòngluàn), the editorial begins by addressing the entire population of China, acknowledging their diverse expressions of grief. Specifically referencing the need to "turn grief into strength," the editorial suggests that the poignancy of Hu's death reaffirms the significance of upholding Party rule. Carried out by "an extremely small number of people," subversive responses, which the editorial describes as mostly verbal denunciations of the CPC, are an example of "abnormal phenomena" to be dealt with swiftly.

Focusing in on the students, the editorial references their assembly at Tiananmen Square on April 22 in an effort to participate in Hu's official memorial. The Party, acknowledging that the state of mourning creates "emotionally agitated" students, demonstrated "tolerance and restraint" toward this gathering, and the memorial was allowed to proceed without difficulty. The fundamental problem, according to

the student movement as "a destabilizing anti-party revolt that must be resolutely opposed."

This puts the government on a collision course with the students, and undermines Zhao's efforts at quiet compromise.

The students become unwitting pawns in a factional struggle and coup.

I report nonstop on the following six weeks of protests. They resemble the 1986–87 demonstrations, but escalate to occupation of Tiananmen, million-person marches, a hunger strike,[122] and martial law. Gabriel is

---

the editorial, is that "an extremely small number of people with ulterior purposes" have taken advantage of students, teachers, and even workers, to promote a "reactionary" message against Party leadership. The editorial describes this small group of people as not grieving, but executing a "planned conspiracy" to "plunge the whole country into chaos and sabotage," in order to "negate the leadership of the CPC and the socialist system." This accusation declares actions like the spreading of rumors, the use of posters, and the forming of independent unions as completely detrimental to the future of the nation. The editorial suggests that "reactionary" behavior could potentially reverse the economic progress made by Deng Xiaoping's program of reform and opening up. According to the editorial, this jeopardizes existing initiatives to control prices, eliminate corruption, and take on political reform. The editorial therefore calls on the population to help stabilize the political status quo by refusing to take part in any disturbances. Illegal unions, rumor-mongering, and "unlawful parades and demonstrations" are presented as not only violations against the state, but also against a student's right to study. The editorial ends by alluding to a general agreement among students and the Party to eliminate corruption and promote democracy, emphasizing the need to end disturbances in order for China to move forward.

122. May 13 Hunger Strike Declaration (1989):
In these bright and beautiful days of May, we are beginning a hunger strike. We are young, but we are ready to give up our lives. We cherish life: we do not want to die.

But this nation is in a critical state. It suffers from skyrocketing inflation, growing crime rates, official profiteering, and other forms of bureaucratic corruption, concentration of power in a few people's hands, and the loss of a large number of intellectuals who would now rather stay overseas. At this life-and-death moment of the nation's fate, countrymen, please listen to us!

China is our motherland.
We are the people.
The government should be our government.
Who should speak out, if we should not?
Who should act, if we should not?

Although our bones are still forming, although we are too young for death, we are ready to leave you. We must go; we are answering the call of Chinese history.

Our honest feelings of patriotism and loyalty to the nation were distorted as "turmoil," and we were accused of being the tools of a "handful" who have "ulterior motives."

my constant companion. I write and he photographs. We're running on two to three hours of sleep per night for forty-five days. I'm drunk with fatigue. Then events turn fatal.

We ask of every Chinese citizen—every worker, peasant, soldier, civilian, celebrity, every government official, policeman, and our accusers—that you place your hand on your heart and ask yourself: What wrong have we done? What "turmoil" have we created? What causes have led us to protest, to demonstrate, to boycott classes, to fast, to hide ourselves? Why did this happen? Our words were not heard in good faith. We were beaten by police when we marched, though we were only hungry for the truth. Our representatives knelt for hours, presenting our petition, only to be ignored by the government. Our request for dialogue has been put off again and again. The safety of our student leaders is now uncertain.

What shall we do?

Democracy is supposed to be the highest of human aspirations and freedom a sacred human right, granted at birth. Today these must be bought with our lives.

We say to our dear mothers and fathers, do not feel sorry for us when we are hungry. To our uncles and aunts, do not feel sad when we leave this life. We have one wish, that the lives of everyone we leave be better. We have one request, that you remember this: our pursuit is life, not death. Democracy is not a task for a few; it takes generations.

May this declaration, written with our lives, break up the clouds that cast their shadows on the People's Republic of China. We are doing this:

1. To protest the government's indifference to the student demonstrations;
2. To protest the government's failure to enter into a dialogue with students;
3. To protest the government's unfair characterization of the student democratic movement as "turmoil" and the further distortion of it in newspaper coverage.

We request:
    a. An immediate dialogue between the government and the students on substantial topics with equal status;
    b. An acknowledgement by the government of the legitimacy of the student democratic movement.

Time of the hunger strike: Begins at 2:00 PM, May 13, 1989.
Place of the hunger strike: Tiananmen Square.

chapter twenty

墨写的谎说，决掩不住血写的
事实

*Moxie de huangshuo, jue
yanbuzhu xuexie de shishi.*

LIES WRITTEN IN INK CANNOT CONCEAL
TRUTH WRITTEN IN BLOOD.

Friday June 2, 1989

The telephone in the UPI office rings. Dave picks up, says a few words, then barks: "Savitt, it's your girlfriend."

I hurry over and pick up. Dede is calling from the five-star Shangri-La Hotel. She and Mrs. Lord are working as paid consultants for the CBS Evening News. As usual, they're my most reliable sources of information.

"There was a fatal accident on the Avenue of Eternal Peace. A military jeep hit and killed four students!"

This was the news we'd been dreading. Until now, the protests have been predominantly peaceful. There were a few skirmishes between tired, frustrated martial law troops and students—I witnessed some myself—but the capital as a whole remained calm, and no one lost their life.

"I knew it," I say to Dede. "You can't have this many people under this much stress for this long, with tanks and troops running around, and not have something bad happen."

"The accident's on *Fuxingmen* Overpass, at the junction between *Chang'an* and the Second Ring Road. The military jeep is surrounded by students and they won't let the driver leave. There are rumors that soldiers are coming to get them out. You and Gabriel should get out there now."

"We're on our way," I say.

"*Zanmen zouba!* [Let's hit the road!]" I say to Gabriel as he shoulders his camera case and I grab my motorcycle keys.

Saturday June 3, 1989

We stay out the whole night and next day. It turns out that the army jeep was the first wave of an attempted assault on the square by soldiers that's repelled by citizens. Near Tiananmen, hundreds of troops are surrounded by protesters and trapped in buses loaded with AK-47s and .50-caliber machine guns.

Those aren't just for show, I think to myself.

Gabriel climbs on top of the bus to shoot inside. He's like a man possessed. Then we speed back to the bureau to file this news and transmit his photos.

6:00 PM June 3, 1989

The sun is going down, and I haven't slept in two days. All I want to do is lie down, but I know I have to keep working.

The phone rings. It's Dede and Mrs. Lord again.

"Get to West Avenue of Eternal Peace right away. The troops and tanks are moving. They have orders to clear Tiananmen before dawn."

"*Cao!*"

"Thanks," I add, and hear her say, "Be careful," as I hang up.

I grab my camera bag and motorcycle helmet, shove my cell phone into the pocket of my dad's old army jacket,[123] and call out: "The troops are moving, I'm heading west."

---

123. I'm wearing it for good luck; it kept him alive in Korea.

"Keep your phone on," I hear Schweisberg say as I sprint out the door.

Gabriel and I have agreed to split up. He'll stay near the square, and I'll head out west to where the military camps are.

I hop on my bike, kick-start the engine, and speed out the front gate of the diplomatic compound. It's ten kilometers (6.2 miles) to the west end of *Chang'an*. I've made the ride in less than fifteen minutes with no traffic. But now the streets are packed with people moving concrete lane dividers into the roadway to block the troops from entering the city.

No car can get through this. Other journalists are going to have a hard time getting to the front line.

Public loudspeakers at every intersection repeat the martial law warning: "Citizens are forbidden to enter the streets or Tiananmen Square. Violators will be responsible for their own fate. Should anyone ignore this order, the martial law troops, people's armed police, and public security officers will use whatever means necessary to enforce it."

I steer into the bike lane and weave through the crowds heading to Tiananmen.

The square is packed with people. They're gathered in groups talking, but appear fiercely determined to hold the heart of the city through the night.

I ride past the portrait of Chairman Mao hanging above the Gate of Heavenly Peace. His suspicious eyes seem to follow me. As I leave the square the number of people in the street thins out. I veer back onto the main road and pick up speed. The landmarks tick by: *Tiananmen* (Gate of Heavenly Peace) West Road. *Xinhuamen* (New China Gate). *Liubukou* (Six Ministries Street Mouth). *Xidan* (West Monumental Arch). *Minzu Gong* (National Minorities Palace). *Fuxingmen* (Glorious Revival Gate—the entrance to the old Imperial City). *Muxidi*—the site of high officials' residences, including the Communist Party General Secretary's chief of staff and family.

I finally arrive at *Gongzhufen*—Tomb of the Princesses[124]—where the Third Ring Road turns south toward the military encampments where I know the tanks and troops are stationed.

---

124. The favored third and fourth daughters of the Qing Dynasty Jiaqing emperor (1760–1820).

It's taken me almost an hour to get here. The grassy roundabout is filled with people discussing the day's events and speculating about what the government is going to do next. Contrary to the festive mood in the square, this crowd is on edge.

I feel my cell phone vibrate and see it's Dede.

"Where are you?"

"*Gongzhufen.*"

"The troops and tanks are coming up the road from the south toward you."

"Thanks," I say and shove the phone back into my pocket.

Mrs. Lord and Dede's intelligence is again impeccable. I ride my bike south with the lights out to avoid detection. I hear a low rumble grow louder, and as I come over a rise I see a line of battle tanks, armored personnel carriers, and thousands of soldiers with bayonet-tipped assault rifles coming toward me. It's the most terrifying sight I've ever seen.

I swing my bike around and speed back toward the intersection.

"*Dabing laile* [The soldiers are coming]*!*" I yell.

I ditch my bike in a clump of bushes. I'm still wearing my motorcycle helmet, and my bandana covers my mouth and nose. Only my eyes are visible; no one can see I'm a foreigner. Suddenly anti-riot troops in black uniforms with metal shields and steel helmets pour into the roundabout from all sides. People start running. I hear the thud of wooden truncheons smacking skulls.

"Fascists!—*Faxisi!*" "Dogs!—*Gou!*" "Beasts!—*Chusheng!*" onlookers cry.

Then the people start fighting back. Young men break sidewalk flagstones into jagged chunks and throw them at the soldiers.

A young riot trooper gets trapped against a metal fence and pelted with bricks and stones until he falls to the ground. I try to help him, but the crowd closes in. They appear to be beating him to death.

Then I hear the unmistakable sound of machine-gun fire. *Pop-pop-pop.* Steady bursts of three shots that means the rifles are on semi-automatic. Red and green tracer bullets streak across the sky. It's eerily beautiful. I can't help thinking of the lines from "The Star-Spangled Banner": "*And the rockets' red glare, the bombs bursting in air. . . .*"

Suddenly a man next to me spins and falls to the ground. I see a red stain spread across his T-shirt.

"Are they rubber bullets?" I ask a guy running by.

"Rubber bullets? Fuck no, they're live rounds." He knows what he's talking about; most people here do mandatory military training and are very familiar with these weapons.

Then the tracer fire moves from over our heads directly into the crowd. People start falling all around me. I hear the *ppppzzzzhhhh ppppzzzzhhhh ppppzzzzhhhh* of high-velocity rifle bullets buzzing past my head. A tear gas canister explodes next to me and I fall to the ground. My eyes are tearing and burning. Gasping for air, I lie paralyzed on the pavement for several minutes. When I can finally see again, the tanks and troops are moving toward the next intersection, *Muxidi*.

I call in the first confirmed death after 10 PM, my voice barely audible above the din of gunshots.

"Dave," I say when I hear my boss's voice. "They're firing into the crowd and a guy's dead."

"How do you know he's dead?"

"Because his brains are splattered on the pavement."

Then the phone cuts off.

A guy my age limps toward me. I see he's shot in the upper leg. His pants are drenched with blood. I tell him I'll take him to *Fuxing* Hospital, a mile away at *Muxidi* Bridge.

I pull my bike out of the bushes and help him straddle the seat. As he leans against me I feel his blood seep into my clothes. I speed off in the bike lane. The tanks and troops are advancing down the main road less than twenty meters away. They're firing into the crowd ahead. If they turn their guns sideways we'll both be shot.

We pass bicycles and flatbed tricycles transporting the wounded.

I speed up to the hospital entrance and half-carry the guy in. The sight inside shocks me. The entrance corridor is filled with gunshot victims. Most aren't being treated. Some are hooked up to IV bags. A handful are covered with bloody white sheets, obviously dead.

"*Jiuming*—help!"

A nurse wearing a surgical mask runs over, and we ease the guy onto the floor.

"He needs to be treated right away!"

"No one's available. The doctors are all operating on the worst cases. We aren't prepared to handle this many gunshot wounds."

I know from my Outward Bound training that the biggest danger of massive trauma is blood loss. If they don't get transfused quickly the victims "bleed out." That's what's happening here. This hospital won't have enough blood for all these people.

"How many wounded?" I ask the nurse.

"All the operating rooms are full. So is the *taipingjian*—rest-in-peace room." *Rest-in-peace room* is the Chinese word for morgue. There must be scores of injured and dead.

I step back through the bodies in the entryway. The stench of blood and open wounds nauseates me.

But there's nothing more I can do here. I should be out reporting.

I run outside, hop on my bike, and take off after the tanks.

The carnage I just witnessed at *Gongzhufen* repeats itself at *Muxidi*. Anti-riot troops try to clear the intersection and are attacked by citizens throwing stones, bricks, bottles, and flaming Molotov cocktails. The soldiers open fire again and all around me people start dropping to the ground bleeding.

"Get her to the hospital immediately or she'll die," I yell to a group carrying an injured young woman.

The tragic scene repeats itself all the way down the ten-kilometer length of the Avenue of Eternal Peace. Thousands of enraged citizens fill the streets, massing spontaneously at each intersection to resist the assault. Incapable of clearing them with tear gas and batons, the soldiers shoot their way through the crowds and dozens if not hundreds fall at every crossroads.

Fuxingmen (Glorious Revival Gate), *Minzu Gong* (National Minorities Palace). *Xidan* (West Monumental Arch). *Liubukou* (Six Ministries Street Mouth). *Xinhuamen* (New China Gate). *Tiananmen* (Gate of Heavenly Peace) West Road. The horrific scene continues. I ride the entire length of the Avenue of Eternal Peace on the sidewalk, as far from the troops as I can get while still catching the action with my camera. Famed photojournalist Robert Capa said: "If your photographs aren't good enough, you're not close enough." He's right, but if I get too close the nervous soldiers will fire at me. The tension sharpens my senses and etches every moment into my memory.

On numerous occasions I make eye contact with soldiers less than twenty meters away. They point their rifles at me several times, but for some reason don't shoot. I guess they're exclusively focused on getting to the square so nothing else matters.

They finally arrive at Tiananmen just after midnight. The tanks and troops begin to fan out and surround the ten-acre square. They line up in straight rows, apparently awaiting orders for the final assault. When the cordon closes the thousands of students and citizens will be trapped.

This is my last chance to join them. I race ahead of the tanks to Justice Lane—*Zhengyi Lu*, an alley southeast of the square. It's part of the old Legation Embassy Quarter.[125] I have close friends who live here and I know the streets well. I ride down the pitch-dark alleyway with my lights out, park my bike in a dark corner where I can retrieve it later, and run onto the square just before the tank line closes.

An emergency message broadcasts continuously from loudspeakers mounted on light poles in the Square: "City residents and students, a counterrevolutionary rebellion has taken place in Beijing. A small number of terrorists has incited students to violently attack the Great Hall of the People and throw rocks and Molotov cocktails at PLA soldiers and the people's armed police, injuring many. Students and residents are asked to leave Tiananmen Square immediately or you will bear the consequences of your actions."

I hurry to the Monument of Revolutionary Martyrs at the center of the square. Several thousand students and citizens remain. Those nearest look at me like they're seeing a ghost. I look down and see I'm covered with blood. Then I remove the bandana covering my face. They're even more shocked to see that I'm a foreigner.

---

125. Where the Boxer Rebellion (1897–1901) Foreign Legation fifty-five-day siege took place.

"*Zenme hui shi?* [What happened?]" they ask.

"What *happened*? Don't you know? They're shooting everyone in sight!"

The students on the square don't know what's occurred outside Tiananmen. I'm the first to bring the tragic news. I'm quickly surrounded and recount everything I've witnessed.

Now they're scared.

"Do you think they'll shoot us?"

I shrug my shoulders and remain silent.

They sit back down on the marble steps of the monument, visibly shaken. I sit with them and take a much-needed rest.

"*Minbuweisi, naiheyisijuzhi* [the people aren't afraid to die, how can you threaten us]?" a female student yells, shaking her fist at the tanks and soldiers surrounding the square.

This gesture of defiance raises her classmates' spirits.

"I was just accepted to medical school. This is an inconvenient time to die!" a male student jokes, and his fellow protesters laugh, relieving the tension.

We sit facing the massed tanks and troops from midnight until 4 AM. Blinding floodlights I've never seen before illuminate the square. I hear the sound of gunfire and see tracer bullets flying overhead. Street battles continue on the roadways adjacent to Tiananmen.

Finally a young professor from Beijing Normal University, Liu Xiaobo,[126] persuades the students that they don't have to sacrifice their lives. He receives their permission to negotiate a settlement with the troops. We watch him cross no-man's-land between us and the soldiers and talk to their commanders. We're afraid he's going to be shot, beaten, or arrested, but he returns after half an hour and reports that he's made a deal. The Martial Law troops will allow a one-time exit out the southeast corner of the square. Anyone who stays behind won't be protected.

The protest organizers, now led by twenty-one-year-old female Commander-in-Chief Chai Ling, gather to discuss their response. There's

---

126. Who in 2009 becomes the Nobel Peace Prize winner and is serving an eleven-year prison sentence for subversion.

intense debate. Some want to leave and live to fight another day. Others want to occupy the square to the bloody end.

"How about a compromise?" Chai Ling proposes. "Those who want to leave can leave, those who choose to stay can stay."

They all agree and communicate their decision to Professor Liu, who goes back and conveys it to the troops. An agreement is finalized. The students are promised safe passage out of the square.

Tiananmen has been occupied nonstop for the past seven weeks. Beijing police stopped working a month ago, and the capital's crime rate dropped. It's the closest thing to selfless community I ever expect to see. Now it's ending in tragic defeat. It feels like the death of idealism and innocence.

4:30 AM June 4, 1989

The students link hands, form two columns, and walk toward the corner of the square. They circle around Chairman Mao's Mausoleum. I walk alongside them. But before all the students make it off the monument, the troops start moving. Their first target is the Goddess of Democracy statue facing Chairman Mao's portrait at the front of the square. A tank rolls forward and topples the twenty-foot papier-mâché sculpture then crushes it.

The tanks and troops move toward the tent city standing between them and the monument. The scene is similar to the one I witnessed earlier—people running chaotically ahead of armored vehicles, shouting, and the staccato burst of gunfire.

Those students remaining on the monument are broadcasting "The Internationale" on the public-address speakers they installed when the protests started.

"*This is the final struggle. Let us come together and create a brighter future for humanity . . .*" reverberates over the hellish scene.

The tanks roll over the tents, crushing anyone still inside, and continue toward the monument. Soldiers fire at the speakers to stop the music. Bullets pierce the metal but the music continues for what seems like minutes. Then the speakers start to drone and finally go dead.

Dawn is breaking as I leave the square with the students. We pass through an opening the soldiers make and then the line of tanks and troops closes behind us.

We head west and begin the ten-kilometer walk back to the university district.

At the first intersection, *Liubukou*, we turn right and head north. Emerging from the narrow alleyway onto *Chang'an*, we see a line of troops running toward us. They fire tear gas and we fall to the ground. Then I hear the terrifying rumble of tanks. There's no place to run. I dive over a lane divider just in time. Those who remain behind are crushed.

I run back to Justice Lane and find my motorcycle. Then I speed to catch up with the survivors continuing their march to campus. I offer a ride to a female student who looks too exhausted to walk. She gratefully accepts.

We retrace my path of the night before. Riding west on the Avenue of Eternal Peace, the scene resembles a war zone. Burned-out tanks, smoldering military vehicles, articulated bus shells, dead bodies. The stench of fire and death is overwhelming.

The chaos stretches the entire length of the avenue. At *Muxidi* we see the extent of the night's violence. Even the high officials' residences have dead and wounded. People gather in groups on the street wailing at the tragedy and cursing the powers that be.

Liumang zhengfu [Criminal government]*!*"

Xiao Hong (Little Red), the girl on my bike, weeps softly behind me.

The overcast sky mirrors the desolate scene all around us. Suddenly a smoldering military vehicle's gas tank catches fire and *kaboom!* it explodes. We both recoil at the loud noise.

I finally make it to the entrance of Beijing University. For the first time there are no guards at the gate. Outside the university health clinic, dead students are on display. They've been shot, parts of their heads and bodies blown away. The dozen corpses are laid out on blocks of ice. People are whispering and crying. Xiao Hong looks away. In a barely audible whisper she thanks me for the ride and drags herself back to her dormitory.

It's afternoon now. My cell phone battery is dead. I can't call in any more reports. I head back to the office.

I ride on the Second Ring Road. As opposed to the city streets, the highway is free of wreckage. But tanks and soldiers have set up checkpoints at every overpass. When they see that I'm a foreigner they wave me through.

I arrive back at the UPI office and stumble through the door. Dave, deputy bureau chief Mark, Delhi bureau chief Landay, and our local staff are all huddled over their computers pounding out stories. The room is choked with cigarette smoke. When they see me they all jump up at once.

"When we didn't hear from you, we thought something happened," Dave says with relief.

"My cell phone died this morning while I was still in the square."

They all look at me strangely. I glance down and see that my clothes are ripped and soaked with blood.

"Are you hurt?" Dave asks.

"This is other people's blood."

They guide me to a chair and someone hands me a cup of tea. I gulp it down. I haven't had any water, never mind eaten, in close to twenty-four hours. I'm exhausted and in shock. But I give them a rundown of everything I witnessed. I find out that what I saw took place all across the capital.

There was a massacre in Beijing.

The Chinese Red Cross reported two thousand dead, with a detailed breakdown of casualties hospital by hospital. Then the military moved into all medical facilities before dawn, stopped the counting, and even fired on and killed medical personnel who were trying to help the wounded.

When I hear this news I start to cry. Then I compose myself and finish my account. But I can barely string thoughts together. I haven't slept in three days.

"Is it okay if I go to sleep?" I ask.

"Sleep. Sleep," Dave says. "We've got things covered, and this story is just getting started."

I stagger across the hall and push open the door of my apartment. I collapse on the bed in my bloodstained clothes and fall into a dead sleep.

Sunday June 4, 1989

I grab a couple of hours of rest. But I can't turn my mind off. I have nightmares about the bloodshed and wake up shortly after midnight, my skin covered in sweat.

I know I won't be able to fall back to sleep, so I wander across the hall to the office in an exhausted daze and see everyone still working.

"How do you feel?" Schweisberg asks.

"Okay, I guess."

"Are you ready to work?"

"Do I have a choice?"

My gruff boss smiles.

We all get an unpleasant surprise when deputy bureau chief Mark DelVecchio walks into the office with an armful of suitcases. His wife is a Beijing native. It's not safe for them to stay and he's returning to the States immediately.

So, now it's just me and Dave staffing the office.

We switch on the TV. I do a double-take when I see a photo of Wang Dan, number one on the government's Most Wanted list of criminals.

There are tanks rumbling up and down the Avenue of Eternal Peace past our office. Getting close to one of these forty-five-ton monsters is a terrifying experience. People are still out on the streets throwing bottles and bricks that just bounce off the armored behemoths, angry and frustrated at being massacred by their own government.

The iconic photograph of the man who stands in front of the tanks, published around the world, is snapped a stone's throw from our office.

Wednesday June 7, 1989

Troops and tanks keep rolling up and down the Avenue of Eternal Peace in front of our office.

Suddenly a burst of machine-gun fire shatters the windows above us, barely missing the heads of the young children of U.S. Embassy personnel who live upstairs. The kids were looking out at the patrolling troops.

That's it.

The U.S. Embassy goes on emergency status and sends all non-essential personnel—including all spouses and family members—home. This means that Dede no longer has a job. She and I decide it will be best if she returns to New York to visit her family—neither of us have been home in the three years since we met—and continue working for CBS there. There's nothing for her to do here.

All Chinese have to provide documentation to their work unit that they weren't involved in the protests. It's a tragic irony because everyone was involved in the protests. Gabriel doesn't have a work unit to lie for him like John does, so we bribe a police officer with a Japanese color television (the equivalent of today's most expensive flat-screen TV) to give sworn testimony that Gabriel wasn't involved in the protests. Of course Gabriel's photos of the massacre are appearing in media all over the world, unattributed. With the sworn testimony, Gabriel secures a passport and exit visa and escapes to France to work for Agence VU photo agency in Paris.

John accepts an offer to study at Pennsylvania State University, with my parents acting as economic sponsors.

Less than a month after the massacre, all my best friends are gone.

Wang Dan goes into hiding but is caught and arrested. He's held in Beijing's notorious Qincheng Prison (where all prominent political prisoners are jailed) and eventually sentenced to four years. Ren Wanding is also arrested and given a seven-year prison sentence.

Fang Lizhi and his wife Li Shuxian take refuge in the U.S. Embassy and, having been granted asylum, will live in the tiny infirmary behind the ambassador's residence for an entire year. The Chinese government has put Fang and his wife Li at the top of the "wanted" list of people responsible for the protests. During his time in the U.S. Embassy, Fang writes an essay entitled "The Chinese Amnesia," criticizing the government's repression of human rights and the outside world's turning a blind eye toward Beijing's abuses. In June 1990, the Chinese authorities allow them to leave the embassy and board a U.S. Air Force transport plane to Britain in a deal secured between Henry Kissinger and China's paramount leader Deng Xiaoping. During his incarceration Fang receives the

Robert F. Kennedy Human Rights Award. After some time at Cambridge University and Princeton, Fang moves to Arizona where he works as a professor of physics at the University of Arizona.

My old friends, political activists Chen Ziming and Wang Juntao, are declared the leading "black hands" behind the movement and given prison sentences of thirteen years each on sedition charges.

Without Dede, I can't sleep. I stare at the ceiling, eyes wide open, images from the massacre playing over and over in my head. I'm afraid that if this relentless insomnia continues I'll lose my mind.

I throw myself into my work, collecting bad news. We hear gunshots outside our office every night. Soldiers patrol in pairs after some were found murdered and floating in the canals downtown. There are heavily armed roadblocks all over town; I know a driver who gets shot and killed fleeing from one.

Martial law remains in force for the rest of the year, rendering Beijing a war zone. Soldiers regularly point AK-47s in my face while I'm out reporting, and I've had my car commandeered by troops needing a ride. There's no normal.

Everyone is suffering some level of post-traumatic stress. I'm not officially obliged to risk my life for UPI, but my role has now assumed war-coverage status. For this I get a raise in pay. These events are a tragedy for everyone but us foreign correspondents. For us it's an opportunity. I hate exploiting others' suffering; I care too much about this place. So I go on working every day. I spend the next months documenting a numbing continuum of executions, arrests, and exiles. I do surreptitious work for Amnesty International and Human Rights Watch alongside my UPI journalism. My byline appears on headlines across the world. I'm featured on National Public Radio and the BBC, and the highlight of my fifteen minutes of fame is an appearance with Ted Koppel on ABC's *Nightline*.

In July, we have an unexpected visitor. President George Bush Sr. can't be seen to shake hands with the butchers of Beijing, so he sends the president who initiated the opening to China—Richard Nixon—to meet with the Chinese leadership and ascertain where the U.S.–China relationship stands and what's really going on here.

I'm designated the pool reporter for Nixon's visit—this task is always delegated to a wire service reporter—and I spend the day with President Nixon driving around Beijing in his limousine. Against his security detail's advice, he gets out on the downtown Beijing shopping street *Wangfujing* and shakes hands and greets citizens. Everyone recognizes him of course. In spite of his disgrace back home, in China he's still a hero for his bold decision to travel to Beijing, meet Mao, and initiate normalization between the PRC and the U.S.

Back in his limousine, I tell President Nixon that we're graduates of the same school—Duke—and that my father was in the same class as his younger brother Ed. Nixon is delighted at hearing this news and for the rest of the day we discuss our shared love of Duke basketball.

"How does it feel to be back in China, Mister President?"

He looks wistful as he meets my gaze.

"It's good to be back, son."

chapter twenty-one

城門失火殃及池魚
Chengmen shihuo, yangji chiyu.
WHEN THE CITY GATE IS ON FIRE, IT BRINGS
DISASTER TO INNOCENT PEOPLE.

June 1990

After working nonstop for the year following the massacre, I take my first trip home. I visit my family in Connecticut, then go see Dede in New York. We've exchanged letters, but this is the first time we've seen each other in a year.

I stay in her parents' Park Avenue penthouse. I've never seen this opulent Manhattan world before. Her father owns the building, and the Lords are their neighbors.

That first night, Dede and I make love like wild animals. We lie clinging to each other and talk about the future. We decide to try to live together again. She has an offer to open the Asia Society office in Hong Kong, and I have a job lined up with *Billion* magazine, a business-and-finance monthly in Hong Kong. We resolve to move together in the fall.

September 1990

Dede and I rent an apartment halfway up Victoria Peak on Hong Kong island. The balcony has a harbor view, and there's a swimming pool and tennis court, just what I need to recover from Beijing.

The weather is nice, the pay is good, and for a while my nightmares fade.

But reporting on initial public offerings and insider trading, the transfer of money from one pocket to another, can't compare to the drama of more than one billion people wrestling with and redefining their national identity.

China is slowly but surely recovering from the Tiananmen trauma. Business is picking up, and I keep getting sent back to Beijing on story assignments.

September 1991

As I spend more time on the road, Dede gets impatient. She finally gives me an ultimatum: get married or move out.

I sleep on the couch and agonize over this decision all night. In the morning I tell her that my work in Beijing isn't done. I see pain and anger in her eyes before she turns away.

She goes to work. I pack all the clothes and books I can fit into a backpack and head to the airport. My old friend John Moffley is head of the United Airlines office in Beijing, and he lets me stay in his apartment with his cook and housekeeper rent-free.

For work I resume reporting for *Asiaweek* magazine. Post-1989 China is different from the China I knew in the early 1980s. There's now an exclusive focus on making money as quickly and ruthlessly as possible. Official corruption is at an all-time high as rapidly increasing foreign investment and aid increases opportunities for graft. Crime rates are soaring and social order is breaking down as increasingly large numbers of rural poor migrate to the capital in pursuit of economic opportunity. The age-old scourges of prostitution and drug addiction return with a vengeance. This plays out in an alarming absence of public debate, as the state maintains its iron grip on all media. Official television, newspapers, magazines, and radio continue to parrot the mind-numbingly uniform Party line.

In this information vacuum I've spotted an opportunity to participate in promoting change. The most knowledgeable and concerned potential audience for news on China—local readers—are neglected. My simple but subversive idea is to establish an independent newspaper in Beijing. There is a growing expatriate community, but also a large and increasing number of English-reading Chinese. So I hatch a plan to publish an underground, independent English-language newspaper.

What's the worst thing that can happen? They shut me down, detain me, and deport me.

I'm so burned out that part of me wants to go home anyway. I have nothing to lose.

There has never been an underground publication in the People's Republic of China except for brief periods during the Cultural Revolution and the 1978–79 Democracy Wall movement. These were mostly homemade *samizdat* mimeographs. I need to find an offset printing plant that's willing to break the law to publish a tabloid-sized newspaper in a quantity of thousands.

I need to find staff. I start hosting weekly newspaper planning meetings at my apartment to try to recruit staff and brainstorm on what kind of content will push the envelope without going over the edge, reportage that is bold and subtle, what the Chinese call *cabianqiu*—ping-pong ball that grazes the edge of the table but is unreturnable and scores a point.

September 1993

The sky is still dark. I get up, shower, shave, and put on a blue button-down dress shirt, pressed khaki pants, and brown leather shoes. The sun is just cresting the horizon as I start my camouflage-green, canvas-roofed Beijing army jeep and head west. I'm an hour ahead of the morning rush hour traffic, and make the ten-kilometer drive to *Wanshoulu* (Longevity Road) in thirty minutes before turning off the main road onto an unmarked dirt track just beyond the Revolutionary History Museum. The road dead-ends at a concrete pillared, metal-gated entrance to a research facility. The high cement walls are topped with jagged broken glass and coils of barbed wire to prevent intrusion. The soldier standing guard with his AK-47 clutched to his chest confirms that this is an important government installation. The sign above the entrance, written in Chairman Mao's highly distinctive calligraphy, reads *Beijing Gaoji Nengyuan Wuli Yanjiusuo* (Beijing Institute of High Energy Physics [IHEP]).

I tell the guard in Mandarin that I have an appointment with Professor Shu at the computer center. After he makes a telephone call to confirm the meeting, he grunts directions at me and then waves me through. I pass a hangar-like white building the size of a football field that I later learn is the institute's positron collider (aka "atom smasher"). Just beyond this is a four-story, white-tiled building that a big sign identifies as the institute's computer center.

I park at the curb, bound up the steps, and stop at the reception desk.

"I'm here to see Professor Shu," I say to the young female receptionist.

She lifts a switchboard telephone, punches a button, and announces, "There's a *laowai* [literally: 'old outsider,' or 'foreigner'] here to see you."

I wince at her casual emphasis on the word 'foreigner,' but then I remember that I'm in a sensitive military facility. I turn my head toward the staircase in time to see an attractive woman in her early thirties in a blue skirt, white blouse, and hair pulled back in a tight bun descend the stairs and cross the floor to shake my hand.

"Welcome to our institute," she says to me in unaccented American English.

I do a double-take. "Where did you learn to speak like that?"

"In California," she replies. "I just returned from a decade at Stanford University, completing a doctorate in computer science. Have you spent time in Silicon Valley?"

"My cousins live in Mountain View, so I've spent a lot of time in the Bay Area and at Stanford," I tell her. "I especially like Lake Lagunitas," I add, referring to the small lake on campus that Stanford students use to suntan and windsurf.

"By the way, my English name is Cindy," she says as she leads me by the arm up the stairs to her office. I nod and smile. "It's weird to be back in Beijing after ten years in California."

"Tell me about it," I respond. "I've been living in Beijing for ten years. That's even weirder!"

We both laugh. She seems to prefer speaking English and I'm happy to do the same. It's a welcome break from speaking Chinese all day every day, but we continue to pepper our conversation with Mandarin words that flow more easily, like *diannao* (literally: "electric brain") for computer and *Zhuxi* (Chairman) for Deng Xiaoping, China's Central Military Commission chairman who had to give the final approval for China's first Internet connection.

"Stanford told us at the beginning of this year that they were willing to extend the trans-Pacific Internet cable to Beijing to facilitate this atomic experiment data exchange," Cindy tells me. "But we needed official permission first. Deng Xiaoping's daughter is the head of the Chinese Academy of Science, our parent government organization. She brought this Internet connection proposal to her father, and it was approved in a matter of days.

"How did you hear about our project?" she inquires.

I tell her that my Duke University classmate, who now works in Silicon Valley, alerted me that Stanford had just established the first trans-Pacific data link with China, and I was curious to see what this Internet that all my American friends are raving about looks like.

"Several years ago we began a collaborative research project with Stanford, sharing data from our atomic experiments. But sharing experimental data by post was a logistical nightmare. So Stanford suggested that we establish an Internet link. Of course this required high-level Chinese government permission—not to mention the Pentagon's approval—but because it's in the cause of furthering our scientific capability, it was approved quickly. We started with a satellite link, but that's extremely expensive to maintain. So just last month an undersea cable connection was made, and China now has its first hardline Internet connection."

As she leads me through a room with a dozen Sun workstation computers on desktops, she adds, "I was brought back from Stanford to oversee this project."

She leads me into an air-conditioned room and shows me the computer center's prized possession, an IBM mainframe computer processing and distributing via the Internet massive amounts of atomic experiment data. "This was donated to our institute by our Stanford colleagues," she explains.

"Can you show me how 'email' works?" I ask, having up until this time only heard about it from my friends and read about it in newspapers.

Watching Cindy send and receive email for five minutes captivates me. Then she asks, "Do you want to email someone?"

I tell her that I want to contact my old Duke classmate Banks Lowman, a graduate student in information technology at the University of Hawaii.

I type out my first fateful message to Banks:

To: Banks Lowman [Computer Science Department, University of Hawaii]

From: Scott Savitt, Beijing Institute of High Energy Physics

Subject: Greetings from China
  Dear Banks: I bet that this is the first email you've ever received from the People's Republic of China. Go Duke! This new technology rocks. We should start a newspaper in Beijing.

I sit and wait. After five long minutes, an email arrives in my inbox:

To: Scott Savitt, Beijing Institute of High Energy Physics

From: Banks Lowman [Computer Science Department, University of Hawaii]

Subject: Re: Greetings from China
  WELCOME TO THE INTERNET!! GO DUKE!!!
P.S. I'LL NEED A LITTLE BIT MORE INFORMATION ABOUT THAT NEWSPAPER.

I can't get rid of the huge grin on my face. I'm spellbound by this new technology. I see so many ways that this networking technology can revolutionize telecommunications, media, and public opinion in a tightly controlled society like China. Presently international telephone calls and even newly introduced fax technology are prohibitively expensive, costing more than US$100 for a single long-distance transmission. A freely available Internet would reduce the cost of international communication to near zero.

"Surely your superiors are aware of the potentially subversive social and political role of this new technology on a closed society like China?" I wonder out loud to Cindy.

She arches her eyebrows and smiles at me. "Let's just say that's not the aspect of the technology I emphasized in promoting it to my superiors."

Cindy leaves me sending email to every old friend I can look up an address for, and goes on her work rounds. When she returns half an hour later I'm still like a kid in a candy store. Seeing how clearly smitten I am, she asks, "Would you like an Internet account?"

I can barely restrain my enthusiasm: "Yes, of course!"

So she sits down and sets up an administrative shell account for me. I'm now one of the first Internet users in China.

As I drive back home, I'm floating on air. This has opened up a whole new vista of possibilities. I can finally see a window of opportunity for helping to change this society for the better after the tragedy of Tiananmen Square. I'm determined to be an Internet activist, hack around the government censors and bring free information to the masses of China. Now the question is, how best to achieve this goal? The answer I come up with for myself is simple but no less subversive: start an English-language newspaper.

I start emailing Banks every day.

So, when are you coming to join the Chinese Internet Revolution?

You've read your John Milton (Areopagitica) and Thomas Paine, you know what history demands of those granted such unique opportunities.

> We're still in our 20s. How many times in your life
> are you going to get a chance to change the world for
> the better?
> Didn't Steve Jobs ask John Sculley [Apple's first
> CEO]: Do you want to spend your life selling sugar
> water [Sculley was then the CEO of Pepsi] or do you
> want to change the world?

Banks, eminently more pragmatic than me, asks all kinds of sensible questions.

> Where are we going to get this newspaper printed?
> What are we going to do for start-up capital?
> What happens if we get shut down before the first
> issue is printed?

These are all very practical points, but no match for someone who competed in Chin's first Ironman Triathlon without training (and finished in respectable time): me.

"Where there's a will there's a way," I tell Banks, and set about researching the answers to his questions.

The funny thing about my relationship with Banks is that he can't say no to me, and we both know that. But it's a godsend that he's more level-headed. As in all start-up enterprises, someone must play the visionary otherwise new ventures would never get off the ground. But someone else must ask the tough questions or too many important details get overlooked. Banks' first concern is about where and how to get the newspaper printed.

I seek out the highest-ranking Communist Party member I know, my friend July Zhou's father, Long March veteran and former chief of staff to the late–Premier Chou En-lai, Zhou Weizhi. I make an appointment through my friend July, and go to meet Minister Zhou in a palatial courtyard near the Forbidden City in central Beijing.

I state my case, and he laughs and reminds me that his two sons, both close friends of mine, produced an independent newspaper in Beijing during the Cultural Revolution, and were thrown into solitary confinement in China's Qincheng political prison by Mao's wife and the Gang of Four for their troubles. They were detained for almost a decade. One would expect a father to be upset by this memory, but Minister Zhou is actually laughing. Talk about whistling past the graveyard and scoffing in the face of death!

Then he offers the same response that I'll hear repeatedly in the days, months, and years ahead as I pursue this quixotic undertaking. He recognizes the noble impulse behind it; he himself will not risk his neck and the safety of his family for such a politically dangerous undertaking. But what he will do is inquire about how the authorities are likely to respond. That's the most I can hope for, and I thank him and take my leave.

Within a week I hear back from July with good news. His father has ascertained that the propaganda authorities who oversee all of Beijing's media will be inclined to take a *kaizhi yan, bizhi yan* ("one eye open, one eye closed") approach to an English-language newspaper published by a foreigner in Beijing. This is as close to a green light as a foreigner is ever going to get. I report back to Banks with the good news. He has to admit that this is a major breakthrough. The next matter is money.

I bite the bullet and decide to approach my attorney father.

"Pop," I greet him long distance in my once-a-month telephone call paid for by my parents, who want reassurance that I'm still alive. "You put [my brothers] Greg and Rick through graduate school [one law, one psychology]. I haven't asked for a penny since I graduated from college. Now I have something I really want to do. What do you say, can you help me out?"

"Here, talk to your mother, let her decide."

I'm secretly relieved because my mom, like Banks, can't say no to me.

Before the conversation is over, I have a commitment of US$50,000. When I report this exciting news to Banks, he has to admit that things are shaping up. Fifty thousand is not a lot of money for a new media venture once you start calculating computer equipment, office and home rents, airfares, printing, and distribution costs and salaries. We know that we're going to have to come up with a means of generating revenue before hard-to-attract advertising kicks in.

The idea hits me. How about marketing email accounts?

Normally I would consider this an ethical breach. Cindy Shu was already sticking her neck out to make an account available to me. But surely these are extenuating circumstances. I'm the only person I know in Beijing with email (the IHEP domain is still the only one active in China). I know that I'm sitting on something of enormous value if I can bend the rules a little (and China is nothing if not the Land of Bent Rules).

I set up a computer as a server in my living room and begin letting friends and neighbors know that I can make Internet access available to them for a price. The demand is overwhelming. Before the end of the first week, the head of the U.S. Embassy's Cultural Section asks if I can provide email access to their entire staff. I sell each email account for US$500, and by the end of the summer have fifty users on the network.

All the pieces are in place for the launch of the newspaper. We've settled on a name: *Beijing Scene*. It's no one's favorite, but it's the one we can all agree on. Katherine points out that no one thought The Beatles, The Who, or Yes were such great names in the beginning either.

Katherine and I reconnected while I was home in Connecticut attending the wedding of my childhood best friend. She was waiting to hear back from Master of Fine Arts programs and thought that China would be a great adventure for an artist/photographer to take a gap year, and she took me up on my offer to return to Beijing with me.

My dad came through with the US$50,000 loan, and we've grossed US$25,000 from the sale of email accounts over the summer. We have an interim graphic designer—now in Seattle producing the award-winning weekly *The Stranger*, but preparing to relocate to Beijing—a business manager (Banks in Honolulu), a photographer (Katherine), an advertising sales director (my friend Michelle, already living in Beijing), and me as editor. I also know that the moment we pull the trigger many of my Chinese reporter friends, underemployed due to the ongoing fallout from the Tiananmen crackdown, will be available to help us get the newspaper started.

There's just one catch.

chapter twenty-two

讓人早死，讓他辦報紙

IF YOU WANT SOMEONE TO DIE YOUNG, MAKE THEM A NEWSPAPER PUBLISHER.

Apple computers aren't available in mainland China.

Due to ongoing Cold War restrictions, they're considered powerful enough to have military applications and can't be exported to Communist countries. Since it's necessary to leave China to purchase them, we decide to meet somewhere equidistant from all of us, and choose Hawaii.

I wire Banks funds and he purchases the equipment in advance. We plan to put the cutting-edge desktop publishing system together in an office in Honolulu, fine-tune it, and test-produce the first issue of the newspaper there. This means we'll have it ready for printing the moment we arrive in Beijing in the New Year.

We decide to take a final Thanksgiving break with family—those of us in China with our makeshift expat families—then gather in Hawaii on December first and spend a month there before returning to Beijing.

Finally the big travel day arrives.

Katherine and I leave a trusted friend, New York City native Beijing University student Andrew Nugent-Head, to watch our apartment and houseplants in Beijing, and board the plane for Hawaii. There's no turning back now. When we touch down in Honolulu the midwinter morning sun shines bright in a clear blue sky. It's sunny and 70 degrees with a cool breeze blowing off the Pacific Ocean. I see Banks's laid-back California beach-boy smile in the crowd and greet him with a big "Aloha!" and Hawaii hug.

This warm ambience couldn't be further from the cold, permanent tension of Beijing.

Banks has rented an office in the warehouse district in downtown Honolulu, a short walk from the beach. I fear that we'll be distracted by the ocean's warm embrace, but it turns out to be just the right mixture of work and play. Katherine and I stay at a comfortable guesthouse on the University of Hawaii campus. We rent bicycles and ride the fifteen minutes to our beachfront office every morning. Dave Kaill—who prefers to be called by his Spanish name, Pablo—arrives the next day, and we all meet in person for the first time. Pablo is six feet four inches tall and has a gruff demeanor, but we come to realize he's a big teddy bear. Banks and Katherine are very good at putting people at ease. I fall into my accustomed, slightly eccentric role as "the China guy."

After all the conflict, violence, social unrest, and upheaval I've experienced over the past decade in China, a month in Hawaii is bliss. Katherine and I get up with the sun and run on trails around the beautiful University of Hawaii campus together. Otherwise I stretch and do slow-motion *t'ai chi* exercises while she works through her yoga poses. The Pacific sea air smells like a beautiful woman. We share a light breakfast of good Kona coffee or Chinese green tea, fresh-squeezed orange and grapefruit juice, and either toasted fresh-baked bread or easily digested Chinese-style rice porridge. Then we hop on our rented mountain bikes and coast down the hill from the university to our beachfront office.

Our makeshift digs take up the entire floor of an empty office building. The economic downturn triggered by the drop-off in Japanese investment means that we're able to rent the office for US$500 a month. Banks has already purchased all the desktop publishing equipment on an academic discount at the university, and the machines are sitting in shiny white Apple boxes stacked in the corner of the room. We get to work unpacking and networking everything together. The initial lineup is ten top-of-the-line Macintosh workstations with keyboards and monitors, a black-and-white and color laser printer (brand-new technology at the time), a high-quality digital scanner for the art director, some new Nikon photo equipment and lenses for Katherine, accounting software for Banks' role as business manager, and some proprietary editorial content management software Banks has procured (this is long before the Internet provides a grab-bag of free software).

The crown jewel is a US$10,000 Lasermaster high-resolution tabloid-sized digital printer, so if worse comes to worst we can print a high-resolution copy of the newspaper ourselves on eleven-by-seventeen-inch tabloid-sized paper, shoot a photographic positive of it, and have printing plates made and newspapers printed from this. This very expensive piece of equipment proves an essential purchase.

We put all the pieces together, and at the end of the first day print out a sample newspaper cover: Hiking the Wild Great Wall. We high-five each other at the surprisingly good quality we're able to produce.

The days fly by and we come to realize that we've put together a talented and compatible team. We have a strong feeling that we're on the verge of doing something important. We give ourselves Christmas Eve off to celebrate—there's no possibility of a White Christmas in Hawaii, but we party together on the beach past midnight—then begin preparing for our January 1 return to Beijing.

There's a big risk involved in our return trip. PRC customs charges up to 150 percent duty on imported computers. For this reason, most foreign business travelers don't declare computers. We can't afford to pay this tax—it will break our tiny budget. So we have to figure out a way of getting the computers in without having customs discover them.

We go to a sports store in Honolulu and buy six big canvas hockey-gear bags. We break all the computer equipment down to its smallest components and cover them with dirty clothes to deter inspection. Then we pack everything up. Pablo, Banks, Katherine—who's very strong from lugging around a shoulder bag full of cameras all the time—each carry one of the bags, making them look like large suitcases.

We board the United Airlines flight in Honolulu and, after nine hours in the air, arrive in Beijing late at night. Evening customs is more lax. I lead everyone to the customs line, carrying a hockey bag in each hand.

"Do you have anything to declare?" the female customs agent asks.

"*Wo shi qiongmanghu* [we're starving peons]," I say to her in unaccented Chinese. "How could we afford anything to declare?"

She compliments me on my Mandarin and doesn't think to check my bags. I pass through undetected, and tell her that Katherine, Pablo, and Banks are with me and she lets them through too. I tell them to hurry and get in a cab and I'll meet them at home. Then I go back for the final two bags.

"Hey, didn't I just see a bunch of similar bags go through here?" a male customs agent says.

Katherine, Pablo, and Banks are almost out the exit, and I call out as nonchalantly as possible in English, "Run!"

The customs agent doesn't understand English, but is now alarmed.

"Let me check these bags."

We prioritized; the most expensive equipment went through first. The couple being stopped now only have easily replaceable computer monitors in them. We just successfully smuggled in forty thousand dollars' worth of computer equipment, the first Macintosh computers in Beijing.

The official impounds the last two bags, but I return the next day and slip him a US$100 bribe to get the monitors out of hock, still a steep savings on the 150 percent duty.

We gather back at our office.

This is my old two-bedroom United Press International diplomatic compound apartment; I've also procured two studio apartments with a "gift" of a bottle of Johnnie Walker Red and Marlboro carton to the Chinese manager. Katherine and I live in one, Banks has the other, and Pablo moves into the back bedroom of the office.

We unpack all the computers from the hockey gear bags and assemble them as we'd done in Hawaii. We pray that everything survived the trip and still works. We let out a group cheer when we hear the familiar chorus of Macintosh gongs indicating that the machines are starting up successfully. The early advantage of Macintosh computers for media is graphic design and networking. It's why Apple still dominates the field, because individual computers can handle large graphics files and be easily networked together with Ethernet cables for file-sharing. We begin the production and printing process for the inaugural issue of the newspaper we prepared in Hawaii.

We work so many hours the first week that people just curl up under their desks for a few hours' shut-eye and then roll over, hit the computer *on* button, and start working again.

It takes us three days to produce the first issue of *Beijing Scene*.

To be safe, we take a high-resolution, camera-ready copy of the black-and-white, sixteen-page inaugural issue of the tabloid newspaper to the film production "service bureau" (as printing press film output operations are formally called) at the state-run Foreign Languages Press Publishing House (FLP) in Beijing. FLP was the infamous publisher of the bestselling book in history, *The Little Red Book of Chairman Mao's Quotations* which sold tens of millions worldwide. Although FLP is still a stodgy official propaganda mill, they produce a large volume of magazines and books as well as internal government publications: *Beijing Review, Beijing Reconstructs, Chinese Literature.* They have state-of-the art desktop publishing equipment, and because China's market reforms now require that each department be responsible for its own profits and losses, they're willing to rent their equipment to outsiders for a fee, no questions asked. We also bring our Macintosh production computer to test whether we can do the production process digitally. This is still the era of dial-up Internet access, so large files like a copy of the newspaper can't be transmitted online; the network connection is much too slow.

The experiment goes smoothly. We output our content from our computer to the service bureau's master computer, only experiencing minor glitches with certain typeface fonts that the two computers don't share and therefore have to be downloaded from our computer to theirs. But otherwise the transfer goes smoothly, although the rendering of the large graphics files takes hours. Once the copy of the newspaper is on the press' film output machine, it produces acetate film positives, ready to be transferred to flexible metal printing press plates at the printing plant.[127]

The next process—printing the newspaper—is tricky. The authorities are very wary of independent publications. The last time they were produced was during the Cultural Revolution. I have Chinese friends who produced independent *xiaobao* (small newspapers) then.

The Communist Party is very clear about the threat of independent publishing. Chairman Mao famously declared: "Political power grows out of two barrels: the barrel of the gun and the barrel of the pen."

Every state-run printer we ask to take the political risk of printing our newspaper says no, so we have to be creative. The solution I come up with is to get the PLA to print our newspaper.

In Communist countries, there's one entity that's above the law, and that's the military. This is especially true in China. Common laws don't apply to military vehicles, military officers, military compounds, and military-run businesses.

So we contract with the People's Liberation Army Publishing House to print 10,000 copies of our first issue of *Beijing Scene* for fifty cents per copy.

I've never seen a printing plant in operation before. It's an amazing process. Giant web presses run off hundreds of thousands of copies of the official *People's Liberation Army Daily* newspaper here every day. For our relatively small print run, a smaller German Heidelberg offset press is used (a machine that still costs several million U.S. dollars). We sit in a glass-enclosed room and watch the first issues of our newspaper rolling off the press. A machine at the end of the assembly line cuts, collates, and folds the pages, and after a couple of hours, when it's done, 10,000 copies lie stacked on wooden pallets.

We recruit local friends, divide into five teams, and take 2,000 copies of the newspaper each, enough to fill a minivan, and begin delivering

---

127. We choose to print in black-and-white because it's cheaper and technically simpler. Color printing, which we will transition to later at the request of deep-pocketed multinational advertisers, requires four pieces of film for each page of print in a process known as CMYK—cyan, magenta, yellow, and black, the four colors used to produce every color in the palette. The black-and-white technique of "spot color" involves occasionally adding a single additional piece of film overlay to a page of the newspaper, like our crimson *Beijing Scene* logo.

them to preselected distribution sites all over town: hotels, foreign embassies, universities, bars, and bookstores. By 5 PM we're finished, and gather at a Sichuan restaurant near our office to share a meal and celebrate. After dinner we walk over to a bar near our office to continue our celebration and wait to see what the response to the first independent English-language newspaper ever produced in the PRC is.

The Mellow Mushroom Bar, located behind the U.S. Embassy, is a scene straight out of a Kubrick film. It eerily, if unintentionally, resembles the creepy Korova Milk Bar from *A Clockwork Orange*. The exterior is unassuming, just a white stucco building with a yellow lantern by the door. But as soon as you enter, you're in a cave-like space with sculpted white walls, like you've entered a giant mushroom. It's illuminated by candlelight with intricately colored glass and ceramic tilework inlaid into the walls, tables, mirrors, ceilings, and floors.

The new venue is jointly owned by a rich young businessman and a couple of artists who teach at the nearby Central Academy of Fine Arts, so that explains the creative design. Our group piles in around a table that resembles a mushroom cap in the back of the bar, and I order a pitcher of Tsingtao draft beer to start the celebration. We fill our glasses and toast each other on a job well done, and then sit back to watch the show.

We've strategically placed a pile of fifty copies of *Beijing Scene* by the door. As patrons arrive—foreigners getting off work from the nearby embassies and young Chinese professionals—we watch them pick up copies of the paper. Conversations about it begin immediately—where it's from, who produced it, why it's not written in Pidgin English like all other government publications here. No independent English-language publication has ever appeared in the PRC; who would dare try it? All that exists is the *China Daily*, a broadsheet often referred to by its expatriate readership as "the most boring newspaper in the world." It's produced by the Communist Party's Central Propaganda Department, and carries lifeless editorials about the superiority of socialism and how happy all of China's ethnic minorities are in their worker's paradise. It also spares no opportunity to attack the United States and other hostile Western forces dedicated to the downfall of China's glorious socialist experiment.

Beijing Scene, in contrast, is tabloid-sized and of superior print quality. An artistic, full-page black-and-white photo of a Chinese woman on a bicycle taken by Katherine graces the cover for a story on sports in Beijing. And at the top is what will become the familiar *Beijing Scene* logo: Beijing outlined in a splash of scarlet.

The stylish cover is just the start of the many differences between our newspaper and those that have preceded it. From the very first word, readers are aware that this is not produced by Party hacks writing in an unfamiliar second language. It's written by young, energetic, native-English speakers with a robust sense of humor and irony. The cover story surveys all the different exercise options in Beijing, from the most modern hotel health clubs and private spas to traditional *qi gong* and martial arts groups that gather in parks before dawn and after work.

There's also an advice column cheekily titled "Ask Ayi" (*Auntie* in Chinese); a tongue-in-cheek, darkly humorous Chinese-language column called "Comrade Language"; a review of the newest films by Chinese directors from Zhang Yimou to Jia Zhangke; and a feature piece on the revival of Peking Opera.

And there are free and paid classified advertisements—free community service ads we've solicited from friends and local businesses.

As pitchers of Tsingtao beer flow, we watch the crowd of young Chinese and Westerners pore over the newspaper, point at passages, laugh out loud, and wonder about the provenance of such a strange and unprecedented arrival. On my way back from a trip to the restroom I eavesdrop on a conversation between a group of young expatriates and their hip young Chinese friends.

"Who could have produced this? It's clearly not Chinese government propaganda!" a young Englishwoman with a plummy Oxbridge accent says.

"There's no such thing as a publication that's not Chinese government propaganda!" her thirty-something male colleague responds.

"I don't care what you say. If this writing's produced by the Chinese government I'll eat this newspaper," the woman retorts.

A satisfied smile crosses my face as I head back to our table. But we're all exhausted from so much travel and work, so shortly after midnight we call it a night—and agree to see each other at a staff meeting at 9 AM.

After my usual predawn martial arts workout at nearby *Ritan*, Altar of the Sun Park, I'm at my desk at 7 AM.

My telephone rings. It's *Wall Street Journal* Beijing bureau chief Jim McGregor.

"Comrade Savitt, congratulations. Whatever happens from now on, you can take pride in having accomplished something historical. . . ."

"Come on. What do you really think?" I ask.

McGregor was in on the secret project before its publication.

"It's incredible. Hey, it might not be the *Village Voice* yet, but neither is the *Village Voice* anymore. It's a damn good independent weekly by any standard, never mind the tremendous obstacles you've had to overcome."

"Thanks, Jim, that means a lot coming from you."

The tenor of this call is important. I know, but haven't told our team, that the most critical audience comprises my fellow Beijing-based foreign correspondents. It's a community of opinion makers. What they say and think about *Beijing Scene* is going to make or break its future, critically and commercially. They'll influence how people in our community react, and how advertisers and investors spend their money.

The phone doesn't stop ringing, with an endless string of congratulatory calls and inquiries about how to place advertisements in the next issue. We have to take the phone off the hook in order to conduct our 9 AM business meeting.

We make a decision. Having intentionally labeled this the inaugural issue, we've committed to a biweekly publishing schedule to give us time to get our production processes in place. We plan and share out assignments for the next issue a fortnight hence and, just like that, my life changes and I no longer have time to bicycle halfway across Beijing to train with my seventy-year-old martial arts master Li Peikun in *Ditan*, Earth Altar Park. The only day I can now spare the several hours required is Sunday, when all his old students return to pay their respects, brush up on their training, and spar with each other.

I now begin my days by lacing up my Nike running shoes or, if I'm feeling lazy, half slipping on my Chinese black cotton rubber-soled martial arts shoes. I run out the back gate of the diplomatic compound and shout a *"Nin zao* [Good morning]*!"* to the rifle-cradling soldier finishing his overnight watch as I sprint by.

I jog the half mile to the embassy district's *Ritan,* Altar of the Sun Park. The park doesn't officially open until 6 AM, but I know a back way in through a maze of administrative offices on the east side of the park.

I go to a grassy area near the park's man-made, koi goldfish–filled pond, and do a series of yoga and martial arts exercises before performing one of the slow, orchestrated *t'ai chi* series of shadow boxing movements my martial arts master taught me. After an hour I run a few laps (1.5 kilometers per hour) around the park then head home. I quickly shower in cold water—a habit left over from living with John—then dry off and throw on some clothes and am at my desk by 6 AM to start the day's work.

The biggest change between my new life as a publisher and my old life as a reporter is the number of administrative tasks I have to attend to. I laugh at the inconveniences I used to complain about in my life as a journalist: filling out expense reports for our bosses back in D.C. and keeping the bureau accounts. I would give anything to have that minimal level of interruption again. Now I have to worry about the office budget, contract negotiations, making sure salaries and bills are paid on time, and, in particular, whether advertising revenue is going to cover the newspaper's mounting expenses.

The good news is that the positive critical response to *Beijing Scene* keeps snowballing. Even though my name appears nowhere on the first issue of the newspaper, Beijing's grapevine spreads the word that I'm the invisible hand behind it.

My old boss, *Los Angeles Times* Beijing Bureau Chief Rone Tempest, stops me on the steps to our building one morning on our way to work. "Only you could have pulled this off, Scott. What you've done is big. Now your only challenge is to stay one step ahead of the Communist Party."

He's right.

The authorities take a hands-off approach to the first issue. There are no government calls, no one comes knocking, and our military printer doesn't receive a visit from the Beijing government. Someone is *kaizhiyan, bizhiyan*, keeping one eye open and one eye closed.

"*Meishi buzhao shi*, if it ain't broke, don't fix it," becomes my mantra. I have so many logistical tasks vying for my attention that I have no time to worry about getting arrested. I've taken a leap of faith, and am prepared for the worst. I know that the newspaper could get raided at any time, and this dream could vanish. There's nothing I can do to forestall that, so my best bet is to concentrate on creating the best newspaper possible.

The better the publication is, the better its chance of commercial success and survival, I reason. I'll be able to protect it with bribes to well-placed officials. The only problem is that our bank balance is diminishing as our expenses increase but our revenue stream isn't keeping pace. We continue to run the private email service, and advertise it in the inaugural issue of the newspaper, but even US$500 doesn't pay for much more than an hour of our business operations and office overhead.

Our advertising sales director, Mandarin-fluent and cheerleader-cute Michelle Kairies, is pounding the pavement twelve hours a day, trying to drum up advertising support. But her prognosis is grim. While everyone in town is obviously talking about and impressed by the new publication, no one wants to be the first to commit money to it. Again and again Michelle hears two concerns: How long are the authorities going to allow this new experiment to continue? Will corporate sponsors get themselves in trouble by sticking their necks out and showing support for such a subversive undertaking?

It's Friday afternoon, and the office phone rings. A local business called the San Francisco Brewing Company, an international chain of microbrew pub restaurants founded by a couple of Beijing-born, San Francisco–bred entrepreneurs named Frank and Eileen Zhao, want to take out a year's worth of full-page display advertisements at US$5,000 per issue, paid in advance. We're saved.

This in one fell swoop underwrites all our costs. We go from operating in the red to being profitable overnight.

We celebrate at the San Francisco Brewing Company restaurant with a round of their microbrewed pale ale. I can only spare an hour of time and one mug of cold beer before I have to return to the office to continue plowing through my relentless workload. There's always another issue of the paper to produce.

chapter twenty-three

喜事

GOOD FORTUNE

My overhead costs are fixed: office and apartment rents, salaries, newspaper printing costs, production equipment upgrade and maintenance, utility and phone bills. I keep all incoming bills in my top desk drawer and delay spending our precious start-up capital until we're threatened with having the water, electricity, or phone service cut off.

We're in one of our regular 7 AM management meetings.

Banks, who has experience working with Silicon Valley start-ups, has seen all this before.

"None of our creditors will put us out of business for late payment, because if they force us into bankruptcy then they'll never get paid," he confidently predicts.

His words prove accurate, but I'm still under constant, grinding pressure. Everyone has committed their time to this venture, but no one else has borrowed US$50,000 from their family and put their professional reputation on the line. I have no choice but to put in the hours to make sure I can make good on this gesture of good faith by my family and friends.

I'm so exhausted from working twenty-hour days for weeks on end that by the time my head hits the pillow, I fall fast asleep.

But I'm following my heart.

I'm one of those people who, since childhood, have always held a job. Since I was eight years old I had a newspaper route, cut lawns, shoveled snow, gave tennis lessons, and lifeguarded in the summer to "learn the value of money," as my parents put it. Since graduating from college the only job I've had is as a newspaper reporter. Unlike so many of my college peers, I didn't go to graduate, professional, or business school and don't go to bed at night reading books about how to be a better entrepreneur. If I'd read those books I would know that the vast majority of start-ups (some statistics place the number higher than 90 percent) fail within the first year. Perhaps if I'd known this, I would have stuck with reporting.

I'm convinced that I'm going to be one of the lucky one out of ten that succeed.

Financial pressure starts to take its toll on our workplace camaraderie. Mercifully for me, since Banks is the business manager people take their troubles to him. And since he so effectively embodies the Hawaii "aloha" spirit that he internalized during his years as a student in Honolulu, he's able to successfully defuse the tension. But there's increasing grumbling about the unrelenting work hours, no prospect for salary raises, and speculation about whether this newspaper is in fact viable. Or is it a noble undertaking that's doomed to failure?

"Maybe we should consider hanging up our pens and calling this quits," advertising sales director Michelle says at one of our regular staff meetings.

I swallow hard.

"I won't quit if I'm the last person left in this office," I tell the assembled staff. "I'll go out and refill every position, beg, borrow, or steal more funds, and keep this going as long as I draw breath.

"This newspaper will fail over my dead body," I hear myself saying, and I wonder whether there might be some ominous prophecy to this statement.

We pass the six-month mark and the twelfth issue of the newspaper. I feel like John Henry, the man who died trying to outwork the steam-powered hammer pounding railroad spikes. My background as a marathon runner and Ironman triathlon finisher gets me through my eighteen-hour workdays. I edit every word published in *Beijing Scene*, including advertising copy; I write or rewrite and revise all of the articles as Beijing's brutal summer peaks in a series of 100-degree July days.

The United Nations International Women's Conference, dedicated to advancing half the world's population, is being held in Beijing. The forty-four-member U.S. delegation coming over includes Secretary of State Madeleine Albright and First Lady Hillary Clinton.

A spike in advertising sales relating to the conference encourages us. I decide to personally deliver copies of *Beijing Scene* and a *Beijing Scene* T-shirt to Clinton, which she puts on and models for her staff and our photographer.

Then I have two new ideas:

1. We're going to make use of all the resources and capabilities we've accrued into producing a *Beijing Scene* guidebook.
2. We're going to increase our frequency of publication to weekly at the end of the summer.

Despite my exhausted staff's initial objection, doubling publishing frequency potentially increases revenue while overhead remains the same. A weekly has more opportunities to generate revenue than a fortnightly. Now that we've gotten the hang of publishing once every two weeks, it's just a matter of maximizing our efficiency to publish every week.

At least this is the logic I use to justify increasing our workload.

Our classified advertising revenue is growing steadily. But we only charge for employment ads, reasoning that classified ads are one of the biggest attractions of the newspaper for readers. We've continued to secure corporate advertisers, but potential customers are still concerned about what fate the Communist Party has in store for us. Hence the decision to publish a guidebook.

Advertisers see a guidebook as safer than a newspaper. A guidebook is a one-off project that readers will continually refer to, and they'll see the business's ad for a longer time than in a disposable newspaper. Advertisers also reason that this is the kind of thing the Chinese government doesn't and can't do well in English. In increasingly cosmopolitan, international Beijing, the general consensus is that the government may be happy to see a group of young Americans doing their propaganda work for them.

230 crashing the party

Another valuable brainstorm I have: instead of just selling copies of the book, why not sell advertising too (I've never understood why books don't contain advertising). We'll sell space in each of the guidebook's chapters to corporate sponsors.

We pull it off.

We charge US$10,000 per chapter and the advertisers go for it. We've sold out every chapter sponsorship; US$120,000 in advertising revenue. United Airlines signs on to sponsor the tourism chapter; the International School of Beijing the education chapter, Gold's Gym the health and fitness chapter, Apple and Hewlett-Packard split the information technology chapter, Hilton Hotels the hotel chapter, and just like that we're well in the black.

September 1 marks our first weekly newspaper. It requires twice as much work as publishing once every two weeks, but the critical advantage is that we can accept, run, and receive revenue for advertising once a week instead of once every two weeks. All of our present advertisers prefer the weekly publishing schedule because many of their events occur on a weekly basis, if not more frequently, and they don't require as much lead time and advance planning to get an announcement for a suddenly planned or changed event into the newspaper.

We publish the first annual *Beijing Scene Guidebook* on the same day we begin weekly publishing. The book is a rousing success. We've secured distribution for the guidebook in hotels, foreign embassies, even the Beijing airport bookshop—which had been reticent to accept and distribute the newspaper. We decide to charge the relatively low price of US$10 for the guidebook, netting approximately US$5 on each sale (book distributors all require a cut of each book that they sell, anywhere from 10–50 percent of the sales price).

Who would have predicted that eight months after we launched the newspaper, we would be making money? Now we might even be able to think about paying ourselves more than starvation salaries.

I'm working at my desk in the back corner of the office—I always like to have my back to a wall and face to the door—it's a survival instinct left over from reporting in dangerous situations. I look up from my pile of work and see the type of person who doesn't often venture into our office. A guy in his early thirties, dressed in a suit and tie.

I decide to check out who he is. I stroll over to where Banks is talking to him. Banks introduces me. He's British.

"Paul Hallett," he introduces himself.

He has an article he would like to submit about teaching himself Chinese from a dictionary that lists Chinese characters according to the frequency of their occurrence in the Chinese language—he only later learns that it's a dictionary of the most frequently used terms in Chinese aquaculture.

I crack up at the absurdity of the idea, but after reading through the piece see that Paul is a clever writer. I ask him if he'd like to sit down and have a cup of tea. He accepts, and we go into the back bedroom of the office-apartment, the room that doubles as our conference room because it's the only place not constantly filled with people all day.

It turns out that Paul writes as a hobby. His professional background is as a certified public accountant and chief financial officer. He's overseen large businesses back in London, and even has the experience of taking companies public.

"You're exactly the type of person this business needs!" I blurt out.

"You're right, it does," he responds, without hesitation, "and it's good that you recognize it."

Paul can see what a diamond in the rough *Beijing Scene* is. It's filled with talented people who are good at their jobs and dedicated to success. It's accomplished the most difficult thing for a new business, growing through the perilous stage of start-up to profitability, and now needs to be run more professionally. He can see the potential of China's newly emerging media industry. Paul's only aim was to submit his article for publication, but by the time our two-hour first conversation is over, I've offered him the job of *Beijing Scene*'s chief financial officer, and he's accepted. His challenge is to turn our amateur-run business into a more efficient, productive, profitable, professional organization.

We shake on the agreement.

With Paul as our new business manager, *Beijing Scene* goes from being a good community newspaper run by writers to a professional publishing operation. He automates all our accounting, invoicing, and advertising systems, batch-faxes sponsorship solicitations to businesses all over China every night, and professionalizes our bookkeeping. Within four months the newspaper goes from just breaking even to grossing US$50,000 per issue.

I'm surprised by a call from my old friend July Zhou. He has a message. Yes, we'll be able to continue to operate, but we'll be hit by a tax. By law, all media in China must be government-owned. Our "tax" is a euphemism for a bribe to be paid to the highest-ranking government official in charge of administering our economic sector (in this case Beijing print media).

What we're facing is a glorified protection racket.

I inform Paul of this news and, to my surprise, he seems to take it in stride. After reflecting on it for a minute, he says, "This is actually really good news."

"How so?" I ask skeptically.

"It means that the authorities are providing us with a mechanism for de facto operating independently," he counsels me in his reassuringly British way.

I trust his business management judgment so much that I don't think twice about it. In fact, I soon come to understand his point. I'd originally hoped that as the result of our venture some progressive-minded Chinese politician would propose and pass a law legalizing independent newspapers or bend the rules just for us. I now see how naïve this is. The best that we can hope for is that a government official realizes there's money to be made, and judges it's worth the risk to provide the venture with political protection.

I follow Paul's instructions.

July informs me that we're to put US$50,000 in cash (all US$100 bills) in a plain brown paper bag and deliver it to him over a cup of coffee at the Beijing Hotel. This feels so strange, like a scene from *All the President's Men*. Paul reassures me that this amount is a reasonable surcharge for the tightly regulated business sector we're in, and the size our publication has grown to. But it's not all we have to pay.

In addition to the US$50,000 one-time bribe, we're required to pay a US$5,000 per issue "administrative fee" to the representative that the Communist Party Propaganda Department has assigned to us. In addition, all of our advertising is required to be routed through their advertising company, Yiren Advertising, so that official government advertising receipts can be issued. Of course, they take a percentage in commission on all of our advertising.

On the appointed day, I take the US$50,000 that Paul has prepared in a paper bag. The bag is surprisingly heavy, like carrying several bricks. I meet July at the Beijing Hotel Coffee Shop and slide the bag with the money across the table. He doesn't look inside or count the money. He simply slips it into his leather briefcase.

"Who's the money going to?" I ask.

"Communist Party Propaganda Minister Ding Guan'gen," he says.

I assume this high-level official must be "taken care of" in order for permission to be granted, but I also assume that people beneath him will be getting a cut, including July's father himself who as a high-ranking retired official draws a government pension of less than US$1,000 per month.

Now that our one-time tax has been paid, we're permitted to publish *Beijing Scene* with an official *kanhao*, publication number.

In addition, and arguably more significantly, we now have an official advertising license number. The advertising license belongs to the *People's Daily*, the official Communist Party mouthpiece commonly known as the throat and tongue of the Communist Party for its official role promoting Party propaganda and policy. We publish both the publication and advertising license information on the inside cover of the newspaper and, at the top, the staff names and advertising contact information. Our existing advertisers and would-be clients are very reassured by this official stamp of approval. They're now convinced we won't be shut down immediately, and any reservations they might have had about doing business with us disappear.

The newspaper starts to be chock-full of advertising. We don't want our advertising-to-editorial content ratio to exceed 40 percent or we run the risk of looking like a supermarket advertising rag instead of a newspaper, so we're now full of long-term full-page display ads. And our classified advertising section keeps expanding.

One day in the office, Banks is playing around on his computer and says to me, "Come here and check out something cool."

I go over to his desk and on his high-resolution sixteen-inch monitor I see a graphic display with the word *YAHOO!* spelled in colorful letters across the top of the screen.

"It's the Internet's first 'search engine,'" Banks explains.

"This is great!"

Banks goes ahead and designs a simple web page for *Beijing Scene*, and the newspaper becomes the first China-based newspaper with a web page (beijingscene.com). The online version of our newspaper will become an increasingly important component of our business as time goes on.

Every Thursday morning at 7 AM after our all-night weekly production process that includes copyediting, final spell-checking, and posting the new issue to our web page, an English-speaking editor from the *People's Daily* comes to our office, sits down, and previews a black-and-white office printout of the week's newspaper. He skims the content quickly, asking questions about the meaning of unfamiliar English words, such as *surfing the web*. He occasionally asks me to change a reference to Chairman Mao or some other marginally politically sensitive comment that might get us and by extension his bosses at the *People's Daily* in trouble, but no major changes are ever requested.

I duly mark the offending sentence with a red marker but rarely make the changes in the final document. No one at the *People's Daily* actually reads the final newspaper. Their English isn't good enough, and they're happy with this new source of revenue.

"I think it's time . . ." Banks greets me one morning.

After more than a year of working on average twelve-hour days, he's decided to return to his life and graduate studies in Hawaii.

We're sad and sorry to see him go, but he's more than pulled his weight in helping get us up and running, and with Paul now in place as CFO, Banks has skillfully replaced himself. All the original founding members of *Beijing Scene* pile into my jeep and drive Banks to the airport to see him off through the same terminal where we arrived, lugging our hockey bags full of Apple computers, twelve months before.

Next to go is Dave "Pablo" Kaill, to be replaced as art director by my old Duke classmate Brian McClain (who has the added attraction and benefit of being a world-class political cartoonist). I first met Brian when we were hallmates my freshman year at Duke and he used to draw a serialized comic called *Kozmic Kat* on the stall walls in the bathroom. It caricatured our misadventures; a group of co-ed classmates getting caught in a speed trap and ultimately jailed in Jacksonville, Florida, on spring break was a classic example. Brian keeps *Beijing Scene*'s Duke connection alive.

Then, to my profound sorrow, Katherine decides that she needs to go back to her graduate studies as well. She's received a scholarship offer to study for a Master of Fine Arts (MFA) degree from Columbia University.

"You know I love doing the newspaper," she tells me when we discuss this big decision, "but it's always been your dream, not mine. This is a once-in-a-lifetime opportunity to study with the best fine art photographers in New York City."

"I know," I say, "and I support your decision."

Katherine stays to spend my late-August birthday with me, my thirty-third, and then I drive her to the airport and watch her disappear into the international terminal and, as it turns out, from my life.

chapter twenty-four

"In business school, do they advise you *not* to start a business in a place you don't want to live?" I half-jokingly ask one of my American friends with a graduate business degree.

"No," says Tom Stahl, another Duke classmate who has an MBA (Master of Business Administration) from Berkeley and works for Bell South in Beijing. "That would come under the heading of common sense."

I've been living in Beijing for thirteen years, nearly half my life, and my entire adult life since graduating from college.

One by one everyone close to me is returning to the States. But I'm attached to this newspaper that the international community in Beijing depends on for its information and entertainment, and, an increasing number of people tell me, for its sanity. I believe fervently in my work— it's a positive response to the tragedy of the Tiananmen Massacre—but I don't see any future for myself here other than an endless series of too-long workdays.

I get out of the city every weekend with my friend Andrew Nugent-Head to hike on the Great Wall.

Looking north, toward Mongolia, I say to Andrew, "At least we can get in some world-class hiking here."

He makes eye contact and points south.

I turn and look back toward Beijing and the malevolent grey-brown smog cloud obscuring the entire capital. The choking miasma is part of our daily lives, with wind carrying pollution from all over the surrounding region as well as dust from the Gobi Desert.

Back in the city, Brian McClain, nicknamed Max, and I are playing hacky sack outside our office with Brian's Chinese design intern, assistant

Liu Jing. The sack goes over my head and lodges in a shrub beneath the giant satellite dish that picks up illegal international television signals for the enjoyment of residents in the diplomatic compound.

As I reach up to grab the sack, my hand brushes across a sticky bud the size of a small banana. A huge marijuana flower bobs in front of my nose. I've long known that hemp grows wild all over China and have seen it regularly in Beijing, but this is something altogether different.

Now, I walk by this spot every single day and practice my *t'ai chi* here every morning, and I've never noticed this plant before.

It's not some wild hemp plant; it resembles carefully cultivated sinsemilla (highly potent seedless marijuana).

I rip the seven-foot plant out by its roots, a surprisingly difficult task because the stem is as thick and woody as a rhododendron, and run inside the office with it. I hang it upside down from the ceiling in the back bedroom of the office, and go back out to talk to Max and Jing.

"Did you guys see what I just saw?" I ask.

Max is cackling maniacally, and Jing is asking "What? What?"

"I swear that plant was not here yesterday!" I say to Max.

"Comrade Jack and his Magic Beanstalk," Max says with a leering grin.

We nickname it Fragrant Hills blend, after the poetic name of the mountains west of Beijing.

Liu Jing has only heard of this stuff, marijuana, and certainly has never seen or tried it. But he's ready to try it now. We wait until the plant is good and dry, a fairly fast process of three days due to the low-moisture of the northern Chinese air, and then "harvest" it. The dried buds fill a dark green industrial garbage bag. We put the leaves and plant stems and branches in a separate bag to make baked goods and medicinal tea from. But it's the buds that we're after. We take Liu Jing out to the pagoda in the small park in our residential compound. Max has purchased a small souvenir opium water pipe at the local Panjiayuan antiques market, made for smoking tobacco out of. But it's not tobacco we cram it full of. We show Jing how to first exhale, inhale the smoke deeply into his lungs, and then hold it as long as possible.

Before long he has the same ruddy complexion as he does when he takes a few shots of *baijiu* grain alcohol when we go to local restaurants, and his eyes are bloodshot red. We all start to laugh. Jing has a wide grin on his face, and he says, "I feel great."

When we're done smoking we go down and play some more hacky sack, hoping that maybe we'll get lucky again. We try to be discreet, keeping our weed indulgence for after-work hours and out-of-doors. Most of our workmates don't know about this discovery and we don't volunteer the information. But it bolsters our stamina and creativity. Max comes up with some of his best cartoon ideas during our after-hours "meetings" and I keep a pocket notebook and mark down funny ideas whenever I have them.

Secretly, I feel a little disappointed in myself. This was one of the reasons that I left the United States and have stayed away so long, the easy availability of drugs and their wanton recreational use. I like China's ascetic approach to intoxicants of all kinds. The general attitude is that they're not worthy of a serious person with serious ambitions. But the constant stress has made me crack. And when this gift from the gods appears, it seems to be a sign—but I'm not sure of what.

Katherine's replacement photographer is a twenty-four-year-old Chinese-American woman named Mary Chang. Mary is pretty and creative and smart, but she's also ten years younger than me. In spite of myself, I fall into a casual sexual relationship with Mary. It's not the same as being together with someone your own age whom you grew up with, but the alternative is being alone here, and that's unbearable.

I'm living in Beijing, but I don't have a real life outside work.

Part of me knows that I'm living on borrowed time. I don't see a way out of this trap. Staff turnover is high. We have a policy that you can leave as long as you're prepared to help train your replacement. But it starts to feel like a merry-go-round. We seem to have a new good-bye party and dinner every other week.

One day I look around and realize that I'm the oldest person in the office. When I started this newspaper I was in my twenties. Now I'm in my mid-thirties. The kids in the office start calling me Grandpa Simpson, after the character on The Simpsons who bores everyone with his long stories about what life used to be like during the Great Depression, before there was electricity.

My stories are about the Tiananmen Massacre.

A decade has passed and the horror has receded to a vague memory. Then the Chinese were poor. Now they're rich. It's like the gold rush. Beijing resembles California in 1849, which is why I'm not entirely surprised when I'm contacted by my old friend Jay McCarthy, an investment banker for Morgan Stanley in Hong Kong.

"Hey, Scott, I've landed a venture capital fund to manage Internet investments in China. Guess what? One of the ventures recommended is *Beijing Scene*."

Wow! This is big news.

It's the first opportunity to reduce some of the stressful, debilitating risk I've continued to shoulder all these years. My family's initial investment has long since been paid back; but all my time, sweat, and blood will be for naught if anything happens to *Beijing Scene* before I sell off some of the ownership. I remain majority owner of the company, but Paul Hallett informs me that now's the time to sell.

Jay's Morgan Stanley fund has investments in a who's who of Internet companies, including all the major Chinese Internet companies, Sina, Sohu, and NetEase, as well as advising a small but as yet unheard of venture called Alibaba.

I let Paul handle all the details while I continue to focus on maintaining the quality of the newspaper. I have to attend regular meetings with Jay and his fund partner Tony Tambunan, a Filipino-American investment banker based in Hong Kong. I find it amusing to observe our different worlds. While the bankers show up at our meetings in six-star Chinese hotel restaurants in silk suits and patent leather shoes, I'm in a tank top, ripped shorts, and flip-flops.

They love coming to our office.

"Where are the adults?" Jay wisecracks.

I'm nominally in charge, but I can usually be seen with my bare feet propped up on my desk hammering away at my laptop keyboard, as often as not with a New York Mets game playing on the small television (night baseball games in the U.S. come on in the morning in China, in my experience the best time to watch a baseball game as a diversion from work).

There's always loud music playing, both Western and Chinese, and laughter. We're a typical new-economy dot-com company, only instead of being in California or New York we're in Beijing.

Paul begins negotiating the investment with Jay and Tony on behalf of Morgan Stanley. They'll buy a 10 percent stake of *Beijing Scene* for US$500,000, with an option to increase their share of ownership later. This values the company we started in our living room five years ago at US$5 million. I'm advised that I could hold out for more, but this is money on the barrelhead. I take Paul's advice and take the deal. What this represents for me first and foremost is security. I'm now comforted that should the dreaded knock on the door from Chinese authorities come, regardless of what happens to me I'll have a cushion to fall back on afterward.

"If the Chinese goons knock down this door I need to be protected," I tell anyone who will listen.

I'm just telling the truth, and the frisson of danger only seems to further compel Jay and Tony to make the deal.

They, of course, have an ulterior motive. They have ground-floor stakes in all of China's leading Internet companies. They see the opportunity to leverage their banking influence and piggyback on their firm's investment and further acquisitions in order to benefit personally.

Beijing Scene is featured in a Morgan Stanley internal report on "Emerging Internet Companies in China."

I'm starting to see behind the curtain of how investment banking really works. The game is fixed. The bankers hold all the cards.

Heads I win, tails you lose.

Once the investment deal is consummated, Jay and Tony begin to pour money into our company at the rate of US$100,000 per month. This means I have to go out and hire a lot more people and expand as quickly as possible. The newspaper grows to fifty employees. We increase the page count to forty full-color pages per week. We redesign and upgrade the website and increase the weekly distribution of the newspaper to 20,000.

I also hire a new managing editor, Sharline Chiang.

Sharline is ABC (American-born Chinese). Her parents were refugees from the civil war in China and subsequent Communist revolution. Her mother's family hails from Hunan and her father's from Shanghai (a volatile combination clear to anyone with passing familiarity with Chinese culture—like a Texan marrying someone from blue-blood New England). Sharline grew up in New Jersey and graduated from Rutgers with a finance degree, but then put herself through Columbia University's prestigious Graduate School of Journalism working for the tabloid *New York Daily News*. When I see her résumé I'm floored by its tailor-made fit: She's completely bilingual in English and Mandarin. On paper she almost appears too good to be true.

I hear the office doorbell ring and get up to answer it. I see a Chinese-American woman in a long wool coat with padded shoulders, an anchor-woman's Connie Chung–style bobbed haircut and heavy eyeliner, and sculpted, rouged cheekbones.

Typical New York professional, I think to myself.

I walk toward her and give her a strong handshake. I take her coat and hang it on the rack by the door. Then I escort her in and show her around the office and introduce her to the rest of the staff.

I trust my gut instinct about things like this and can tell right away that Sharline will fit in. After chatting for half an hour in the breezy, easy way that fellow journalists from diverse backgrounds are able to, telling each other war stories, me about Tiananmen and her about covering the Colombo Mafia crime family in New York City, I ask if she wants to go get some lunch.

Over sushi and sake in the little no-name Japanese restaurant behind our diplomatic compound, I pop the question:

"Do you want to be *Beijing Scene*'s managing editor?"

"Sure," Sharline answers without hesitation. "But there's one little hitch."

"What's that?" I ask.

"I have a yearlong contract with the government-run *China Daily* newspaper that says if I break my contract for whatever reason I have to leave the country immediately."

"Oh," I reassure her, "that isn't a problem, we handle tricky political situations like that all the time."

So Sharline and I make arrangements for her to give notice at *China

Daily. We'll fly her out to Hong Kong in accordance with her *China Daily* requirement, and then she'll fly back in with some equipment that we need to pick up and start working at *Beijing Scene* right after the Thanksgiving holiday.

The problem is that Sharline suddenly gets the urge to tell *China Daily* the truth about what she's planning.

She calls me late at night at our office from her *China Daily* apartment scared and confused.

"They threatened me with arrest if I break my contract," she moans, clearly frightened.

"What in God's name possessed you to tell them the truth?" I ask her.

It's the usual lull between Thanksgiving and Christmas. Even in China, this hyper-commercialized American holiday schedule has begun to take root, especially among the businesses that advertise with us. I have to recruit a few young strong guys from our office to go to Sharline's apartment at the *China Daily*, pack all her belongings into my jeep, and sneak her out in the middle of the night. This includes Sharline's friend Antonio Roque, a Salvadorean war refugee who now teaches bilingual education in a Los Angeles public high school and just arrived in Beijing to visit Sharline during his winter school break.

Sharline is scared to death, but I reassure her that we've done this before and that it's the only way to get her out of her contract with the government.

"Never tell the truth," I tell her as I speed around traffic barriers, trash can fires, and random drunks and homeless people in her north Beijing neighborhood's late-night street-food market.

"I don't know, in the United States I was always taught that truth is the best policy?" she defends herself.

"Well you're in Communist China now. In wartime, truth is so precious it must be attended by a bodyguard of lies," I quote Winston Churchill's famous line regarding the necessity of deception surrounding the Allied plan for its Normandy invasion of Europe the following year.

We get back to the *Beijing Scene* office, grab a spare key, and take Sharline to an apartment I've rented for her a couple of blocks down the Avenue of Eternal Peace. She can pass as a local, and the apartment is in a regular Chinese residential apartment building. It takes a few trips to lug all her stuff up the six flights of stairs. How does someone who's been here less than six months acquire more belongings than I have after thirteen years?

At last Sharline is safely settled in, and we say good night to her and I head back to work. It's nearly dawn and there's another issue of the paper to put out.

"See you at the office," I call out as I close the security gate behind me and wait to hear the deadbolt lock on her door.

The next morning, Sharline is duly chagrined.

"Sorry for my stupid impulse to try to be truthful with a duplicitous system," she says to me with her head lowered like a chastised pet.

"It happens to the best of us," I reassure her, and I tell her to forget about it and get to work.

For the first time since *Beijing Scene*'s inception, I have someone who has the journalism skills to replace me in my editorial role on the newspaper. This means I can spend more time focusing on strategy and tactics for staying alive in these shark-infested waters—Beijing's increasingly lucrative and crowded media-land.

Sharline obviously has much more to learn about the dog-eat-dog aspects of daily life in Beijing.

After finishing the editing of a piece, I look up—she's sitting at the desk opposite me—and say: "Just pretend you're back in New York, but multiply Manhattan's cutthroat, calculating insanity by a factor of ten."

chapter twenty-five

擦邊球
Cabianqiu

A SHOT IN PING-PONG THAT GRAZES THE EDGE OF THE TABLE (AND CAN'T BE RETURNED)

To mark my thirty-sixth birthday, another zodiac year and the end of my third time around the twelve-year Chinese astrological cycle, I make some lifestyle resolutions. I vow to abstain from intoxicants, specifically the Fragrant Hills weed in our office freezer and African voodoo black hashish that young African diplomats smuggle in safely through their embassy pouches that's allowed me to maintain my insane workload and confront the ugly reality of this big, overcrowded, polluted city as I grasp blindly for a sense of community, shared vision, and surrogate family. This newly resolved abstinence isn't difficult for me.

It leverages the same single-minded determination, bordering on obsessive-compulsive, with which I approach everything in life. When I self-medicate, I do it reliably, daily, like clockwork. So when I abstain from that, I just hit the off switch. So now I'm back to running every morning instead of taking a water pipe hit before work.

I'm out on one of my evening strolls through the scenic old Yabaolu district across the Chaoyang Bridge from my apartment and office when I run into a Chinese family out for a surreptitious walk with their unregistered little lion dogs.

Dog registration is another of the catch-22's that China's Communist system is rife with. During one of Chairman Mao's Cultural Revolution anti-pest campaigns, dogs were targeted as a bourgeois luxury and ordered killed on sight. Posses of men with clubs roamed city streets, seizing and beating to death in front of their horrified, traumatized owners any unlucky canine that was discovered. Bounties were paid for dead dogs delivered to government headquarters. Dog ownership died out except in the distant countryside where the Communist Party's reach was limited.

After the economic reforms of the 1980s, people started having disposable income again and slowly dog ownership began making a comeback. The government saw an opportunity to raise revenue from it. In 1992 all dogs above fifteen inches in height were declared illegal within Chinese city limits. And all dogs under fifteen inches had to be registered for an annual fee of ¥5,000 (US$650). In addition a whole battery of expensive tests and vaccinations had to be procured. None but the wealthiest Chinese could afford this, so dog owning went underground, albeit in a thinly veiled way. People walk their dogs before dawn and after dark, keeping a constant eye out for police and government informants.

As I look closer I realize that the smaller one strongly resembles the Tibetan temple dog that I once took care of for my artist friend Ching-Ching while she was ill.

The family says that they can't keep the two-month-old puppy, and that I can have it if I want to. I decide that this is the universe's way of rewarding me for my new clean lifestyle.

The dog is named Nao Nao (pronounced *Now-now*), and though sad to be separated from his adopted family, he senses that I'll be a good caretaker. I pick him up and carry him in my folded arms for the mile-plus hike back to the office.

The whole gang is beavering away, working late as usual, and of course everyone goes gaga over the puppy. It's clear I'm the only one with experience raising a dog and that the primary caregiving responsibility is going to fall on me. The puppy earns the nickname Democracy Dog.

Beijing's oppressive summer heat breaks and we're rewarded with brisk clear autumn weather. I'm sober and happy. I love the routine that dog ownership brings. Just like me, a dog wants to get up at the crack of dawn, get outside and enjoy the early morning—before the cars, coal smoke, and crush of people.

I bring Nao Nao in my bicycle basket to my *t'ai chi* class every morning. He plays in the enclosed grass area while I practice with Master Li on the adjacent pavement. Afterward, it's back to the office for the same old daily grind of writing and editing, broken up by several dog walks during the day around the diplomatic compound playground and grassy lawn area behind our office building, then home after dark for dinner and a movie before passing out from exhaustion and starting the same routine all over again early the next morning.

Beijing Scene is more successful as a business than at any time in its six years of publishing. We're the leading English-language newspaper in China, and, perhaps more importantly, the leading bilingual (English and Mandarin) website in China—because online publishing is politically safer. Our investors Jay and Tony are positioning us to merge with, or be acquired by, one of the other China-based Internet companies they've helped get started, the web portals Sina, Sohu, and Netease. I continue to work as hard as ever, but I start to see light at the end of the tunnel.

I'm also the happiest I've been in my personal life in a long time. I've struck up a new relationship with Sharline. We spend New Year's Eve together, ringing in the new millennium. First we join a raucous party at the Swiss ambassador's residence. Then we go to a rave in a converted bomb shelter called the Beijing Underground Bar where six-foot-tall, rail-thin Chinese and Mongolian models with shaved heads are putting on a strobe-lit fashion show.

I sit in a back corner nursing a Tsingtao draft beer. *At least the beer is good*, I think to myself, something that hasn't always been true in the years I've been living in China.

Sharline's friend Antonio sits beside me. Like Sharline, he's a decade younger than I am, but we have a lot in common. We both play guitar. We have the same taste in Beat and bohemian American and European literature. He's a very talented writer and artist, as well as a good athlete, a scholarship wide receiver at Whittier College, and a valuable addition to our regular pickup basketball games in the diplomatic compound.

In other words, Antonio is a real friend. I have work colleagues and professional acquaintances, but have had no real friends here since John left for the United States following the massacre.

Antonio and I laugh about the six-foot bald model show we're watching.

"You couldn't make this up," I whisper to him. "No one would believe it."

"Tell me about it," he says as he sketches in his ever-present black clothbound artist's journal. "I've been writing letters home to my buddies in L.A. who come from pretty rough barrio neighborhoods, and they can hardly believe what I'm describing."

Beijing is becoming more and more like the dystopia described in the Philip K. Dick novel that became the cult film *Blade Runner*. Never mind that it was set in Japan in the indeterminate future. Twenty-first-century China is a closer fit. The best and the worst of humanity are crammed into this forty-square-mile grid. You can find unimaginable wealth cheek by jowl with desperate poverty—very similar to the United States, the development model that Beijing's leaders seem to be emulating.

Sharline is dancing by herself on the dance floor, swaying in front of a giant speaker that towers over her. I don't know how she can stand the volume. I have no idea what kind of music is playing; it sounds like a recording of a blast furnace in an iron works factory.

I know I sound like an old fogey, and that I'm getting too old for this lifestyle.

I make a decision, and tell Sharline and Antonio that I'm going to leave early to get some sleep so I can get up bright and early for work the next morning. They both shrug their shoulders and I tell them to call me if they can't get a ride home and need me to pick them up. But on my way out of the underground club I turn my cell phone off. Uninterrupted sleep is the one thing I know I need to keep this work pace going.

Sharline's first cover story for *Beijing Scene* runs in January 2000. "Double Vision: Pulitzer Prize–winning photojournalist Liu Heung Shing approaches images of the East with a Western aesthetic."

Liu is an old friend, longtime professional colleague, and neighbor, and he readily agrees to my request for Sharline to interview him for the 2,000-word feature story. The issue features one of Liu's famous black-and-white photographs on the cover, of Chinese workers in peasant straw hats and Mao suits sitting in front of bamboo scaffolding rolling cigarettes after taking down the iconic portrait of Mao that hangs over Tiananmen Square. The removal is for cleaning, but the double entendre that this is what it will also look like when the photo of the Great Helmsman comes down for good is clear to all. The face of the Chairman towers over the workers, as it did in Chinese life for so many decades after the Communist revolution, but for the first time the workers are not intimidated and appear quite relaxed, even smiling. The image seems to sum up the mood of the post-Mao period.

When the first papers come in from the printer, Sharline is ecstatic.

"My first newspaper cover feature!" she says excitedly. "Even though I can't put my name on it [she's using her mother's maiden name Ellen Chen as her byline for fear of reprisal from *China Daily*], I know it's mine. I can send it to my parents to demonstrate that their daughter isn't a good-for-nothing after all."

Her words are said casually but I can hear the pain behind them. This kind of conflict is true of most immigrant families, but Chinese parents seem especially tough on their children, and especially their daughters.

All the *Beijing Scene* staff members gather around Sharline and congratulate her. The issue looks great, definitely one of our best.

After work I walk Sharline home from the office to her apartment half a mile down the Avenue of Eternal Peace, and she invites me up. Antonio is still at the office working on his own first cover story, on the shamanistic culture of the Naxi ethnic minority of far southwest China, and his guitar is lying in its case against the wall. I take it out and start playing quiet music while Sharline prepares tea.

"I'm really excited about this opportunity," Sharline says to me from the small kitchenette. "I paid so much to go to Columbia Journalism School, and didn't have that much to show for it until now.

"My mom pushes me constantly, but I'm more laid-back, like my dad. It drives my mom crazy because if she hadn't been forced by China's revolution to go into exile and start over from scratch in a foreign country, she would have risen up the career ranks with her determination." I detect an undercurrent of disappointment in how her career has worked out until now. She's come close to landing jobs with one of the Big Four U.S. newspapers (*The New York Times, Los Angeles Times, Washington Post,* and *Wall Street Journal*), but always just missed on the final round of interviews. "Now my mom focuses all her ambition on me and my career, and I can't help but disappoint her. She regularly compares me to her friends' kids who are successful, married, and giving their parents grandchildren; and most importantly buying things like cars and houses for them as good filial Chinese children should. And look at me, living in a shithole apartment in Beijing. . . ."

"Hey, this is a pretty nice Beijing apartment," I try to get her to smile.

She does, but fleetingly. "All the time when I was growing up, when my mom got mad, or even just in passing, she would say that she wished I was a boy."

Sharline erects a four-by-six-foot whiteboard on the office wall and has issues of the newspaper charted out months in advance, a level of organization that with all my administrative and political obligations I was never able to accomplish.

And Sharline and I are getting ready to move in together.

We've rented a spare apartment in the diplomatic compound from *Newsweek* magazine and are fixing it up with furniture from Ikea.

Everything is going smoothly, which is why I expect trouble around the corner.

The first hint of difficulty is an emergency message from Los Angeles. Antonio's mother, the woman who brought him across the Rio Grande River on her back when he was a child, and raised him by cleaning rich people's homes and hotel rooms in downtown L.A., has been admitted to the hospital for emergency surgery. Although Antonio is having the best time of his life in Beijing, he has to book a plane ticket home to take care of his mom. The entire staff takes him out for a going-away dinner and celebration, but a writer has blown an assignment on a cover story profiling the Chinese environmental nonprofit Friends of Nature, and I have to stay up all night conducting phone interviews and writing up the story for tomorrow morning's deadline.

I don't even get to go to my own best friend's going-away party, I think and shake my head. This sums up my lack of balance between work and social life.

The next day I drive Antonio to the airport and give him a big hug good-bye. I watch him walk through the security checkpoint—another good friend gone.

Sharline and I feel even more isolated without Antonio, and turn to each other for emotional support. After work I watch with exhaustion as she sews curtains for our new apartment.

"What, haven't you ever seen anyone sew curtains before?" she laughs self-consciously.

"No," I admit to her. "I've missed all those normal details of life living here in this time warp, remember?"

chapter twenty-six

秋後算賬
Qiuhou suanzhang
SETTLE ACCOUNTS AFTER THE HARVEST

Nao Nao is sitting in his usual spot, on the ledge of our second-floor office balcony doing his watchdog duty. The sky is overcast. The newspaper went off to the printer overnight and I'm waiting for the new issue to arrive.

Nao Nao's ears prick up, and I see he's staring at something unusual. I crane my neck and see dark blue police vans pulling into the parking lot in front of our building.

I wonder where they're going? I think, and then with sudden dread realize: *They're coming here.*

Before I have a chance to react, dozens of uniformed and plainclothes police crash through the front door, round up the Chinese staff, and take them in the back room to interrogate them. Then they begin itemizing and confiscating all the newspaper's equipment: computers, printers, scanners, cameras, a complete archive of all two hundred issues of the newspaper, research files, reference books, even wastepaper baskets.

I barricade myself in the bathroom and call our Chinese partners to find out what's going on.

They make quick inquiries, then call me back and tell me that China's Ministry of State Security (the PRC's KGB) is carrying out the raid and there's nothing they can do.

I curse myself. Here I am, sitting on tens of thousands of dollars in the office safe, and hundreds of thousands in the business bank account. I could have easily spread some of that money around to politically well-connected Chinese and averted this raid, or at least guaranteed advance notice of its planning.

Why didn't I do more to protect myself?

I should be scared, but I feel calm. I've expected this moment every day for the six years since I started this newspaper.

A burly, leather-jacketed cop raps on the bathroom door with his electric cattle prod and orders me out.

I do as I'm told. I'm carrying my Apple laptop containing the entire digital archive of the newspaper. We've long vowed to keep a copy of it safe off-site in case of a police raid, fire, or robbery, but never got around to doing it. I clutch the black laptop to my chest like a football.

The officer grabs me under the armpit and leads me into the back bedroom for a private interrogation. I notice that the vertically hinged window is open. While the officer is closing and locking the door behind us, I take two running steps, jump up onto the four-foot-high ledge, and as he grabs the back of my brown leather jacket and it rips in his hand I leap from the second-story window. I land safely on my bare feet in the wet, grassy area fifteen feet below and don't look back. I take off running toward the nearby exit of the diplomatic compound, the computer still safely in my arms.

I know that in order to come after me the cop will have to go back out the front door of the apartment, and by then I'll be out of sight in the maze of alleyways that lead from the compound in all directions.

I don't stop running until I reach our nearby bank branch, CITIC (China Industrial Trust and Investment Corporation). I go into the office of our private banker, an attractive young woman in her mid-twenties named Miss Cui.[128] She raises her eyebrows at my appearance: torn jacket, bare feet, and dripping with sweat. But polished professional that she is, she asks no questions and follows my instruction to wire all our office funds to a bank account in the States.

---

128. Pronounced *ts-way*.

My mind is eased at having accomplished this critical task. After stashing the archive computer at my apartment, I head back to the office to deal with the fallout. By the time I get there the police and state security officers are gone. All that's left is a shell. The place has been stripped bare. Not a single electrical device remains in a room that was buzzing with normal business activity. Broken cords dangle like spaghetti strands where dozens of top-quality Macintosh production machines were networked together an hour ago. Also gone are all the expensive laser printers, scanners, digital photography equipment, and all the cash and the safe it was in.

The crowning blow is seeing that the only physical archive of *Beijing Scene*, Volume 1 Issue 1 to Volume 6 Issue 12—two hundred issues in all—has been seized. I shake my head in despair.

Seven years of hard work down the drain.

I feel like crying, but am too exhausted.

I whistle for Nao Nao. He appears from underneath a desk and I say a prayer of thanks that at least they spared him. He follows me on the walk home.

Nothing good can survive here, I cynically say to myself on the way back to our apartment, even though I don't really believe it but just feel this way this moment.

Sharline jumps up as I open the door—I called from the bank and told her about the raid—and after hugging me and scooping up Nao Nao she asks: "What are we going to do now?"

"I've been thinking," I say out loud. "With the Internet growing so fast, you and I could do this on a much smaller and safer scale. Get rid of all the overhead—there are fifty people drawing salaries right now—move into a smaller place, and just do a web-based version ourselves."

I pour myself a cup of tea, take a deep gulp, and continue: "You don't need a dozen licenses and to pay off every crooked cop and politician in the city to do that, just half of them," I joke.

Then I notice that Sharline is crying.

"You didn't expect this raid to happen?" I'm genuinely surprised.

"How could I?" she responds, wiping away her tears.

I realize how stupid my question is.

"I've only been here for six months. You've been here seventeen years."

I see her point. It's almost impossible for me to remember that far back. But of course there was a time when I didn't know about China's dark side either, and only saw the shiny, happy masses going about their socialist business.

What I'd do to have a little of that innocence back.

Sharline and I agree that I'll contact our investors, and then see if our Chinese partners have any good ideas about how to extricate ourselves from this mess. Meanwhile Sharline will get in touch with our Chinese and Western staff and tell them that they can take a paid vacation. Even though US$30,000 was confiscated from the office safe, we still have plenty of funds. Missing an issue or two of the newspaper isn't a big problem, but we won't be able to keep all the employees if we don't find a way to bring new revenue in soon.

Word of the raid travels fast.

Everyone I contact already knows about it. Our Hong Kong investors say they're going to see if they can pull any strings and engineer a merger with one of their Internet investments here. We have extensive talks with one of them, NetEase (now NYSE-listed), but it becomes clear that there's no way I'm going to retain control of my company in a merger, and nobody wants to be politically tainted by associating with me anyway.

I find myself running around like this for weeks. It becomes increasingly clear that no matter what I do I'm a marked man. I've done hundreds of favors for people over the years—especially the years running the newspaper—but as soon as I say the words "Ministry of State Security raid," no one wants to have anything to do with me.

I start to think that maybe it's time to consider heading home. *Qiang da chutou niao*—the lead bird always gets shot by the hunter, they say here, and I feel like I've got a few slugs in me right now.

It's been a long day of knocking on doors and I'm driving in early afternoon traffic along the Avenue of Eternal Peace. I pass the forty-foot-tall, garishly colored portraits of the four fathers of Marxism: Karl Marx, Friedrich Engels, Vladimir Lenin, and Joseph Stalin. They're erected in Tiananmen Square every year on May 1, International Workers' Day.

I smile.

Only in China do you see giant portraits of the mass murderer Stalin.

I can't help thinking of a couple of old jokes. One is someone wondering whether this is an advertisement for men's facial hair: Marx has a full beard, Engels a half-beard (sideburns cut), Lenin a sharply sculpted goatee, and Stalin his trademark woolly mustache.

The other joke was told to me by our old UPI translator Yale. He was leading a group of American senior citizens around Tiananmen Square one May Day when the portraits were up.

One of the older women asked in a thick New York accent: "Hey, Yale, I always heard about that Gang of Four, but I never seen 'em!"

I'm still smiling to myself when out of the corner of my eye I see a uniformed traffic cop leap off his pedestal in the middle of the crowded intersection and jog in my direction. I can't be sure that he's coming toward me, but I certainly have good reason to be concerned. I look back over my right shoulder to see if I can change lanes and pull over. Whether he's coming for me or not, I want to get as close to the safety of the side of the road as possible.

My worst fear is realized when I hear him blowing his whistle and pointing for me to pull over.

I start to pull over to the side of the road and most importantly, get out of the way of all the cars that are dangerously swerving around me. Then the cop does something really unexpected: he jumps on the hood of my car. This I've never experienced before, and I have no idea how to react. My first instinct is not to stay sitting in the path of moving traffic, especially with a cop on the hood. So I continue to slowly pull over to the shoulder of the road.

The U.S. Embassy warns its citizens about situations like this. Americans have been attacked by angry Chinese crowds at traffic stops. The embassy advises that under certain circumstances, using one's own discretion, it might be advisable to show your foreign passport through your closed window and drive to the U.S. Embassy. If the police want to follow you they can, and if it's an important-enough matter they'll find you one way or another.

I didn't judge this to be that serious a situation and did pull over. But my last interaction with cops had seen me leaping out a second-story window to flee an interrogation, and I had an unregistered dog in the car with me and wanted to protect Nao Nao.

I get to the side of the road and the cop jumps off the hood and comes running to the driver's side door. He yells at me to turn off the engine and get out of the car. I dutifully obey. Nao Nao knows something's wrong and is cowering under my seat. I give him a reassuring pat and softly say "Good dog," then get out of the car to deal with the cop. An angry crowd of more than a hundred people has formed and is pressing in around me.

"Who do you think you are, foreign bastard?" one guy yells. He reaches out and grabs my T-shirt and when I pull away it rips off in his hand.

I'm starting to worry that this could escalate. More people crowd in to witness the entertaining drama of a cop and foreigner having it out.

"*Rangkai* [get back]*!*" the cop yells, and lucky for me he's authoritative enough for the crowd to move back a step. But we're still surrounded by a riled-up, leering mob of mostly young Chinese men. The cop is understandably angry. But I still can't understand why he jumped on the hood of my car when I was pulling over like he told me to. I guess I'll find out.

There's always a delicate give-and-take in situations like this. Sometimes it's best to feign ignorance of Chinese. Few if any traffic cops speak English, so without a translator, Chinese police often have no recourse but to let foreigners go with a finger-shake warning.

But my gut feeling is this isn't the best way to handle this situation. So I immediately launch into the most abject, polite Chinese apology I can: "Ten thousand pardons! Are you hurt? This was really a misunderstanding! I'm so sorry! I hope you're okay?"

The combination of the cop and crowd hearing me speak fluent Mandarin, and my obvious concern for his well-being, deescalates the situation.

Now that my ability to speak Mandarin has been established, the cop can return to his accustomed officiousness: "Show me your driver's license and registration!" he demands.

I unlock the car door and lean over to the glove compartment. I rummage for my registration with my left hand while reassuringly patting Nao Nao with my right and whispering, "It's okay, everything's okay."

I find the registration card, pull it out, and hand it to him. The cop is immediately reassured that the car is properly registered to me. I then pull out my wallet and show him my Chinese driver's license. He scrutinizes it, but points out to me that it's just past expiration. I explain to him that I've completed the formal renewal process but just haven't gone to the Beijing Motor Vehicles Department to pick up the new license. This is a technical infraction but a very minor one, normally entailing a citation that can even be rescinded with proof that the renewal is successfully completed.

But just to be safe, the cop takes out his walkie-talkie and calls in to his station chief. I hear him read my ID information into the walkie-talkie: "S-A-V-I-T-T. *Meiguoren* [American]. Thirty-seven years old. General Manager, *Beijing Scene* Publishing Company."

The walkie-talkie squawks and squeals a few times as he waits for a reply.

Half a minute of silence goes by and then the station chief barks something I can't catch and the cop walks away from the crowd and plugs his other ear to hear better. He nods his head repeatedly, then abruptly clicks off the walkie-talkie and comes back to me.

"My chief wants to talk to you in the station."

He instructs me to drive my car and follow him on his motorcycle to the nearby Beijing Municipal Public Security Bureau headquarters. Of course I consider making a run for the U.S. Embassy, but on the capital's crowded streets a car could never outrace a motorcycle, and all I know I'm facing is a minor traffic violation. Not following his instructions now would constitute a much worse offense, never mind the danger of playing Mad Max on the streets of Beijing with a motorcycle cop in pursuit.

We pull into the police department parking lot. The moment we get inside the station, I know something's terribly wrong. There's a whole retinue of police brass there to meet us. I'm immediately taken into an interrogation room where they have a thick file on me on the table. I can see by reading upside down that it has records of my reporting, including my chronicling of Tiananmen, and has nothing to do with this traffic incident.

This has been my deepest fear since arriving here and hearing John's horror stories about the police. I've foreseen this event in regular anxiety dreams I wake up from in cold sweats. Now my worst fear is coming to pass: A police interrogation that pieces together all my past subversive activities.

The interrogation room is a typical Chinese office: cheap wooden desks scarred from decades of use, puke-green paint covering the bottom half of the wall, intended to cover up scuff marks and dirt but in its institutional ugliness emphasizing it, giving way to darkened whitewash along the top half of the walls. One bare fluorescent tube light intermittently buzzes in the fixture hanging slightly askew overhead, its dangling wires dangerously exposed. I'm left alone in the room for what seems like an hour. I've seen enough cop shows and grown up around police stations (when I was a kid my dad represented the New Haven Police Department) to think there's a good chance I'm being monitored through a one-way mirror or a video camera. I glance around and do see a wall mirror above a sink that could serve this purpose, but know that these things can be easily disguised. Due to my familiarity with police stations from my childhood, and having seen the inside of plenty during my years of reporting here, I'm not intimidated and know the best way to act: with abject deference.

Cops like nothing better than beating humility into uncooperative suspects. I have no intention of giving them that satisfaction.

Finally the door opens and an obese officer swaggers in. He sits down, makes a big show of frowning and demonstrating his clear distaste for this situation and me, and then says, "My name is Sergeant Wang."

He starts to thumb through my file and comments, "We have many witnesses saying that you tried to run the police officer over."

"What?" I bellow.

I can barely believe what I've just heard. I know that they can pin any crime on me; this is the nature of the Communist system. John taught me early on: *yujia zhizui, hehuan wuci*—if you want to frame someone with a crime, there will always be a ready charge. In spite of this cynical view, I didn't see this coming. But it's obvious there's no use playing the ignorant foreigner anymore. From the file I can see that they probably know more about me than I know about myself.

Still, I try to protest my innocence as deferentially as possible: "It's a misunderstanding. I was just trying to pull to the side of the road."

Sergeant Wang frowns. This interrogation is clearly frustrating him. He reminds me of a Chinese version of the *NYPD Blue* cop Andy Sipowicz (a show I've seen on bootlegged Chinese DVDs). Sergeant Wang is clearly not a happy man, and will enjoy nothing better than taking that dissatisfaction out on me. I pride myself on being able to elicit sympathy and even affection from most Chinese I interact with, they can't help but be flattered and entertained by an American who has learned so much about their culture and language. But there's one type of Chinese man that's immune to these charms, and that's Sergeant Wang's type.

"I don't like Americans."

No beating around the bush.

"You drive around in your army jeeps acting like you own this place," he continues, sounding like we're in a Communist propaganda movie. "You take our jobs, sleep with our women, enjoy our food, and then trash-talk us in your newspapers."

I can see that I have either been very unlucky in the type of interrogator I've been assigned, or Sergeant Wang was chosen intentionally for his xenophobia. My instinct says it's the latter. Wang is clearly the type of Chinese guy who detests foreigners. He's probably about the same age as I am, even though he looks significantly older. It's not hard to imagine why he would envy and resent the life I lead here and what I represent, and enjoy nothing more than destroying that. He continues to act like he's playing a part in a 1950s Cold War drama when the relationship between China and the U.S. resembled that between the U.S. and present-day North Korea or Iran.

"And you Americans bombed our Chinese Embassy in Yugoslavia and killed four of our diplomats," he adds, referring to the supposedly accidental bombing of the Chinese Embassy in Belgrade during last year's U.S. bombing campaign.

Wang resumes interrogating me about the traffic incident, but intersperses his queries with questions it's clear he already knows the answers to.

Slowly leafing through my file, he looks up and asks, "Who were your Chinese partners on your newspaper?"

This is a question I've been dreading.

"I'll tell you anything and everything you want to know about me, but I'm not going to talk about anyone else."

"Hmmm, that's an admirable stance," he says. "But I hope you realize that unless you give us other names you're going to bear the full brunt of any punishment yourself."

"Yes, I realize that," I say, "but I want to state clearly that I won't talk about anyone else's actions or involvement but my own."

Sergeant Wang slaps his hands on the desktop loud enough to startle me, and then gets up and leaves the room. Perhaps to confer with his superiors, I guess.

I take the opportunity to take a few deep breaths to relax myself and take stock of my situation. The traffic stop didn't seem to be staged, but of course the truth of that is impossible to know. But clearly once the police realized who I was, they saw it as an opportunity to interrogate me and hopefully gather some actionable intelligence on my publishing activities, perhaps implicating some other foreigners or vulnerable Chinese. But I've clearly frustrated them by refusing to rat on my friends.

I'm starting to feel really exhausted.

The interrogation room door suddenly swings open and Sergeant Wang swaggers back in. He puts his hands down on the desk in front of me but remains standing.

"I'm told that the last time you were being questioned by the police you resisted and jumped out a window?"

I nod in acknowledgement.

"That's a crime," he says, and he lets this ominous information sink in.

Then he smiles.

"Is your dog legally registered?"

This statement takes me by surprise. It's a low blow.

"No, my dog isn't registered."

"Well, if you don't start cooperating and giving us information on other people, we'll have no choice but to kill your dog."

Kill my dog?

Here comes yet another in a long string of death threats I've faced in China. But threatening my dog is different. I know how much Sharline loves Nao Nao; he really is like our child. If I let anything happen to that dog, I know it will be the death of our relationship. And I want so much for that to work out, to gain some sense of stability and normalcy in my otherwise chaotic life.

But my childhood lessons from my father about not squealing on other people is too deeply ingrained to ignore, and I know from painful experience in China that it won't do any good anyway. They'll take what I give them and use it to punish and squeeze similar confessions out of others I sell out, and then kill the dog anyway.

I guess it should offer some comfort that I've learned the harsh realities of this modern world—you can trust or help no one but yourself.

"Sergeant Wang," I say with heavy fatigue in my voice. "You obviously have the power to do whatever you want to with my dog. And you can threaten me all you want. But I won't sell out and talk to you about my friends."

Sergeant Wang smiles sadistically, as if he welcomes this answer.

"I have to admit that I admire you for sticking to your principles," he purrs.

Then he turns toward the door and calls out, "Officer Lee," and his assistant pops his head in the door. Wang tosses him my car keys, "Go get the foreigner's dog out of the car."

The next few minutes drag by in excruciatingly slow motion.

Officer Lee goes out the door and arrives back a minute later, carrying Nao Nao by the scruff of his neck. Nao Nao makes eye contact with me, silently pleading for me to hold and protect him like I've done every day of his life since he was a puppy.

It tortures me that I can't protect him.

Officer Lee hands the golden-colored Tibetan dog to Sergeant Wang, who strokes him in his lap in front of me like an evil Nazi interrogator.

"Are you sure you won't change your mind?" he taunts me.

I don't even look up, just shake my head.

Sergeant Wang smiles at me and makes a mock hand motion of breaking a small animal's neck. He then calls Officer Lee back in, shoves Nao Nao at him, and orders, "Sha ta. Kill the dog."

I can't look up as Nao Nao is taken away for the last time. Officer Lee walks out the door and around the office corner, and I hear Nao Nao let out a piercing, high-pitched squeal of pain.

I'm completely numb and beyond anger.

I find myself repeating the words of Jesus on the cross: "Forgive them, Lord, they know not what they do."

This is what everything in China leads to, I think to myself.

Why does everything in my life lead to the death of the things I most love?

And some flame that has stayed alive inside of me, a belief in a better future and passion for fighting for what's right, is extinguished.

chapter twenty-seven

不見棺材不落淚
Bùjiàn guāncái bù luòlèi.
DON'T CRY UNTIL YOU SEE THE COFFIN.

Sergeant Wang keeps me sweating in the interrogation room long past midnight. I try to use my cell phone to call Sharline and let her know where I am. She'll be sick with worry. I never go out at night and never go anywhere unexpectedly but to work.

I can't get any reception in the subterranean room.

Finally Sergeant Wang returns with two of his henchmen, uniformed young police officers. He tries to act formally and police-like in spite of his massively protruding "banquet belly" (as my friends and I call the huge pot bellies that distinguish corrupt Chinese officials).

He clears his throat and says, "By the power vested in me by the constitution of the People's Republic of China and our country's criminal code, you're hereby formally detained."

Despite my numbness over the death of my beloved dog, Nao Nao, my torn shirt, battered physical state, and physical and mental exhaustion, this announcement greets me like a punch in the face.

I've been held and questioned in Chinese police stations many times while reporting in places as far-flung as the border with Siberian Russia, Muslim Chinese Central Asia, and the Himalayan plateau of Tibet. I've spent nights in jail cells before leaving town at dawn—most police don't want anything unusual happening on their watch and in general don't want trouble with foreigners from the capital, never mind foreign reporters that can really make trouble. But I've never been criminally detained in my life until now. This is an important distinction from an arrest. I don't have to be charged with a crime, just suspected of an unnamed one. It's the critical loophole that allows the Chinese police to detain any individual anytime they want for any reason.

Sergeant Wang tells me to put my hands behind my back and, as I do, he clamps handcuffs on my wrists, also for the first time in my life. Sergeant Wang makes sure that he closes them tight enough to cut off the circulation in my hands, which start to throb and ache.

The two uniformed police officers lead me back out of the station to a waiting police van with a barred and blackened-window backseat. It's nighttime, but Beijing is always lit up enough to make out directions, which I carefully watch through the van's windshield. The van pulls out of the police headquarters and heads west on Beijing's Second Ring Road. When we arrive at the centuries-old Yonghegong Lama Temple, a favorite weekend destination of mine in Beijing, we exit the Ring Road and enter a narrow alleyway. After a couple of blocks the van takes a sharp left turn and we're driving along an alley no wider than this single vehicle. We finally arrive at an unmarked green metal-hinged double door that a plainclothes guard opens up and lets the van through.

I realize that, like the bat cave, we've come in through the vehicle entrance of the Beijing Number Three Detention Center, also known as Artillery Alley (Paoju) Prison. It's part of my job as a reporter to know the background of Beijing's jails and prisons, not to mention my personal fascination with the gulag systems of the Soviet Union and the PRC. Mao based his prison model on the penal system of Lenin, Stalin, and Beria's Russia. The van pulls up at a building entrance and my door is unlocked and I'm led out.

The uniformed prison warden is here to receive me. I have no idea what to expect. But I'm not scared, because as far as I'm concerned all of China is a big penal colony. This is just another layer of the repressive apparatus. And I don't believe that I'm in any kind of imminent danger, or just don't care anymore. The police hand me over to the jail supervisor, a hard-assed looking guy with a crew cut in his mid-thirties who leads me by my handcuffed hands into the bowels of the ugly utilitarian building. Unpainted poured concrete floors, puke-green lower and dirty whitewashed upper walls, all completely institutional. I'm led up a flight of stairs and then down a long hallway with jail cells on both sides. This hallway is completely empty.

The VIP wing, I guess to myself (which turns out to be true).

The cell at the far left end of the hallway is opened and I'm led inside. It's dingy even by my low expectations. There's nothing but a grass mat on the concrete floor and no window, a real dungeon chamber.

The guard leaves me without a word and I hear the lock click shut behind him as he closes the cell door and I hear his metal-studded boots click as he disappears down the hall.

I'm so exhausted I curl up on the bamboo mat, pillow my head with my hands, and fall asleep.

I open my eyes, momentarily disoriented. I have no idea where I am. I was dreaming of being back in New Haven, Connecticut, near Yale University, walking down Congress Avenue, a low-income African-American neighborhood, after dark. Yale, like quite a few other elite American universities including Columbia, is located in the middle of a ghetto. I regularly found myself in this situation taking the bus home from music or tennis lessons at Yale. The trick is to look like you're there on purpose and know what you're doing, and to show no fear. The moment you look scared or vulnerable is when someone sees you as an easy victim.

I shake my head to wake up, unnerved by the bizarre parallel between my dream and reality.

I stand up and my legs almost give way. I have no idea what time it is as there's no natural light, only the naked floodlight bulb in the rusty ceiling fixture ten feet above my head. But my internal clock is pretty reliable, and I guess it's early morning.

I take this opportunity to do a slow set of martial arts breathing exercises. This is the first morning in years, indeed in almost two decades, that I've woken up with no work to do. This might not be the first place I would pick to take a vacation from my overwhelming workload, but it's a vacation nonetheless. And because I know many stretching and moving meditation exercises that are designed for a conscribed space, I'm actually quite happy to be locked in a room alone to concentrate on my practice.

I finish my stretches, do several different slow flowing *t'ai chi* forms, focusing on practicing as meticulously as possible because it's clear that the one thing I have is unlimited free time.

I'm sitting in silent meditation when I hear the cell door lock click open. It's the guard, holding a plate of food for me. What he can't know is that I never eat in the morning. I only eat one meal a day, usually in the early evening. Especially in the summer heat, all I have during the day is fresh fruit. But the guard is holding a plate full of very unappetizing dirty rice, wilted vegetables, and a few pieces of gristly bony meat.

And a thought occurs to me.

I clear my throat and say in my clearest Mandarin: "As long as you hold me here, I won't eat."

The guard looks at me like I'm an alien from another planet. Not eating is unimaginable to an average Chinese person. After Chairman Mao's misrule caused widespread famine and food shortages, most Chinese live to eat. It's the primary social activity for most families, and how all business is conducted here. Going without eating to the average Chinese person like this prison guard is the definition of insanity.

I know the Chinese word for *hunger strike* because the student protesters used this tactic to great effect during the Tiananmen protests. Many argue it was the last straw that initiated the government's use of the military to massacre the protesters. The hunger strike elicited so much general sympathy from the population—watching one student after another taken away on IV drips to be treated in the hospital for weakness from not eating for more than a week—that the government was finally forced to take drastic conclusive action because they were losing the battle for the hearts and minds of the populace.

I repeat to the guard: "*Jueshi* [I'm hunger-striking]."

He raises his eyebrows in surprise, but then shrugs his shoulders.

"It doesn't matter to me if you eat or not," he says and leaves the tray of food on the floor and backs out the door, and I hear the loud metallic lock click back into place.

It's my thirtieth day in jail.

A month of my life locked in this closet-sized room. If this goes on much longer, I'll have to take drastic action; perhaps a self-inflicted wound to get me to a hospital.

I haven't eaten for a month.

The prison guards have threatened to force-feed me, but haven't yet followed up on their threats. My rib and hip bones are protruding. I'm five foot eleven and when I got here weighed a fit 150 pounds from regularly playing basketball and running an average of twenty miles per week. Looking down at my shrunken waist, I guess that I've lost more than twenty pounds.

Yet I've taken this opportunity alone to reflect on my past two decades in China. I've resolved to make some dramatic changes in my life, namely to leave and return home to the U.S. I don't yet know what I'm going to do there or what the future holds, but I'm going to try to pick up my life's thread where it left off when I arrived here seventeen years ago.

My reflection is interrupted by the sound of the lock being opened. It takes significant effort to push myself up to a sitting position. The door opens and there stands my old nemesis, Sergeant Wang, in his green police uniform smoking a cigarette.

He takes a deep drag as he scrutinizes my pathetic state. Then he exhales a lungful of smoke and says, "Get up."

He follows this with the words I've been praying for.

"You're leaving."

It takes all the effort I can muster to stand up. I'm still wearing nothing but the flip-flops, filthy cargo shorts, and torn, bloody white T-shirt I was taken into custody in.

Fortunately I've secreted the minuscule journal I've been keeping in the one place I hope they don't check, between my shriveled butt cheeks.

I follow Sergeant Wang and the prison guard down the hall, shuffling slowly, barely strong enough to lift my feet off the ground.

My departure is unceremonious. No good-byes, no speeches. I follow Sergeant Wang and the prison guard down the stairs of the prison and out the door of the steel-barred building. I reflexively lift my hand to shield my eyes from the sun. This is the first time that I've seen the sky in a month.

In the police van, I still have some illusion that they're going to send me back to my old apartment.

"We're taking you straight to the airport," Sergeant Wang growls at me, "where you'll be escorted onto the plane in handcuffs, and then they'll be removed. You're being formally deported from China."

What happened to Sharline? I wonder, catching sight of myself in the van's rearview mirror. I'm shocked to see that my beard has turned completely white. Even my hair is streaked with white.

I arrive at the airport surrounded by uniformed police to see Sharline pulling a cartload of our luggage. We make eye contact and I can see that my problems aren't over. She's clearly livid at what I've put her through. I'd be angry too if I were her. She came to China seeking her roots as an only child of Chinese immigrants, looking for a career opportunity as an experienced journalist, and look what her relationship with me has brought her: failure and heartache.

The police don't let us talk.

They wait until the United Airlines flight to San Francisco is fully boarded, then, for the sake of ultimate humiliation, escort me on board in front of all the other passengers, where they then unlock and remove my handcuffs, and allow me to sit down next to Sharline.

"Hi," I croak.

The United Airlines plane is bound for San Francisco, the closest port of entry in the United States. My confiscated money has been used to purchase the tickets.

Sergeant Wang shakes his head in contempt.

"*Zaijian*, see you again," he says, then turns and disembarks the plane.

I would probably cry if I could feel anything. My ears have a constant ringing and I feel dizzy and disoriented.

A flight attendant asks me if I want anything and I manage to blurt out, "A glass of water, please."

The plane begins to taxi, and I look out the window at the bright white, hot, and humid Beijing midsummer day—my home for almost two decades—and then as the airplane taxis out to the runway, I see the permanent brown smog blanketing the hills to the west of Beijing.

Zaijian, I say to myself.

See you again.

Scott playing guitar at Beijing Teacher's College, June 1983

Beijing International Marathon, October 1986

High school prom with Karen, May 1981

Beijing Christmas, 1985

With Gabriel at Great Wall, Summer 1986

U.S. Ambassador Winston Lord and Bette Bao Lord, 1986

Chinese fortune teller

Contemporary Chinese painter Fang Lijun, Beijing 1987

Student protest leader Wuerkaixi in Tiananmen Square, May 1989

Student protest leaders Chai Ling (L) and Li Lu in Tiananmen Square, May 1989

Nobel Peace Prize laureate Liu Xiaobo announcing hunger strike in Tiananmen Square, June 1989

Famous Taiwan singer Hou Dejian in Tiananmen
Square, June 1989

Largest-ever protest in the PRC, May 4, 1989

Protesters cheering each other on the Avenue of Eternal Peace, May 4, 1989

Largest-ever protest in the PRC, May 4, 1989

Largest-ever protest in the PRC, May 4, 1989

Scott on Monument to People's Heroes a
month before the crackdown, Tiananmen
Square, May 1989

Goddess of Democracy statue in Tiananmen Square, June 1989

Hunger strikers meditating in Tiananmen Square, May 1989

Hunger striker being rushed to hospital, Tiananmen Square, May 1989

Student protester in Tiananmen Square,
May 1989

Protesters sitting on Monument to People's Heroes, June 3, 1989

LA soldiers entering Tiananmen Square, June 4, 1989

Armored personnel carrier set on fire by protesters in Tiananmen Square, June 4, 1989

PLA soldiers occupying Tiananmen Square, June 4, 1989

PLA soldiers occupying Tiananmen Squre, June 4, 1989

Crushed protesters and bicycles at Liubukou intersection, June 4, 1989

Makeshift morgue at Fuxingmen Hospital, June 4, 1989

Protesters throwing rocks at Ministry of Public Security, Tiananmen Square,
June 4, 1989

Cui Jian in Tiananmen Square, Beijing 1987

Nao Nao the dog looking at photo of Scott and Beijing Scene staff, 2000

Beijing Scene staff celebrating Chinese New Year, 1995

Scott and Katherine, 1994

Paoju Prison in Beijing, Summer 2000